James Hobson Aveling

The History of Roche Abbey

From its Foundation to its Dissolution

James Hobson Aveling

The History of Roche Abbey
From its Foundation to its Dissolution

ISBN/EAN: 9783337326227

Printed in Europe, USA, Canada, Australia, Japan

Cover: Foto ©ninafisch / pixelio.de

More available books at **www.hansebooks.com**

Yorkshire.

THE
History of Roche Abbey,

FROM ITS

FOUNDATION TO ITS DISSOLUTION,

BY

James H. Abeling, M. D.

"When the substance of these fabricks shall have passed away, their very shadows will be acceptable to posterity."—*Fuller.*

Worksop:
ROBERT WHITE, PARK STREET.
MDCCCLXX.

To

The Right Honourable The Earl of Scarborough,

This Volume

Is,

By his Lordship's permission,

Dedicated

By one of the many thousands who would

Gratefully acknowledge the kindness which permits them

to visit and enjoy

The Picturesque Beauties of the Valley

and

Ruins of Roche.

THE PREFACE

"THE art of phyfic, which I have profeffed (with competent fuccefs) in this county, not being able for any long time to continue the people living in it, I have charitably attempted, notwithftanding the difficulty and almoft the contrariety of the ftudy, to practice upon the dead, intending thereby to keep all which is, or can be, left of them, to wit, the fhadow of their names, (better than precious ointment for the body,) to preferve their memory, as long as may be, in the world, though for this latter undertaking I expect no more glory than I have gotten riches by the former," thus wrote *Dr. Thoroton*, in the preface to his "Hiftory of Nottinghamfhire." Almoft the fame words are repeated by *Dr. Burton*, in the preface to his "Monafticon Eboracenfe," And now for the third time they appear in this preface, becaufe they exactly exprefs the feelings of the Author.

As far as he is concerned, the prefent "undertaking" is purely a work of love, at the fame time he has fpared no expenfe in collecting materials and no time in endeavouring to place them before the public in an acceptable form. His aim has been to make the volume intelligible to the general reader, and with that view all charters have been tranflated and foot-notes have been appended where obfcurity feemed to exift. The Author, however, cannot think his work anything like perfect; ftill he has the fatisfaction of knowing that feveral documents have been refcued from oblivion which were faft becoming unreadable from extreme age, and that fome points of doubt with regard to the hiftory of the Monks and their Abbey which have hitherto exifted, have been finally fettled.

In thanking his numerous friends for their kind affiftance the Author is met at once by the melancholy fact that during the time this Volume has been going through the prefs, two from whom he received a large fhare of help, are no more. To that good and learned man, the Rev. J. Eaftwood, M.A., he was efpecially indebted for many ufeful fuggeftions and for carefully correcting all the tranflations; and to Mr. W. M. Campfall he muft always feel thankful for the fervice he rendered in preparing many architectural drawings. To the Earl of Scarborough, the Author is greatly obliged for his kindnefs in allowing excavations to be made, to determine the ground plan of the Abbey, and to Mr. G. Naylor Vickers he is indebted for affiftance in carrying them out. He would alfo wifh to exprefs his deep fenfe of obligation to the Rev. John Stacye for his invaluable aid, and to Mr. Theophilus Smith, to Mr. W. Swift, Mr. J. Bohler, The Rev. J. T. Jeffcock, F.S.A., Dr. Sykes, and Mr. C. Jackfon for the kind affiftance they have each rendered.

Contents.

List of Subscribers - - - - - -	viii
Reference to Plates - - - - - -	xii
Introduction - - - - - - -	xv
The Abbots - - - - - - -	1
The Possessions - - - - - - -	97
The Architecture, Monastic Buildings, and their Remains	161
Addenda - - - - - - -	179
The Flora of Roche - - - - - -	181
Index - - - - - - - -	189

List of Subscribers.

His Grace The Duke of Norfolk, E.M.
His Grace The Duke of Devonshire, K.G., L.L.D.
His Grace The Duke of Newcastle.
The Right Honourable The Earl of Scarborough.
The Right Honourable The Earl de Grey and Ripon, K.G.
The Right Honourable The Earl of Effingham.
The Right Honourable Lord Wharncliffe.
The Right Honourable Lord Foley.
The Right Honourable Lord Halifax.

Abbot, G. L.	Sheffield.
Aldam, W.	Frickley Hall, Doncaster.
Anderson, Sir C. H. I, Bart.	Lea, Gainsborough.
Appleton, Rev. J., M.A.	Worksop.
Aveling, Stephen T.	Lessnes Heath, S.E.
Aveling, Thomas	Rochester.
Aveling, Miss	Needham Hall, Wisbeach.
Baines, William L.	Bawtry.
Barber, Fairless	Castle Hill, Rastrick.
Baxter, Dudley R.	Doncaster.
Bent, Rev. G.	Worksop.
Bentley, Robert J.	Finningley Park, Bawtry.
Binney, J.	Sheffield.
Bower, E. C.	Wadworth Hall, Doncasrer.
Bragg, William, F.R.G.S.	Shirle Hill, Sheffield.
Brereton, Charles	Beverley.
Brodhurst, G.	London.
Broomhead, Barnard P.	Sheffield.
Broomhead, John	Blyth.
Broughton, John	Peterborough.
Brown, Sir John	Endcliffe Hall, Sheffield.
Brown, John	Misson.
Catling, Mrs. Robert	Needham Hall, Wisbeach.
Chaloner, Edward	Hermeston Grange, Worksop.
Chrimes, Richard	Moorgate Grove, Rotherham.
Close, Thomas	Nottingham.
Cocking, Charles C.	Wath-upon-Dearne.
Coney, John	Awkley, Doncaster.
Corbitt, William	Rotherham.
Coulson, Mrs.	Bellaport Hall, Market Drayton
Coupland, J. M.	Tinsley.

LIST OF SUBSCRIBERS.

Dawson, George	Thorncliffe.
Depledge, John	Thorncliffe.
Drabble, James	Carlton.
Drury, Robert	Sheffield.
Dunn, Miss	Bideford.
Dunhill, John	Cliftonville, Brighton.
Ellenberger, Dr.	Worksop.
Emsley, Samuel	Sheffield.
Frith, John	Sheffield.
Flockton, Thos. J.	Sheffield.
Foljambe, F. J. Savile	Osberton.
Forrest, Charles	Lofthouse, Wakefield.
Fowler, William	Whittington Hall, Derbyshire.
Free Library	Sheffield.
Gardner, Samuel	Archer House, Abbeydale, Sheffield.
Gatty, Rev. Alfred, D.D.	Ecclesfield.
Guest, John	Moorgate Grange, Rotherham.
Habershon, Matthew Henry	London.
Hadfield, M. E., F.I.B.A.	Sheffield.
Hailstone, Edward, F.S.A.	Horton Hall, Bradford.
Hatfield, George	The Hermitage, Doncaster.
Haywood, George	Moorgate, Rotherham.
Hogg, John	Doncaster.
Holmes, H. T.	The Laurels, Shortlands.
Holmes, George	Harthill.
Horncastle, John	Edwinstowe.
Hotten, John Camden	London.
Hoyle, F. W., F.G.H.S.	Eastwood Lodge, Rotherham.
Hoyle, W. Dickon	London.
Hoyle, W. P.	Ferham House, Rotherham.
Hubbard, Edward Isle	Rotherham.
Hugo, Rev. Thomas, M.A., F.R.S.L., F.S.A.	West Hackney, Stoke Newington.
Huntsman, Benjamin	West Retford Hall.
Ingleby, William	Sheffield.
Jackson, Charles	Doncaster.
Jackson, Rowland	Leeds.
Jackson, Samuel	Attercliffe.
Jeffcock, John	Cowley Manor, Sheffield.
Jeffcock, John T.	Cowley Manor, Sheffield.
Jenkinson, William	Sheffield.
Jewitt, Lewellyn L., F.S.A.	Winster Hall, Matlock.
Jubb, James Shemeld	Morthen Hall.
Latimer, William	Anston.
Lawton, Miss M.	Sheffield.
Laycock, R.	Wiseton, Bawtry.
Leader, J. D.	Sheffield.

Lincoln Diocesan Architectural Society	Lincoln.
Linley, Robert	Netherholme, Worksop.
Livesey, Rev. J.	Sheffield.
Longden, Henry	Sheffield.
Lowther, Sir Charles, Bart.	Swillington House, Leeds.
Makin, W.	Attercliffe.
Marrian, Thomas	Sharrow Grange, Sheffield.
Massey, Henry	Worksop.
Metcalf, A.	Retford.
Miles, Mrs.	Firbeck Hall.
Milner, Henry B. W.	West Retford House.
Moore, Rev. Edward, F.S.A.	Spalding.
Moore, Thomas	Sheffield.
Morris, Richard M.	Worksop.
Munk, W., M.D.	London.
Natorp, Gustavus	New York.
Newton, Thomas	Chapeltown.
Newton, W.	East Retford.
Nicholson, G. P.	Wath-upon-Dearne.
Padley, James Sandby	Lincoln.
Parker, Thomas W.	Rotherham.
Peacock, Edward, F.S.A.	Bottesford Manor, Brigg.
Pearson, Thomas J.	Worksop.
Peech, John	Wentworth.
Peel Park Library	Manchester.
Perrot, Eugene H.	Rotherham.
Plant, Edwin	West Retford.
Ramsden, Robert J.	Carlton Hall.
Rawlinson, Robert, C.B., C.E., F.G.S.	London.
Reed, Mrs.	Elm.
Roberts, Samuel	Queen's Tower, Sheffield.
Robinson, Mrs.	Rotherham.
Rodgers, Jeremiah	Doncaster.
Rodgers, Thomas	Sheffield.
Rolleston, George, M.D. F.R.S.	Oxford.
Rotherham Library	Rotherham.
Rotherham, Mrs. A.	Throapham.
Rotherham, Mr. Alexander, Jun.	Throapham.
Sales, J.	Rotherham.
Sanderson, George	Manchester.
Science and Art Department	South Kensington.
Sheffield Library	Sheffield.
Sheardown, J. B.	Doncaster.
Shillitto, F. W.	Rotherham.
Shortridge, William	Chipping House, Heeley.
Shuttleworth, J. J.	Bath.
Sisk, Rev. T. Ignatius	St. Bernard's Abbey, Leicestershire
Siddall, Joseph	Wath-upon-Dearne.
Smith, R. Moffatt,	Manchester.
Smith, Theophilus	Sheffield.

LIST OF SUBSCRIBERS.

Smith, John Russell	London.
Spurr, H. A.	Blackburn.
Stacye, Rev. John	Sheffield.
Stevenson, W. H.	London.
Swift, William	Sheffield.
Sykes, Dr.	Doncaster.
Tasker, Rev. C. W.	Glossop.
Teulon, W. M.	London.
Tipping, Rev. Vernon	Lawton.
Thompson, Lady Mary	Sheriff Hutton Park, York.
Trollope, The Rev. Archdeacon, F.S.A.	Leasingham.
Tylden-Wright, F.G.S.	Woodlands, Worksop.
Vickers, Edward	Brighton.
Vickers, G. Naylor	St. Petersburgh.
Vickers, Henry	Holmwood, Ecclesall.
Vickers, T. Edward	Bolsover Hill, Sheffield.
Wake, Bernard	Sheffield.
Wake, William	Sheffield.
Walker, Thomas	Woodlands, Doncaster.
Ward, A. J.	Sheffield.
Wardell, James	Leeds.
Watson, Henry E.	Park Cottage, Worksop.
Webster, Henry	Sheffield.
Weightman, J. G.	Collingham.
Weldon, John	London.
Weldon, Walter	London.
Wentworth, Godfrey	Woolley Park, Wakefield.
Whall, John	Worksop.
Wilcockson, W. H.	Nottingham.
Willoughby, The Hon. and Rev. C. J.	Wollaton.
Winn, C.	Nostel Priory, Wakefield.
Wise, John R.	Edwinstowe.
Wood, John	Sheffield.
Yates, James	Oakwood Hall, Rotherham.

Reference to the Plates.

FRONTISPIECE.—General View of Ruins from south-west.

PLATE   I.—Plan of Abbey Grounds, shewing old boundary wall.

       II.—Ground Plan of Abbey Church (restored), the dark portions indicate the present remains.

       III.—Elevation of interior of North Transept (east wall), with plan of Piers.

       IV.—Perspective details of Capitals, &c.,
- Fig. 1. Centre Pier in east wall of north transept, from north-east.
- „ 2. Side of south-east Tower Pier from south transept chapel.
- „ 3 and 4. Cap and Base from north window in chancel.
- „ 5. Cap from south window in chancel.
- „ 6. Corbel Pillar supporting the groined roof of chancel (north side).
- „ 7. Ditto ditto (south side).

       V.—Fig. 1. Enlarged Plan of Tower and Nave Piers.
- „ 2. Enlarged Plan of Piers to north transept chapels.
- „ 3. Section of Capital of transept Pier.
- „ 4. Section of Base to ditto.
- „ 5. Section of Arch Moulding to same.
- „ 6. Section of Groined Moulding in aisles (transverse).

       VI.—Fig. 1. Plan of Pier (displaced).
- „ 2. Section of Tower Arch Moulding.
- „ 3. Ditto of String inside chapter house.
- „ 4. Plan of West Door Jamb (clear opening of door, 5ft.5in.).
- „ 5. Section of Moulding, now in possession of Mr. Crossley, of Maltby.
- „ 6. Section of Mouldings to Jamb of Doorway into chapter house.
- „ 7. Section of String of chapter house (exterior).
- „ 8. Section of Base Mould of chapter house (exterior).

REFERENCE TO THE PLATES.

PLATE VI.—Fig. 9. Section of String (triforium).
- „ 10. Section of Parapet (chancel).
- „ 11. Section of Label.
- „ 12. Section of String (clerestory).
- „ 13. Section of Groin Moulding (transept, &c.).
- „ 14. Section of Groin Moulding (diagonal).
- „ 15. Section of Groin Moulding (early decorated), found in Chapter House.
- „ 16. Section of String (interior).
- „ 17. Section of Base Moulding.
- „ 18—22, Sections of Bases to Window Shafts, &c.
- „ 23. Section of Base to west Door Jamb.
- „ 24. Section of Capital.
- „ 25 and 26. Sections of Window Shafts.

VII.—Fig. 1. Section of Arch Mould (transitional), found near chapter house.
- „ 2. Section of Cap and Base to Shafts (decorated).
- „ 3. Elevation Section of Corbel, next entrance from Abbey Buildings to south transept.
- „ 4. Section of Piscina Mould.
- „ 5. Section of Window Jamb Moulding (transitional).
- „ 6. Section of Angle Shaft.
- „ 7—9. Sections of Window Jamb Mouldings in south chapel (decorated).
- „ 10. Section of Arch Moulding (decorated).
- „ 11. Plan of Window in south Transept chapel (decorated).
- „ 12. Elevation of Window in ditto (restored).

VIII.—Fig. 1. Present condition of Easter Sepulchre (?) in north wall of chancel.
- „ 2. Piscina in south wall of north transept chapel.

IX.—Various ancient incised Masons' Marks found on Roche Abbey.

X.—Fig. 1. Secretum of Roche Abbey.
- „ 2. Matrix of the same.
- „ 3. First common Seal of Roche Abbey.
- „ 4. Last ditto, attached to the Surrender Deed.

XI.—Fig. 1. Fragment of Capitals of West Door Jamb, found near the quarries, together with portion of String.
- „ 2. Cap and Base (perpendicular).
- „ 3—6. Various Fragments (transitional).

XII.—Fig. 1—5. Fragmentary portions of the Easter Sepulchre, (?) &c., (decorated), discovered in excavating below it.
,, 6. Ancient Copper Key found in ruins (Weight, 2¾oz).

XIII.—View of Abbey Gatehouse, from south-east.

XIV.—Plan of Abbey Gatehouse.

XV.—Fig. 1. Plan of Jamb Mouldings of Gatehouse.
,, 2. Section of Arch Moulding of Gatehouse.
,, 3 and 4. Sections of Base Mouldings of Gatehouse.
,, 5. Section of Groin Moulding (transverse).
,, 6. Section of Groin Moulding (diagonal).
,, 7—9. Capitals.
,, 10 and 11. Corbels.

PLATE II.

ROCHE ABBEY.

GROUND PLAN OF ABBEY CHURCH, RESTORED.
THE DARK PORTIONS INDICATE THE PRESENT REMAINS.

SCALE OF FEET.

ROCHE ABBEY   PLATE IV.

Roche Abbey

Plate VI

ROCHE ABBEY   PLATE VII.

ROCHE ABBEY   PLATE VIII

ROCHE ABBEY　　　　　　　　　　　　　PLATE IX

ROCHE ABBEY. PLATE XI

FIG 1.

FIG 2.

FIG 3.

FIG 5.

FIG 4.

FIG 6.

Roche Abbey

Plate XIII

ROCHE ABBEY. PLATE XIV.

PLAN OF ABBEY GATEWAY.

SCALE OF FEET

The Introduction.

THE INTRODUCTION
ROCHE ABBEY.

IN the beginning of the twelfth century, after the Crusaders had taken Jerusalem and had completed the massacre of its inhabitants, after they had fallen down, their swords still streaming with the blood of women and children, before the holy sepulchre, weeping in the ecstasy of their devotion; and after Robert, Duke of Normandy had lost his crown by loitering upon the road, to espouse Sibylla, the daughter of an Italian Count: Henry I. foreseeing that his usurped crown would sit uneasily, endeavoured, by a charter which he then passed, to gain the confidence and love of his subjects.

He, in this charter first makes great concessions to the church, promising "that at the death of any Bishop or Abbot he never would seize the revenues of the See or Abbey during the vacancy, but would leave the whole to be reaped by the successor; and that he would never let to farm any ecclesiastical benefice, nor dispose of it for money." The King had also another object in conciliating the favours of the clergy and especially of Anslem who, from his zeal and piety of character, had obtained great authority in the kingdom. Henry proposed to marry Matilda, daughter of Malcolm III. King of Scotland, and niece to Edgar Atheling, but as that princess had been brought up in the nunnery of Rumsey, the legitimacy of the act became a matter of doubt and the religious prejudices of his subjects had to be overcome; which difficult task the church alone could perform.

The concessions contained in this charter, and other things tending to give confidence to the clergy, caused religious houses to spring up so fast, that during the thirty-five years in which Henry reigned no less than one hundred and fifty were established. Five new orders also came into England during this reign, and one of these was the Cistercian, to which order the monks of Roche Abbey belonged.

Of all the orders which sprung from the Benedictines, the Cistercian was the most popular. Their first monastery was at Cisteaux—now Gilley-les-Citeaux—about twelve leagues to the north of Chalons-sur-Saone. To this place Robert, Abbot of Molesme, having obtained the Pope's sanction, retired together with twenty-one of his brethren. Cisteaux at that time, 1098, was a dense and tangled wilderness, inhabited only by wild beasts, but Robert de Molesme disgusted with the laxity of those he had left, was determined, most effectually, to separate himself from the world. The more wild and uninviting the place, therefore the more tempting was it to this ascetic Abbot. He immediately commenced cutting away the thorns and crowded trees, and under the protection of Otho, Duke of Burgundy, and the Bishop of Chalons, soon laid the foundation stone of the first Cistercian Abbey.

The first Abbey of this order in England seems to have been at Waverley, in Surrey, founded about the year 1128, thirty years after Robert de Molesme's entrance into the wilderness of Cisteaux. *Mr. Rastal*, however, in his Chronicles says that "the order of Cysteaux was first brought into England by Walter Espeke, who founded the first Abbey of that religion at Ryvall." Although this abbey may not have been the first in England, it was, doubtless, the first in Yorkshire.

The rules of the Cistercian order were very strict, but did not last so long. Their houses were to be built in solitary places, and to be dedicated to the Holy Virgin. All secular affairs were to be placed in the hands of lay-brothers. Their revenues were to be divided into four parts—to the bishop a fourth; to the priests a fourth; to the exercise of hospitality a fourth, and a fourth for widows and orphans, the sick, and repairs of the church and cloisters. They were not to possess any churches, altars, ovens, mills, towns, or serfs. They were not to permit any women to enter their Abbeys or any dead to be buried there. They were to wear no leather, linen, nor fine woollen cloth, neither were they, except on a journey, to put on any breeches, taking heed to deliver them up, fair washed, upon their return. They were to have two coats with cowls, which they might lessen but not augment, and in which habit they were to sleep. They were to observe strict silence, save to their Abbot or Prior; to "devise extraordinary afflictions for their own bodies, to the intent their souls may be advantaged;" to fast, to prostrate themselves before visitors, and to wash their feet.*

The Cistercians were sometimes called "White Monks" owing to the colour of their habit, which consisted of a white cassock with a narrow scapulary. According to a legend of this order this colour was assumed at the wish of the Virgin Mary, intimated in a vision to St. Bernard. When they were at work or abroad a black gown fastened about the waist with a black girdle of wool was worn over the white to protect it from dirt. They also wore a cowl and a hood of black. The lay-brothers and novices were always clad in a dark colour.

---

* Peter, of the Grandimont order, wore upon his naked body a coat of mail; his bed was made of a hard board, having neither straw nor coverlet; "with often kneeling, kissing of the ground, and beating it with his forehead and nose, he rendered his knees and hands hard like a *callus*, or horn, and his nose crooked."

The Cistercians performed their devotions seven times in the twenty-four hours, as follows:

    Nocturnal . . . . . at 2 a.m.
    Prime . . . . at 6 a.m.
    Tierce . . . . at 9 a.m.
    Sexte . . . . at noon.
    None . . . . at 3 p.m.
    Vespers . . . . . . at 6 p.m.
    Compline . . . . . . at 7 p.m.

The vestments, utensils, and ornaments of the church were ordered to be very plain. The crosses were to be of painted wood uncarved, and the candlesticks of iron. Pictures and painted glass were not to be allowed.

From the following history the reader will learn that this humility and self-denial did not last long. Wealth, even when it entered the walls of a monastery could not leave luxury without; nor could the monk exercise the power which the ignorance and superstition of the people allowed him without pride. Not many years had elapsed from the institution of the order, before the Cistercian Abbot might have said with the Benedictine, "my vow of poverty has given me 100,000 crowns a year, my vow of obedience has raised me to the rank of a sovereign prince."

When the bold usurper, Stephen, obtained his throne the power of the church had become so great that the mitre might be said to rule the crown, and it is doubtful whether that monarch would have so easily received from the prelate the rite of royal unction and consecration, had it not been for the interest and assistance which he obtained through his brother Henry, who was at that time Bishop of Winchester.

Stephen, like his predecessor, well knowing the importance of securing the good-will of the clergy, lost no time in passing a charter in which he made most liberal promises to the church; and hoping still further to steady his tottering crown, pleased the Pope by desiring him to ratify, by a bull, his groundless title.

Religious houses, during the reign of Stephen, continued to be established, notwithstanding the misery and confusion in which the kingdom was involved, even with greater rapidity than in the time of Henry. "Emperors and Empresses, Kings and Queens, Dukes and Duchesses, exchanged the sceptre and the ducal coronet for the crosier, deserted their thrones and honours in order to assume the titles of ecclesiastics and to wear their habits, and instead of labouring to conquer the world, forsook it, and thereby gained a greater victory—a victory over themselves."

During the short space of eighteen years and nine months which Stephen reigned, no less than one hundred religious houses were founded. At this period the Cistercians gained the summit of their popularity, no fewer than thirty-two abbeys of that order having been added to the thirteen already existing. Among the thirty-two Cistercian Abbeys founded in the reign of Stephen, was one vieing with others in magnificence and interest, the Abbey of Sancta Maria de Rupe, or Roche Abbey.

The Abbey of Roche was situated near the south-eastern extremity of the county of York, within a short distance from the boundary of Nottinghamshire: its site being about nine miles from the towns of Doncaster and Worksop, somewhat less from that of Rotherham, and still nearer to the once celebrated castles of Tickhill and Conisbrough.

It seems desirable for a more distinct understanding of the following history of the place, that a slight sketch should be premised of the general history of the adjoining district and its early lords, some of whom were among the founders and principal benefactors of Roche Abbey.

Previously to the Norman Conquest the lands in this neighbourhood were held by a variety of proprietors, of whom the chief were Earls Harold and Edwin, respectively Lords of Conisborough and Laughton. Shortly, however, after that great event, almost the whole of the manors about here became the prey of three great companions in arms and also family allies of the Conqueror, these were Roger de Busli, Robert, Earl of Morton, and William de Warren— of these Roger de Busli held the largest share, if we include his manors in the county of Nottingham, where he was lord of not less than 170 estates, and also many in the county of York. The head of his fee was, at first, placed at Blyth, in Nottinghamshire, but afterwards removed to Tickhill where he commenced the erection of a castle, on a site which had formerly been occupied as a Brigantian stronghold. The castle of De Busli soon rose to such importance as to give a new name, that of Tickhill, *i.e.* The Wick Hill or Castle Hill, to the vill, to which it was adjacent, which had previously been called Dadesley, under which designation it appears in the Domesday survey. It is a remarkable fact, however, and one worthy of observation, that this castle, which conferred a name on the town with which it was connected, and on the Honour of which it formed the head: in the earliest documents in which it is mentioned, is called the castle of *Blythe*, that is, no doubt, the castle of the *honour*, not of the vill of Blythe. This latter place, Roger de Busli had given as endowment for a Priory of Benedictine Monks, which he founded there in A.D. 1088. He died in A.D. 1099 leaving a son of the same name, who did not long survive him, and died without offspring. After the death of the latter, the extensive fee which they had enjoyed was, for some time, either in the hands of the crown, or of persons to whom it was temporarily assigned by the sovereign, till it was restored to a descendant of the house of De Busli in the person of Alicia, Countess of Augi or Eu, who held it in the reign of Henry III, and whom we shall hereafter meet with in our history. This great lady derived her pedigree from Beatrix, the sister of Roger de Busli, and although she did not appear to have had so good a title to the honour as the representatives of the male branch of the family, who derived their origin from Ernaldus a brother of Roger, who disputed it with her, yet she contrived to maintain her position, chiefly it would seem by royal favour, until, according to *Dugdale*, she forfeited it about 37th Henry III.[*]

Among the numerous manors which Roger de Busli held hereabouts, Maltby, in which the Abbey of Roche was mainly seated, formed a not unimportant one. Previously to the Norman Conquest, it had been the property of one Elsi, but at the time of the great survey it was held, in part, in demesne by Roger himself, and the rest was cultivated by his villeins and borderers. Shortly, however, after that date, it appears that Roger subinfeuded his brother Ernaldus here, as also at Kimberworth and other places, where his family held, on the whole, as much as six knight's fees. At Kimberworth the descendants of Ernaldus had long a mansion and a park; they possessed also Sandbeck, immediately adjoining our Abbey, with which valuable estate we shall find one of his race, the great heiress of the house, Idonea, the widow of Robert de Vipont endowing the brotherhood of Roche. Richard de Busli, the co-founder of the Abbey, was the grandson of Ernaldus. He was not only liberal to this house, but also a benefactor to a kindred establishment, that of Kirkstead, in Lincolnshire, the monks of which had already gained a footing on the confines of his estate at Kimberworth, where they had a small establishment and some property, at the place afterwards called Thundercliffe Grange. To these brethren, about the year 1160, he granted sufficient land for the erection of four ironworks, two for smelting the ore and two for forming it into bars, together with liberty to dig for ore in any part of his Kimberworth manor: they were also to have liberty to pasture their horses and cattle there, and to collect dry wood. There is little doubt, that the building erected by the monks at that time, as a stable for their beasts, and residence for their forgemen exists, little altered, at the present day. It stands, in a very elevated situation, adjoining the road from Rotherham to Wortley, within a short distance of the "Keppel Column," and is well worthy of observation, as a very ancient and curious structure. Maltby, and the other estates of this branch of the De Busli family, continued in the hands of persons of that name till the reign of King John, when they passed by the marriage of Idonea, the heiress of the house, with Robert de Viteri Ponte or Vipont, into this latter name. Here they continued for three generations, till they again passed by the marriage of two co-heiresses, Isabel and Idonea, into other families; the former, being the elder sister, having in 52nd Henry III married Roger son and heir of Roger Lord Clifford; the younger, 1st Roger de Leyburn, and 2ndly John de Crumbewell, who had in her right the manor of Kimberworth. She died without issue, and it would

---

[*] Rot. Fin. 37th Henry III., Baronage, vol. i., p. 137.

appear before her death had conveyed the manor of Maltby to her nephew, Robert de Clifford, and in this great family the manor was vested, with slight intermissions, till the reign of Queen Elizabeth, when it was sold in 1587 by George the 3rd, Earl of Cumberland, of that race, to Sir Edward Stanhope, whose son again sold it to Sir Nicholas Saunderson, from whom it has descended to its present noble owner, the Earl of Scarborough. The family connexions of the De Busli race will perhaps be more clearly understood from the following pedigree derived from *Thoroton's* "History of Nottinghamshire."

Another great lord of the soil in this neighbourhood at the time of the Domesday survey, as we have already intimated, was Robert, Earl of Morton, the half-brother of William the Conqueror. He held a vast number of manors in Yorkshire, the greater part of which were apportioned to two subinfeudatories, Richard de Surdeval and Nigel de Fossard. Some few, however, he retained in his own hands, and of these was the one with which we are now principally concerned, that of Hooton, afterwards distinguished from several others of the name, within a short distance, by the addition of Levet, from the name of the family which subsequently possessed it. This small manor detached from his other estates, and surrounded by those of Roger de Busli, had strangely escaped the rapacious maw of that great leviathan of manors hereabouts. It was held in demesne by Earl Robert, and cultivated by his villeins and

---

[a] Excerpta 6 Rot. Fin. Henry III. vol. i. p p. 357, 371.
[b] ,, ,, vol. ii. p. 410.

borderers, but it did not long continue in his possessions, for it was soon forfeited together with all his other English estates, and appears then to have become vested in the family of Fossard, who thus were elevated to the position of chief tenants. They did not, however, occupy the land themselves, but subinfeuded the house of Vesci, Lords of Rotherham, and these again invested with the actual possession of the soil, a family named Fitz-Turgis. The first person of this race of whom we find mention is Richard Fitz-Turgis, also named De Wickersley, from his having become possessed of the manor of that place, which he held of the Lords of Bentley, the Newmarches, and they again of the castle of Tickhill. It was this Richard, who was so happily joined in the bonds of christian brotherhood, but too rare in such cases, with his neighbour De Busli, Lord of Maltby, whose estate there was separated from his own, only by a small brook, as heartily to co-operate with him, in the foundation of the Abbey of Roche. He was succeeded in the estate by a son, who was also a benefactor to the house, and the latter by a daughter named Constantia his sole heiress, who carried the property into the family of De Levet by her marriage with William de Levet. With the Levets the manor continued till the time of Henry V. about which period they disappear. It then seems to have become the property of the Cliffords, and is mentioned among the places of which Thomas, Lord Clifford died seised in 1454. From that time its descent, it is believed, has been the same with Maltby, to the Earl of Scarborough.*

The other principal fee in this neighbourhood whose lords were special benefactors of Roche, was that of Conisborough. This manor with its numerous dependencies, as already intimated, had before the Conquest been the property of Earl Harold, afterwards King of England, but after that event became the portion of William de Warren, who married Gunnora, the daughter or rather daughter-in-law of the Conqueror. The lands of his Yorkshire fee lay not only at Conisborough and in various townships extending to the extreme confines of the county southward, but also beyond Doncaster, where Hatfield and a large surrounding district was dependent upon it: there being, however, an extensive tract of country intervening which was not in Warren's possession. And it was, as we shall see, at Hatfield and its neighbourhood that the Abbey of Roche was specially benefited by that great family. The manor of Conisborough remained in the family of Warren till the time of Edward III, when their possessions came into the hands of the crown. It was settled on the Princes of the house of York, and became the property of Edmund of Langley a younger son of the King. At the castle here it would appear that he sometimes resided, and here his second son Richard, who enjoyed the title of Earl of Cambridge, was born. This Prince married, as his second wife, Maud a daughter of Thomas, Lord Clifford, who as we shall find in our subsequent history, made

* Hunter's "South Yorkshire," vol. i. p. 265.

her will at Roche Abbey, in which she directed that her body should be buried there.

It appears unnecessary to pursue this general history any further, so much, however, it seemed desirable to premise, in order to enable the reader more intelligently to peruse the following history.

This history will be found digested under the three following principal heads.

    I.—The Abbots.
    II.—The Possessions.
    III.—The Architecture, Monastic Buildings, and their Remains.

And under these heads, it is trusted, that a full and accurate account will be furnished respecting the venerable and interesting Abbey of Roche.

The Abbots.

List of the Abbots of Roche Abbey.

1. Durandus 1147
2. Dionysius 1159
3. Roger de Tickhill 1171
4. Hugh de Wadworth . . . 1179
5. Osmund 1184
6. Reginald 1223
7. Richard 1238
8. Walter 1254
9. Alan 1268
10. Jordan . . . . . ∗∗∗
11. Philip . . . . . ∗∗∗
12. Thomas 1286
13. Stephen 1287
14. John 1300
15. Robert 1300
16. William 1324
17. Adam de Gykellswyk . . 1330
18. Simon de Baukewell . . 1349
19. John de Aston 1358
20. Robert 1396
21. John Wakefield . . . 1438
22. John Gray 1465
23. William Tikil 1479
24. Thomas Thurne . . . 1486
25. William Burton . . . 1488
26. John Morpeth 1491
27. John Hessington . . . 1503
28. Henry Cundal, surrendered in . 1538

THE ABBOTS.

Durandus.

1147—1159.

URANDUS, bearing in his hand a cross of wood, and followed by twelve monks,* in imitation of Christ and his twelve Apostles, might have been seen, in the middle of the twelfth century, wandering about a desolate and trackless forest—which, at that time, covered the South of Yorkshire—in search of unappropriated land in a retired situation, where he might lead a holy life, and by labour win from the earth the little sustenance which his abstemious habits demanded. With much "Travail and hungre, thurste, and colde," he might have been seen to enter a nameless valley, whose tangled slopes were sheltered from the inclemency of the North by a range of lofty gray and venerable looking rocks. And as the good Durandus entered, we still may picture the flash of joy which crossed his weary countenance when he became convinced, from its wildness and extreme solitude, that the long-sought resting place had been found. And as he stood elated at the fitness and beauty of the spot, imagination still may show us the monks approaching, one, with tidings of a spring, surpassing in purity any he had before met with; and another, with awed and eager step, relating that, wandering near, he has found hewn out upon a rock, by God's own hand, an image of our Saviour on a Cross! And may we not still in our

* "For thretteene is a convent as I gesse."—Chaucer.

minds fee Durandus and his twelve bowed down before that myftic rock in filent thankfulnefs and deep devotion?

This valley, fo peaceful and retired, and contrafting fo ftrongly with the turmoil and buftle of the world, and the horrors of civil war (at that time being carried on between Stephen and Matilda,) is fituated in the parifh of Maltby, and the ftream which paffes through it formed the boundary line between the lands of Richard de Bufli, and Richard Fitz Turgis, lords of Maltby and Hooton. In this valley—this lonely and beautiful wildernefs—Durandus and his followers fettled down under the title of "Monachi de Rupe," or 'Monks of the Rock,' living for a time in rude huts under trees, and depending partly upon their own exertions and partly on the charity of others for their fupport. How long the community remained in this condition is not known, but it is not probable that their privations lafted long, for in thofe days the endowment of a religious houfe was looked upon as a high privilege, and lords of the foil loft no time, when an opportunity prefented itfelf of doing that which they believed would both immortalize their names and fave their fouls!

Upon the 30th day of July,[a] in the year of grace 1147, the Houfe of Roche was founded by Richard de Bufli and Richard Fitz Turgis. The following are tranflations of the foundation charters:—

Charter of Richard de Bufli,[b] concerning the Foundation of the Abbey of Roche.

"BE it known to all who fee or hear thefe letters that I, Richard de Bufli, with confent of my wife and heirs, have given to God and St. Mary, and to the Monks of the Rock, for the falvation of my foul, and the fouls of all my anceftors, the whole wood from the middle of the road from Eilrichethorpe to Lowthwaite, and fo far as the water which is the boundary between Maltby and Hooton, and the two farts[c] which belong to Gamul, with a great culture which is there adjacent and common of pafture for a hundred fheep, in number fix fcore, in the foke[d] of Maltby, by this tenure, that they build their Abbey on whichfoever

---

[a] Mr. Hunter makes this date "June," but he is evidently in error, for the paffage in the "Succeffio Abbatum," "tertio kalendas Augufti," can mean nothing elfe than the third day from the kalends of Auguft.—"South Yorkfhire, vol. i. p. 269."

[b] Richard de Bufli was grandfon of Arnaldus, who was brother to Roger de Bufli, an eminent Aorman, who followed the Conqueror, and obtained great poffeffions.

[c] A piece of wood land turned into arable.   [d] Territory.

side of the water they pleafe, according as the fituation of the place fhall be more fuitable, Richard de Bufli and Richard Fitz Turgis agreeing between themfelves that both fhould be the founders of the Abbey, on whichfoever's property the Abbey may be built, as a perpetual charity, free and quiet from all fecular fervice or gift. Before thefe witneffes, Adam de Newmarch, Hugh de Stainton, Odo Filius Johannis, Willielmus Filius Raveni, Jordan Painel, Gamel Filius Befingi, Hugh de Langthwaite, Robert de Scalzebi, William le Buteiler, William de Mileri, Robertus, Filius, junior, Richard Barbot, Gervafe de Barneby, Swein, fon of Tor and Jordan, his fon."

The Charter of Richard Fitz Turgis, respecting the Foundation of the Abbey of Roche.

"BE it known to all who fee and hear this Charter, that I, Richard Fitz Turgis, with the confent of my wife and heirs, have given to God, St. Mary, and the Monks of the Rock, for the falvation of my foul, and the fouls of my anceftors, the whole land from the borders of Eilrichethorpe, as far as the brow of the hill beyond the ftream which runs from Fogfwell, and fo to a heap of ftones which lies in the fart of Elfi, and fo beyond the road as far as the Wolfpit, and fo by the head of the culture of Hartfhow to the borders of Slade Hooton; all that land, and all that wood below thefe bounds and common of pafture of all my land, and fifty cart loads every year in my wood of Wickerfley, where I fhall provide, or fome one on my behoof, for a perpetual charity, free and quiet from all fecular fervice, on this condition—that they build an Abbey on whichever fide of the water they pleafe, according as the fituation of the place fhall appear beft, Richard Fitz Turgis and Richard de Bufli agreeing between themfelves, and conceding that both be founders of the Abbey, on whofefoever fide of the water it may happen to be. Before thefe witneffes, Adam de Newmarch, Hugh de Stainton, Odo Filius Johannis, Willielmus Filius Raveni, Jordan Painel."

In thefe fancy-bazaar and begging-letter days it is difficult to enter into the feelings of two men, who, in the twelfth century, were fo much in earneft, and fo full of faith, that they could without hefitation give up fo large a portion of their poffeffions for the purpofe of building and endowing a monaftery, wherein a few strolling monks, who had chosen to settle upon the borders of their estate, might live and worship God after their own fashion. Two great inducements for such a sacrifice are, however, prominently mentioned in both charters. The first is—"the salvation of their souls and those of all their ancestors" (no small boon!); and the second is, the honour of being founders. The whole of their lands and woods were given to God, St. Mary, and the Monks of the Rock, "on this *condition*, that both be founders."

The building of the Abbey, doubtless, commenced at once, as both wood and good building stone were to be procured on the spot in abundance, no delay would be occasioned in collecting materials. Durandus would, therefore, have the pleasure of seeing the first stone of his Abbey laid, and of dedicating it, as was the Cistercian custom, to the Blessed Virgin Mary. At the laying of the foundation of Croyland Abbey, which took place a few years earlier, the pious Abbot Toffred began by saying prayers, and shedding a flood of tears. Then those who had come to assist in the ceremony each laid a stone, and upon it deposited a sum of money, a grant of lands, tithes, or patronages, or a promise of stone, lime, wood, labour, or carriage, to assist in building. Richard de Busli and Richard Fitz Turgis most likely followed the liberal custom of the stone-layers at Croyland, and Robert de Scalzebi and Adam de Newmarch probably followed their good example, they having been two of the earliest benefactors of the house, and, as the reader may have noticed, two of the witnesses to the foundation charters.

It has been a subject of doubt from which abbey Durandus and his monks came, and some, not content with the sufficiently difficult task of deciding from which of the British abbeys they were derived, have gone so far as to suggest the possibility of their foreign origin.

These doubts, however, need no longer exist, as there is sufficient evidence to prove beyond a doubt from whence they came. From the narration of Hugh, a monk of Kirkstall, which is printed in the *Monasticon Anglicanum*, vol. v., p. 299, we learn the following:—

In the fifth year of the foundation of Fountains Abbey, a nobleman, Ranulph de Merlay, came to visit that abbey, and seeing the conversation of the brethren was struck with compunction, and under the Lord's inspiration, for the redemption of his soul, assigned a certain place in his patrimony for building a monastery. The Abbot of Fountains accepted the offering, and the building having been arranged in due form, he constructed an abbey which he called Newminster. And this was the first daughter of the Church of Fountains, as yet the only one of her mother. In the fifth year of its foundation a convent was sent out from Fountains to Newminster, with Abbot Robert, a holy and religious man, formerly monk of Whitby, who joined himself with those who left St. Mary's Abbey, York, to found Fountains. Thus Newminster had its beginning. And this was the first plant which proceeded from our vineyard. The holy seed flourished in the soil, and as if received into the bosom of a fertile ground, forthwith increased into a stalk, and from a few grains arose a copious crop. For emulating the fecundity of her mother, she brought forth three daughters—Pipewell, Salley, and Roche.

The truth of this narration is corroborated in many ways. Dr. Whitaker, in his *History of Craven*, p. 36, gives a charter,[a] shewing that Swain Fitz Swain sold to Robert, the Abbot of Newminster, some land to build an abbey upon of the Cistercian order (Salley Abbey.) In the *Monasticon Anglicanum*, vol. v. p. 34, there is also a charter proving that the original monks of Pipewell came from Newminster: and the evidence is completed by the letters[b] of the Abbot of Newminster to the Archbishop of York, requesting him to confirm the election of the Abbots of Roche. The Abbot of Newminster, in one of these, styles himself "*Father Abbot and immediate Visitor of the Monastery of Roche.*" Henry, prior of Roche was elected abbot of Newminster in 1216.

The Abbey of Newminster is situated at a short distance from Morpeth, in Northumberland. One doorway alone of the original building remains. From this monastery then, the "Monks of the Rock" came, sent forth by St. Robert,[c] the first abbot of Newminster, a Yorkshireman by birth: and it is not unlikely that he assisted them as he did the monks of Salley in their early poverty.

After having lodged for some time in huts, living on "boiled leaves and herbs," as the monks of Fountains had first done, and with the prospect of winter before him, how gladly must they have received the message of the lords of Maltby and Hooton, offering to build and endow them an abbey! How speedily, too, must the scene have changed! Where a few silent monks had been dwelling in

---

[a] Dr. Whitaker has mistaken the meaning of the words "novi monasterii" in this charter, and places Robert, the Abbot of Newminster, at the head of the abbots of Salley.

[b] See page 62.

[c] The life of St. Robert is given in Alban Butler's "Lives of the Saints," under June 8th. Should it not be June 7th?

solitude, a throng of noisy workmen now appear. And instead of the peace which had hitherto reigned, the rattle of carts, the tramp of horses, and the sounds of pickaxe and spade are heard. It must have been an anxious and a happy time for the good Durandus, as he walked among the labourers, watching their daily progress, and pondering upon the glory of the future. In the crash of falling timber, and in the sounds of mason's tools chipping and shaping the fair white stone, he, perhaps, foresaw his beautiful abbey already standing, capped with pinnacles and towers, surrounded with fruitful gardens, orchards, and barns well stored! Death, however, prevented the good old abbot from seeing all his wishes fulfilled. In 1159, after he had held his abbacy twelve years, Durandus died.

Rest, Durandus! The materials of the crumbling abbey will soon fall over thy mouldering bones. The trees thou felledst have been replaced, and now, with outstretched arms, these younger sons of the forest reclaim the ancient soil. Yea, in the very fane where noble arches sprung, rough branches wave; now flowers only cense the air; and for the solemn mass, now noisy jackdaws sit and mock with scornful laughs!

> "The owl of evening and the woodland fox
> For their abode the shrines of Waltham choose.
> Proud Glastonbury can no more refuse
> To stoop her head."

Dionysius.

1159—1171.

IONYSIUS was elected second Abbot of Roche in the year 1159. Who he was, or from whence he came, are matters of doubt; but there is reason to believe that he was one of the original followers of Durandus, and perhaps, sub-prior to the community previous to his election to the abbacy.

The twelve years during which Dionysius governed the abbey of Roche, exactly coincide with the period during which Henry II. and Thomas à Becket were struggling for the ascendancy. And strange to say, this Royal quarrel threatened at one time to seriously affect the happiness of the poor "monks of the Rock;" for Henry, hearing that Thomas à Becket (who had fled the country) had assumed the habit of the Cistercian order, and was living with Gwarine, Abbot of Pontiniac, wrote to that abbot and threatened to drive out from his realm all the monks of his order if he continued to harbour him in his abbey. Happily for Dionysius and his monks however, Thomas à Becket left Pontiniac, and so the king had not the chance of putting his threat into execution.

The life of Dionysius as abbot must have been very quiet and prosperous. Property came flowing in, and the possessions of the abbey were becoming rapidly more extended. In the time of Alexander, Abbot of Kirkstal, who lived contemporaneously with Dionysius, Henry de Laci, lord of Pontefract, granted and confirmed the donation which Richard de Wickersley, and Roger and Jordan Hoten, made to the Monks of the Rock, of common pasture of all the territory of Hotun. The following charter of Richard de Busli, son of the founder, was probably also granted at this time:—

Charter of Richard de Busli, of Elrichthorpe.

"TO all the sons of Holy Mother Church, as well present as future, Richard de Busli, greeting! Be it known to all that see and hear thefe letters, that I, Richard de Bufli, with the advice and confent of my wife and heirs, have given to God, St. Mary, and the Monks of the Rock, for the falvation of my foul and thofe of all my friends, Elrichthorpe, and whatever belongs to it in all things. And I have granted to them the land of William de Alz which my father gave them, and the land which the aforefaid monks have of my Knight of Scalzebi.—Witneffes, William, his fon and heir; R., his fon; Ralph, the prieft; Hugh, the clerk of Rotherham; Robert de Bufli; William de Sandebi; Mr. William de Duningeton; Richard Baret; William Barbot; and Ralph de Turlavefton."

Dionyfius, fave attending a general chapter now and then, and looking after his revenues, could have had little elfe to do than to fuperintend the building of his abbey, the walls of which by that time muft have reached a goodly height. A few pointed arches, were perhaps, already completed, and had received their fhare of admiration and aftonifhment, for in thofe days the pointed arch was a great novelty, the round or Norman arch being the form, which had up to that time been ufually employed.

Dionyfius ceafed to be abbot in 1171.

Roger de Tickhill.

1171—1179.

HANKS to the cuftom which the monks had when they left the world of leaving their furnames behind them, and of affuming by way of diftinction the names of the places from whence they came, we are able to learn that by this time, the Monks of the Rock had begun to receive brothers from the towns and villages near them; and that Roger, the third abbot of Roche, came from the neighbouring parifh of Tickhill.

The building of the Abbey muft have been carried on very actively during the time of abbot Roger; and we find from the following charter of John, fon of the founder, that the Houfe of De Bufli ftill remained firm friends to the monks:—

The Charter of John de Busli, the son of Richard de Busli.

"TO all the fons of Holy Mother Church, prefent and future, John de Bufli, greeting! Know that I have granted and confirmed by this my charter, to God, St. Mary, and the Monks of the Rock, for the falvation of my foul, and the fouls of my father and mother, and all my anceftors and heirs, all the donations and liberties, without refervation, which Richard de Bufli, my father, gave them, and confirmed by his charters; fo that the ditch of the aforefaid monks as it has been made around the wood fhall remain for good and peace, without any clamour, common from me and my heirs, except the aerie of fparrow-hawks, which the aforefaid monks have granted me. I have granted alfo, to the aforefaid monks, to make ditches and enclofe their fields between the wood of Maltby and the fields of Sandbec, below their boundaries at their pleafure, keeping the two roads untouched, to wit, Bolgate and the road which comes from Blythe. All thefe I have granted and confirmed to the aforefaid monks, for a pure and perpetual charity, free and quiet from all secular service, and from everything which belongs to the estate; so that I and my heirs shall warrant and defend that charity against all. Before these witnesses, Nicholas, the parson of Tickhill; Humphrey, the clerk; William, chaplain of the castle; Robert Fitz Payne; Ralph, his son; Hugh Scausby; Hugh, the son of Robert; Robert of Bereus; Hugh le Engleis; and Thomas, the servant. In the court of Tickhill."

Works on falconry name the kind of hawk assigned to different ranks. The sparrow-hawk is that assigned to the priest.* A hawks aerie was returned in Domesday-Book, among the most valuable articles of property which a person could possess; and doubtless this one was much prized by John de Busli. From it probably he obtained the sparrow-hawk, which had to be rendered yearly by the De Busli's to the Fossard's for the tenure of Bawtry. And this may have been one cause for retaining it.

Blythe mentioned in the above charter was one of the five places licensed by King Richard I. for tournaments, and Roger de Busli placed a colony of monks there; "founding the priory not improbably" says Mr. Hunter, "that there might be those at hand who could minister religious consolation to the knight who might chance to be mortally wounded in those dangerous encounters, or medical assistance, for the monks were often skilled in the healing art, to those more slightly injured." Matthew Paris tells us of a tournament which was held here in 1256; "about Whitsuntide," says he, "a general tournament was held at Blythe, according to the laws and discipline of chivalry, at which the King's eldest son Edward attended in linen clothing and light armour to be instructed in the laws of chivalry. Many nobles who endeavoured to gain knightly renown there, were unhorsed, beaten, crushed and trampled under foot; of whom one was William Longsword, who never afterwards recovered from the effects of his injuries."

Roger de Tickhill was abbot of Roche for eight years. He ceased to be abbot in 1179.

* "There is a Spare-hawke; and she is an hawke for a preest." Dame Julyan Bernes on Hawkynge, WYNKYN DE WORDE, 1496.

Hugh de Wadworth.

1179—1184

HUGH DE WADWORTH, Mr. Hunter says—"appears to have been an active superior, as in his time the Confirmation from the Pope was obtained, and Roxby grange bought." But that indefatigable historian is in error when he states that this abbot obtained the Confirmation charter. This writing is addressed to Osmund, the next abbot, and bears a date two years later than that of Hugh de Wadworth's death.

There can be little doubt but that Abbot Hugh came originally from the neighbouring parish of Wadworth, and not improbably he was a member of the family of that name, which at that time resided at Wadworth. He certainly had one great family likeness to them, namely, that of borrowing money from the Jews at York. Peter de Wadworth fell into sad trouble with these Hebrew gentlemen, and was helped out of his difficulties and assisted in his "great necessity" by the monks of Roche, who had previously received great favours from the family.

The only act which can positively be ascribed to Hugh de Wadworth, is the rather discreditable one of having involved the Abbey in great debt to the Jews of York, for the purpose of purchasing Roxby grange, in Lincolnshire.

He held his abbacy five years, and ceased to be abbot in 1184.

Osmund.

1184—1223.

OSMUND had the most prosperous and the longest reign, save one, of all the Abbots. He came from Fountains Abbey, where he had held the office of "Cellarer," in the year 1184. Ambitious and active, all things prospered in his hands, and under his rule the Abbey became speedily rich and powerful.

His first great act was that of obtaining from Pope Urban III. a Confirmation of all the gifts which the monastery had up to that time received. The following is a translation of it:—

Confirmation of Pope Urban iii.

"URBAN bishop, servant of the servants of God, to his beloved sons, Osmund, abbot, of Roche, and his brethren as well present as future, professing a regular* life—salvation in Christ. To all those who choose a religious life it is fitting that apostolical guardianship be at hand, lest, haply the attacks of any one's temerity should either call them off from their purpose, or (which God forbid!) break in upon the strength of their sacred bond. Therefore, beloved sons in the Lord, we favourably assent to your just requests, and after the example of our predecessor, of happy memory (Pope Lucius;) take under the blessed Peter's and our own protection, and fortify by the privilege of this writing the aforesaid monastery of Roche, in which ye are bound under a divine servitude; in the first place decreeing that the monastic order which is acknowledged to have been instituted in the said monastery according to the rule of the Lord and the blessed Benedict, and the institution of the Cistercian brothers, be inviolably observed in the said place for all time. Next, that whatever possessions and whatever goods the said monastery possesses at present,

* i.e. Monastic.

or in future, by the grant of Pontiffs, largefs of Kings or Princes, offering of the faithful or in any other juft modes by the help of the Lord it may obtain, remain firm and entire to you and your fucceffors, according to the very words in which we have thought right that thefe things fhould be expreffed.

Of the gift of Richard de Builli, (called alfo Bufli,) and Richard de Wikerflai, the place itfelf in which your Abbey ftands.

Of the gift of Lord King Henry II., one hundred acres in Lindric, near the faid Abbey.

Of the gift of the fame perfons, the grange of Aggecroft with its appurtenances.

Of the gift of the fame Richard de Bufli and Hugh de Drigwrt, Lambecroft (Lambcote) with its appurtenances.

Of the gift of Leo de Manners, Brancliffe with its appurtenances.

Of the gift of William Avenell, Anes (Oneafh) with its appurtenances.

Of the gift of Walter de Scoteni, Rokefby (Roxby,) with its appurtenances.

Of the gift of Ralph Tortemayns, Todwick with its appurtenances.

Of the gift of Symon, fon of Symon, land in Inffeby with its appurtenances.

Of the gift of Hamelin Bardolf and Robert Fitz Eudo, land in Winterington with its appurtenances.

Of the gift of Robert de Scalcebye and Adam de Newmarch and Roger de Mar, Newfome with its appurtenances.

Of the gift of William Vavafour, Thurnfcoe with its appurtenances.

Of the gift of Gervas de Barnby, a grange in Barnby and Bramwith.

Of the gift of Thomas de Armthorpe, a grange in the faid town.

Of the gift of Robert Fitz Payne, Wellingley with its appurtenances, and all the lands which ye have in the territory of Wadworth.*

Of the gift of William de Moles and William Fitz Gerard, Sezacres with its appurtenances.

Of the gift of Simon de Plefley, Afhover (Derbyfhire,) with its appurtenances.

Of the gift of Robert, fon of Glai, land and wood of Cumrefbruig (Coningfborough,) as far as to Witewell between the road and the brook.

* The gift of Eudo son of Godfery de Wadworth, says Dr. Burton.

Of the gift of William the Fleming, all the land which Ligulf held and a certain essart between Hestwell and the essart of Orm, the man of Adam Fitz Swayn, with all appurtenances.

Of the gift of Gerard de Stirap, turbary in the territory of the same town.

Verily, let no man presume to extort from you tithes of your labours, which with your own hands or at your own expense you cultivate, as well from lands cultivated as uncultivated, or of the nourishment of your animals, under pain of &c. Given at Verona, by the hand of Albert, priest of the Holy Roman Church, cardinal and chancellor, the seventh day of April, in the fourth indiction, in the year of the incarnation of our Lord MCLXXXVI, but in the first year of the pontificate of the most Holy Pope Urban III."

Having obtained this important charter which not only confirmed the possessions of the monks, but exempted them from paying tithes, Osmund next applied to King Richard, and obtained from that monarch a remission of the 1300 marks borrowed from the Jews of York by his predecessor Hugh de Wadworth. The Jews were so hated at this time that this dishonest interference of the King would be looked upon rather as a virtuous action than otherwise. The sums which the Jews lost in this way must have been enormous.

Osmund also obtained from King Richard a charter which confirmed to the monks the Abbey and all that belonged to it, and granted to them many rights and privileges, not the least important of which was that of allowing them to hold a court of their own, in which they might judge thieves, trespassers, &c. The following is a translation of it:—

Confirmation of King Richard i.

"RICHARD, by the grace of God, King of England, &c., all, &c., know that I have granted, and by the present charter confirmed to God, and the Church of Saint Mary of Roche, and the monks serving God in the same, the Abbey itself, with all its appurtenances, to wit, whatever they have in the territory of Maltby and Hooton, and in the grange of Brancliffe, and whatever they have in the territory of Takewith, Bramley, and the grange of Lambcotes, and whatever they have in the territory of Stainton and Wadworth, and the grange of Wellingley, and the grange of Newhum, and whatever they have in the territories of Scoreby of Marr, Thurnscoe, Armthorpe, Barnby, Bramwith, and the grange of * * * with all their appurtenances; and whatever they have in the territories of Ashover, Torworth, Fairwath, Oldcotes, Stirap,

Winterington, Rifby, and the grange of * * * with all their appurtenances; and all the poffeffions which the faid monks have, or which they may hereafter reafonably acquire, in granges, houfes, buildings, men, fervices, rents, lands, meadows, paftures, commons, woods, ponds, waters, ftews, mills, fifheries, turbaries, in-ways and paths, free introits and exits, and all other poffeffions and liberties, within the towns and without, and in all other places, as the reafonable charters and handwritings of the donors and vendors teftify. Wherefore, I will, and firmly enjoin, that the aforefaid Abbey and monks, have and hold all the aforefaid, well and peaceably, fully, entirely and honourably, in free and perpetual almoigne, free and quiet from all gilds, fcutages, pleas, quarrels, fummonfes, county meetings, wapentakes, trithings, aids to fheriff, and all other aids and all other charities, and from frankpledge and murder, and all other cuftoms and occafions which appertain to me. I grant alfo, that the faid monks fhall have the rights of a Court of their own, over all their tenements, and men with foke, and fac, and toll, and theam, and infangthef. And I enjoin alfo, that the faid monks and brethren be free and quiet from all toll and cuftom which belongs to me throughout my realm, of all things which they fhall buy or fell for their own ufe, or caufe to be carried out or brought in by land or water. And I forbid there being put in any plea concerning any tenement of theirs except before me or my Chief Juftice. Witnefs, the King."

Ofmund alfo obtained a further confirmation from the Countefs of Eu, of which the following is a tranflation:—

Confirmation of the Countess of Eu.

"TO all the fons of Holy Mother Church, prefent and future, Alice, Countefs of Eu, formerly wife of Ralph de Ifondun, Earl of Eu, greeting! Know all of you that I in my widowhood, and being in full power over my own body, for the welfare of the foul of the faid Ralph my lord, and for the welfare of my own foul, and that of Ralph my fon, and all my anceftors, and heirs have granted, and by this my charter have confirmed to the Monks of the Abbey of St. Mary of Roche, the fite of the faid Abbey, and the grange of Aggecroft, with the appurtenances, and the wood of Lindric as it is bounded by a ditch, in pure and perpetual alms, and moreover, all the lands and poffeffions which they hold in the Barony of Tickhill, with the appurtenances, liberties, commons and eafements in woods and plains, and in all places as the reafonable charters of the donors and vendors thereof contain and teſtify. Witneſs, Lord William Earl Warren, my uncle; Philip de Ulecotes; William de Creſſi; Maveſin de Herſy; Baldwin his brother; Mathew de Shepeley; knights. Given at Tickhill in the year of grace 1219."

In the ſeventh or eighth year of Oſmund's preſidency he was made proctor for Cardinal Stephen of all his rents in England, in ſuch ſort, ſays a valuable old deed giving the liſt of the early abbots, " that he received of the goods of the ſaid Cardinal at different times of the year by annual payments to the amount of 400 marks, out of which money they provided handſomely for themſelves, and were enriched to ſuch an extent that they were reckoned wiſe men, and lacking no temporal good." The monks had alſo from this ſame Cardinal the prebend of Laughton.

Roche Abbey ſeems not only to have been fortunate at this time in having an illuſtrious abbot, but alſo in poſſeſſing monks of more than ordinary ability. The names of the four following have been preſerved :—

HELIAS, who was elected abbot of Kirkſtal in the year 1209. The following account of him is copied from a deed quoted by Stephens from *Thoreſby's MSS*. "Helias of worthy memory, formerly monk of Rupe, an induſtrious man, and well verſed in temporal affairs, having taken upon him the government, had enough to do according to time and place to gather what had been ſcattered and to preſerve what had been gathered, and the Lord was with him. Nor did he want tribulation at his firſt promotion; for the noble Roger Lacy, patron of the monaſtery, being ill adviſed by ſome perſons, conceived ſo much anger againſt the ſaid abbot, that he would not vouchſafe to ſee nor admit him into his preſence; but the Lord in whoſe hand are the hearts of princes and their councils, aſſuaged his paſſion and rancor, and converted it into perfect favour and affection, for he afterwards was very familiar and intimate with the abbot, and not a little promoted the affairs of the houſe." Helias held the abbacy of Kirkſtal twelve years.

HENRY, who was elected abbot of the monaſtery of New-minſter, near Morpeth in Northumberland.* This Abbey was founded for Ciſtercian Monks from Fountains; and the connection which exiſted between it and Roche points ſtill to the ſuggeſtion already made, that the original monks of Roche came from Fountains. Henry, who had been prior of Roche was elected abbot of Newminſter in 1216.

* Chronicle of Melroſe, p. 194.

THEODORE, another monk who lived during the reign of Ofmund, and was probably of high ftanding; he took precedence in figning before Henry, prior of Workfop, a deed in which a fon of Girard de Furnival gave to the monks of Kirkftal the moiety of a mill at Hanfworth Woodhoufe.

REGINALD, whofe name appears coupled with that of Ofmund in 1202,* was probably the monk who was elected abbot of Roche after Ofmund.

In 1223 Ofmund died after a reign of thirty-nine years.

* Fines Ebor in the Augmentation Office, IV John.

Reginald.

1223—1238.

DURING Ofmund's time King John granted a charter to the Church, giving to chapters and convents the power of electing their Heads without his interpofition. And though this privilege was foon interfered with by the Pope, it feems probable that the chapter of Roche exercifed their power in the election of Reginald, for we find in the *"Fines,"* before mentioned, that he was a monk of great importance in Ofmund's time, and confequently the one whom from his experience the community would wifh to have at their head.

During the abbacy of Reginald the Abbey increafed confiderably both in wealth and lands, and in 1231 a new confirmation charter was obtained from Henry III., of which the following is a tranflation:—

Confirmation of King Henry iii.

"HENRY, by the grace of God, King of England, Lord of Ireland, and Duke of Normandy, and Aquitaine, and Count of Anjou, to Archbifhops, Bifhops, Abbots, Priors, Counts, Barons, Judges, Vifcounts, Provofts, Servants, and all Bailiffs, and his faithful fubjects, health! We have infpected over a charter which King Richard, our uncle, made with the Abbey and monks of Roche, of donations, fales and grants reafonably made to them in thefe words:—

Richard by the grace of God, &c., to Archbifhops, &c., health! Know that we for the fafety of our foul and the fouls of all our predeceffors and succeffors have granted, and by this prefent charter have confirmed to the Abbey of Roche and the monks of the fame, ferving God according to the Ciftercian order, all donations and fales reafonably made to them, viz: the Abbey itfelf of Roche, with all its appurtenances, tenements and poffeffions which are in the counties of York, Nottingham and Lincoln, to wit, thofe which they them-

selves hold in the territory of Maltby and Hooton with the wood of
Lyndric as it is inclosed by the ditch near the said Abbey, and as it
is inclosed by the same ditch towards Bernehill, and from the said
ditch towards Bernehill, and from Bernehill towards the Mill of the
same monks as it is included, and all possessions which they have in
the territory of Anstean (Anston,) Tathewic (Todwick,) Bramleye,
Braithwell, Stainton, Tikehill, Doncaster, Cuningesburgh (Conisbro',)
Stansale, Wellingleye, Wadeworth, Thirnscohot (Thurnscoe,) Mar,
Newhus (Newhall,) Scalceby (Scawsby,) Askern, Wareleye, Alnel-
thorpe (Armthorpe,) Sandale, Barneby, Bramwick (Bramwith,)
Steinford (Stainforth,) Wykersley, Tange, Sonke, Blide (Blythe,)
Farwath, Tordwith (Torworth,) Ulcotes (Oldcotes,) Babry (Bawtry,)
Scirap (Stirap,) Anes (Oneash,) Aexoure (Ashover,) Lyncoln, Wyvels-
worth, Riseby, Wytrinton, and the grange of Rokesby (Roxby,) with
all appurtenances, in granges, sheepfolds, houses, buildings, men, rents,
services, vassals, lands, meadows, pastures, commons, woods, coppices,
brushwoods, heaths, pools, waters, stews, fisheries, mills, saltsprings,
marshes, turbaries,[a] twiggeries, with free ingress and egress, and all
other possessions and liberties within cities, boroughs and towns and
without, as reasonable charters or deeds of their donors, sellers,
granters or exchangers testify of the possessions which they have, or
which in future they may reasonably add to them, of whatsoever fee
they may be. Wherefore, we will, and firmly enjoin, that the said
Abbey and the monks shall have and hold all the aforesaid well and
peaceably, entirely and honourably, as a free and perpetual alms, free
and quit from all gilds,[b] danegilds,[c] corngilds,[d] themantale,[e] scutages,[f]
scotages,[g] hidages,[h] carucages,[i] shires,[j] assises, pleas,[k] summonses of quest,
armies, miscellaneous suits, counties,[l] wapentakes, trithings,[m] and from
every mixed and common assise, and from fine which belongs to
murder and larceny, and from aids to the sheriff and his bailiffs, and

---

[a] "Turbary," right of cutting turf. In 13, Henry III., William, son of Richard de Barneby granted to abbot Reginald, and his monks, for himself and his heirs, that whenever it should happen that he pared peats or dug turfs in his wood, with one or more of his men, it should be quite lawful for the said abbot and his successors to pare sods and dig turfs in the same place, to the extent of half the number of the said men, of one, to wit, or more, without impediment.—"Fines Ebor."

[b] "Gilds," payments.

[c] "Danegilds," Danegeld, a tribute imposed in Saxon times, to get a fund either for appeasing the Danes, or for repelling their invasions; some say for one purpose, some for another. King Egelred seems to have paid the Danes at five payments, 113,000 pounds, besides granting a yearly tribute of 48,000 pounds.

[d] "Corngilds," Horngeld, a tax on horned animals.

[e] "Themantale," or tenmentale; the Saxons divided their hundreds into tens, or tithings, the head-men of which, took oath of allegiance for the rest.

[f] "Scutages," Scutage, a tax upon every shield; that is, upon those that held lands by Knight's service.

[g] "Scotages," Scotage, a customary contribution (or shot) laid upon persons according to their several abilities.

[h] "Hidages," Hidage, a tax upon every hide of land; a sort of land tax.

[i] "Carucages," Carucate, a tax upon every plough.

[j] "Shires," the duty of attending upon the Sheriff, when he holds his courts.

[k] "Pleas," a plea. An assembly of Nobles for judicial purposes.   [l] "Counties," comitatus, a county meeting.

[m] "Trithings," trithing, the proper form of riding, meaning a third part; as morthing means the moor division.

from all things to them pertaining, and from all other aids, and from the guardianship and working at castles, walls, ramparts, stews, pools, bridges, causeways, and other inclosures, and from warpenning,[a] averpenning,[b] thethingpenning,[c] hengwith,[d] flomenwith,[e] blodwith,[f] leirwith,[g] flemenfrith,[h] * * * * forstal,[i] haimsoken,[j] and from franc-pledge,[k] lastage,[l] stallage,[m] carriage,[n] parnnage,[o] and from all occasions which relate to us. And from essarts,[p] and rewards, and wastes, and inspections,[q] and pleas of forest,[r] in such manner however that if they shall cause any damage in our forests, beyond those liberties conceded to them from us by our letters, we will that they be reasonably punished. We grant also, to them, that the said monks shall have the liberty of holding their own court over all their lands, with soke,[s] and sake,[t] toll,[u] and theam,[v] and infangthef,[w] outfangthef,[x] and every kind of forfeiture of themselves, their lands and men in whatever place they occur. Because, we will that they should hold all their property and possessions as freely and quietly as any other church in all our land, which holds more freely and quietly by (than other.) We enjoin, also, that the said monks and their brethren shall be free and quiet from all toll,[y] passage,[z] pontage,[ab] and every other custom which pertains to us everywhere in our power, of all things which they shall buy or sell for their own use, or shall cause to be conveyed or carried away by land or by water. And we forbid their being placed on trial or answering with respect to any of their possessions, except before us or our Chief Justice or by our special mandate; and that no one shall oppress or disquiet, vex or disturb them, their property or possessions against the liberties of

---

[a] "Warpenning," money paid to the Sheriff or other Castellan, instead of actual watching and warding over camps, and keeping sentry.
[b] "Averpenning," a tax paid to be free from the duty of supplying beasts of burden for the king on his travels.
[c] "Thethingpenning," or tithingpenny.
[d] "Hengwith," or haugwith, a fine for hanging a man out of your own jurisdiction, or for letting him go.
[e] "Flomenwith," flemenwith, a fugative. It is explained by Spelman as "mulcta fugetorum."
[f] "Blodwith," a fine for shedding blood.
[g] "Leirwith," a fine for lying with a person unlawfully, whether by force or otherwise.
[h] "Flemenfrith," the sustentation of exiles.
[i] "Forstal," the fine for occupying the street before another, and so preventing him from getting his wares to market.
[j] "Haimsoken," a fine for a violation of the peace, or an assault, by forcible entry into a person's house.
[k] "Franc-pledge," a token of freedom which the possessor had to shew every year.
[l] "Castage," bottomry.   [m] "Stallage," rent paid for the right of keeping a stall in a market.
[n] "Carriage."   [o] "Parnnage," a sum paid for the right of feeding hogs in the king's forest, on acorns, &c.
[p] "Essarts," clearing forests.   [q] "Inspections," periodical perambulation of forests.   [r] "Forest," wastes.
[s] "Soke," the right of holding a court within your own lordship, for doing justice between your vassals.
[t] "Sake," the lord's right of settling controversies within his manor.
[u] "Toll," the right of holding a market in your manor.
[v] "Theam," the right of taking cognizance of bail forfeitures.
[w] "Infangthef," the right of judging a thief caught within the abbots manor.
[x] "Outfangthef," the right of judging a thief caught without the manor. "Infang" when the thief is one of your own vassals. "Outfang," when he is not.
[y] "Toll," a tax exacted by the lords from those who traded in his market.
[z] "Passage," turnpike toll.   [ab] "Pantage," bridge toll.

their charters on pain of forfeiture of ten pounds. Signed by Mafter Malgerio, of York; Mafter Roger Richmund; Vivian, Archdeacon of Derby; Robert of Thornfham, then Steward of Anjou; William de Rupibus; Girard de Furnivale; Girard Brochard, and many others. Given at Sufa by the hand of Mafter Docelin, then fulfilling the office of our chancellor, on the * * day of February, in the tenth year of our reign.

We alfo, holding the grant and confirmation of the aforefaid King Richard, our uncle, ratified and granted for us and our heirs, as the faid charter which the faid Abbey and monks of Roche have, reafonably teftifies, grant and confirm the fame. Witnefs, the venerable fathers, P. Wynton, (Winchefter,) and W. Karleol, (Carlisle,) Bifhops; Hugh de Bargo, in the county of Kent, Chief Juftice of England; Ralph, fon of Nicholas; Godfrey de Cramcumb; John, fon of Philip; Ralph * * * Richard, fon of Hugh; Alfred le Cauz; Henry de Chapel and others. Given by the hand of the venerable father Ralph, bifhop of Chichefter,* our chancellor, at Winchefter, on the twenty-firft day of January, in the fixteenth year of our reign."

If the reader will ftudy carefully this important charter he will obtain pretty correct views of the poffeffions, privileges and powers of the monks of Roche about this time. The preceding lift of ancient terms here interpreted, is very complete, and gives a good idea of the numerous taxes which were inflicted upon people in thofe days.

A general difcontent in religious matters feems to have prevailed in England about this time, the people were diffatiffied with their priefts, and the priefts with the pope and the heads of the church.

Jacke Upland in the name of the people was afking fuch queftions as the following:—

"How many orders be there in earth? If Chrift's rule be moft perfect why ruleft thou thee not thereafter? Maketh your habit you men of religion? If fo, the better your habit the better your religion! What betokeneth your great hood, your fcaplery, your knotted girdle and your wide cope? Why make ye you as dead men and be not dead, but more quick beggars than ye were before? Why make men believe that your golden trentall fong for ten fhillings or five at leaft will bring fouls out of hell or out of purgatory? If this be truth, certes, ye might bring all fouls out of pain, but ye are

---

* Ralph Owille bifhop of Chichefter, was appointed Chancellor A.D. 1226, but the feals were taken from him in the 22nd year of the King's reign though he ftill remained Chancellor.

not, therefore ye are out of charity! Why busy ye not to hear the shrift of poor folk as well as rich lords and ladies, since they must have more plenty of shrift fathers than poor folk have? Why make ye not your feasts to poor men and give them gifts as ye do the rich, since poor men have more need than the rich? &c., &c."

Money was as it ever seems likely to be, the root of a great deal of evil. The Church fleeced the people and the Pope fleeced the Church.

Speed gives this description by a monk of the governors of the Church of Rome at this time—"not seeking to winne mens souls but their money; oppressing the religious by punishments, usuries and simonie, without any care of justice and honesty."

The following quotations from a political song in the time of Henry III. are also in the same strain.—" Rome lying in the depths of turpitude, ranks virtues beneath filthy lucre." "Before the Cardinals and before the Patriarch a pound overcomes the Bible." "The archcishop tread under feet the necks of the clergy and extort tears in order that they may be dried with gifts." "If anyone begins to complain of an iujury, they immediately stretch their ear to the cause, and their hand to the gift."

But besides the "rivers of silver" which flowed out of England into the Pope's purse—which the people felt severely—there was another hardship, which they found it difficult to bear. They complained that "the church and kingdom of England is grieved, that the patrons of the same cannot present as they wont into their church, for the Pope's letters. But the churches are given to Romans which know neither the realm nor the tongue thereof; both to the great peril of souls and robbing away the money out of the realm." Also, "that in the benefices given to Italians neither the old ordinances, nor relief to the poor, nor hospitalities, nor any preaching of God's word, nor care of men's souls, nor service in the church, nor yet the walls of the church be kept up and maintained."

It can be well imagined that these Italians were not beloved, and that no opportunity was lost for illtreating them. In 1232 says Fox, there was "a general spoile of the Roman parsons in England," all their barns were wasted and the corn distributed among the needy, the Italians hiding themselves in monasteries and cells, thinking it better to lose their goods than their lives.

Under a threat from the Pope, the King ordered the Archbishop of York and others to find out and punish those in the north, who had been guilty of this work of spoliation. Among others was one

Robert Twing, "a comely young man and a talle fouldiour, who of his own voluntary accord, with five others fervitures, whom he took with him abroad to work that feat, came to the King, openly protesting himfelf to be the author of that deed doing, and faid he did it for hatred of the Pope and the Romaines; becaufe that by fentence of the Bifhop of Rome, and fraudulent circumvention of the Italians, he was bereved of the patronage of his benefice." The King recommended him to go to the Pope, and gave him letters certifying his right, and begging for him the Pope's indulgence. The Barons alfo fent letters by him complaining of their rights of prefentation being infringed. The miffion was moft fucceffful, and he returned with a fatiffactory anfwer to the Barons, and a countermand to the Legate and Archbifhop of York, not to infift upon his former order, but to give inftitution to the clerk prefented by the faid Robert Twing.

Fortunately for the wealth of Roche Abbey, Reginald continued to hold the proctorfhip for Cardinal Stephen, of all his rents in England, which Ofmund had, and out of which payments the "fucceffion of abbots" fays the monks provided for themfelves handfomely. The office of Proctor however was anything but a pleafant one, and Reginald, though probably quite eafy as far as money matters went, muft have lived anything but the quiet life we are led to imagine in wandering through the peaceful and fecluded valley which was his home. Befides the troubles of his proctorfhip Reginald had a long feud with the Prior of the Holy Trinity of York, and the Prior of Drax, about the prefentation to the Church of Roxby. Each could produce charters fhewing his indifputable right to it, and the jury who had to determine the queftion (although Reginald made two attempts to get it fettled) could not come to a decifion. It is however probable that the Prior of the Holy Trinity of York was the one who eventually made the prefentation.

The following legend is given by *Matthew Paris* as having occurred in the year 1236:—

Legend.

"About this fame time, in the month of May, near an abbacy called Roche, in the northern part of England, there appeared bands of well-armed Knights, riding on valuable horfes, with ftandards and fhields, coats of mail and helmets, and decorated with other military equipments; they iffued from the earth, as it appeared, and difappeared again into the earth. This vision lasted for several days, and attracted the eyes of those who beheld it, as if by fascination; they rode in arrayed troops, and sometimes engaged in conflict, sometimes as if at a tournament, they shivered their spears into small fragments with a crash; the inhabitants saw them, but more from a distance than near them, for they never remembered to have seen such a fight before, and many said that the occurrence was not without its presage. This occurred more plainly in Ireland and its confines, where they appeared as if coming from battle, and dragged their horses after them wounded and broken down, without a rider, and the Knights themselves were severely wounded and bloody; and what was more wonderful, their track plainly appeared impressed on the ground, and the grass was borne down and trampled on. Many people on seeing this vision fled before them in alarm, and betook themselves to the churches and castles, thinking that it was not an illusion, but a real battle. These occurrences came to our knowledge some years after they happened, from a report and true account of the event obtained from the Earl of Gloucester, and by the evidence of many other persons.'"

This legend is very similar to that of the spectre horsemen of Southerfell in Cumberland. Troups of horsemen were there seen, and "they seemed to come from the lower part of the fell, becoming first visible at a place called Knott; they then moved in regular order in a curvilinear path along the side of the fell, until they came opposite to Blakehills, when they went over the mountain and disappeared. The last, or last but one, in every troop, galloped to the front and then took the swift walking pace of the rest."

The same kind of apparitions are said to have been witnessed above Vallombrosa early in the fourteenth century. On the night of an extraordinary deluge, says Giovanni Villami, "a hermit, being at prayer in his hermitage above Vallombrosa, heard a furious trampling as of many horses; and crossing himself and hurrying to the wicket, saw a multitude of infernal horsemen, all black and terrible riding by at full speed. When in the name of God he demanded their purpose; one replied, 'we are going if it be His pleasure to drown the city of Florence for its wickedness.'"

In Suffolk there is also a legend of this kind. At the little village of Acton the park gates were wont to fly open at midnight "withouten hands," and a carriage drawn by four spectral horses and accompanied by headless grooms and outriders, proceeded with great

[a] Matthew Paris, Bohn's Translation, page 33. [b] Notes and Queries, Vol. vii., page 304, 1st Series.

rapidity from the park to a spot called "the Nursery corner" and were then lost sight of.[a]

A similar cortège to this last, used to be seen near Bury St. Edmunds. It went from the parish of Great Barton across the fields, regardless of fences, and proceeded to a deep hole called "Philis's Hole."[b]

Reginald ceased to be abbot of Roche in 1238.

[a] Notes and Queries, Vol. v., page 186. [b] Notes and Queries, Vol. v., page 365.

Richard.

1238—1254.

FROM two old charters we find that during the reign of abbot Richard, the Abbey larder was pretty well supplied with the good things of this life, and both for feast and fast days the brethren were well cared for. The first charter was granted by the King in 1250, and was one of free warren in all their demesne lands of Roche, Armthorpe and Brancliffe. This was a privilege rarely granted to any but the lords, and the Abbot of Roche was not returned as lord of Armthorpe until 1317. The other charter was obtained from William, Earl of Warren, son of Hameline:—

Charter of William, Earl of Warren.

"WILLIAM, Earl of Warren, to his fishermen, of Brademer, health! Know that I, by an impulse of charity, have given to God and the Church of St. Mary of Roche, and to the monks, servants of God in that place, the tithe of the whole of the residue of all my eels from all my fisheries, which are of the parish of Hatfield, Thorne, and Fishlake, with the exception of the full tithe of my eels which belongs to the monks of Lewes, as a pure and perpetual charity. Wherefore, I command you, that you make them have the aforesaid tithe without any delay or difficulty, and in testimony of this thing, I send you these my letters patent. Farewell!"

In 1244 we find Richard acting as one of the executors of the will of William Percy, and undertaking to pay into the treasury "one pound, which the said William owed the King for his relief, and thirty pounds which he owed to the King for an aid granted to the King towards marrying his eldest daughter!"

We find from the "*York Fabric Rolls*"* published by the *Surtees Society* that the chantry of St. Mary Magdalen in the crypt of the

* Page 294.

Cathedral Church of York, was founded about 1240, for the foul of Galfrid de Norwich, late Dean of York, by Richard, abbot of Roche, Simon, precentor of York, Peter de Munkegate and Robert de St. Paul, his executors. In 1364 there was no fervice at this chantry on account of the rebuilding of the choir, and the chaplain celebrated at St. Andrew's altar.

We alfo find from the fame "*Rolls*"[a] that the abbot of Roche made a bequeft of 3*s*., by the hand of Thomas Sbyfon to the fabric of York Minfter, probably in fupport of the above chantry.

ROBERT, according to a deed of Sibilla de Sancta Maria now in the poffeffion of Mr. Mitchell of Sheffield, was Cellarer of Roche Abbey at this time. The deed is dated at Rotherham in 1239, and contains befides the name of Robert, that of William de Rupe, who was probably a monk of Roche.

Richard prefided over the abbey fixteen years, and died or refigned in 1254.

[a] Page 32.

Walter.

1254—1268.

WALTER, or Walter de Wadeworth, as his name is given in an old charter, was elected head of Roche in 1254, and if we may judge from the small scraps of history remaining he must have led a much more active life than his predecessor, and it might be added one of far less comfort, for we find him in 1256 applying to the Pope and obtaining from him the following bull :—

Bull of Urban iv. to the Abbot and Convent of Roche, concerning not paying usury to their Creditors, certain compacts notwithstanding.[a]

"URBAN, bishop, servant of the servants of God, to his beloved sons, the abbot and convent of the monastery of Roche of the Cistercian order, in the diocese of York, health and apostolical benediction! As your petition exhibited to us contained 'certain persons (traders in lucre in the cities of the diocese and the province of York) who have extorted much from you by usurious richness, asserting that you are bound to them for certain sums of money, very frequently disquiet you with regard to such moneys, by demanding payment for the same.' Wherefore, you have humbly supplicated us of our paternal care to see and take measures about these things. We therefore, yielding to your supplication by the authority of these presents grant you power to deduct from the sums of money of this kind for which you are bound to laymen, what has thus been extorted, on such sort that ye be not at all bound to make satisfaction for these (sums) themselves, or may be compelled to pay them against your will, but that the said laymen be bound to reckon them up towards the principal; that you also may be able to refuse the interests

[a] Lambeth Library; No. 654, Art. 53. (In dorso) Urbanus contra usurarios special.

promised to them, and redemand those which you have paid up to this time, even though you have granted and given over to them your own or any other person's letters for payment of these very interests to those same laymen, or anything else in lieu of them and not requiring them again. Moreover we thought fit that ye be absolved from all letters and apostolic indulgences already obtained, or yet to be obtained, also from the aid of the canonical and civil law and all exceptions whatsoever, and ye have also given your oath. Let no man therefore whatever infringe the letter of this our grant and absolution, or by rash daring go against it. But if any one should presume to attempt to do so let him know that he will incur the wrath of Almighty God and the blessed Peter and Paul his Apostles.

Given at the Old City, (Civita Vecchia) February * * in the second year of our Pontificate."

Besides this bull, which appears rather arbitrary, Walter seven years afterwards obtained the following :—

Bull of Alexander iv. to the Monastery of Roche, of the Cistercian order in the Diocese of York, to allow them to celebrate sacred offices in their cities, towns, granges and houses.*

"ALEXANDER, bishop, servant of the servants of God, to his beloved sons, the abbot and convent of Roche, of the Cistercian order in the Diocese of York, health and apostolical benediction for their devotion! We yielding to your prayers, by the authority of these presents grant to you, for yourselves and your households, licence to celebrate sacred offices in your cities, towns, granges and houses without incurring any penalty at law. Let no man therefore whatever infringe upon the letter of this our grant, or rashly dare to go against it. But if any one should presume to attempt to do so let him know that he will incur the wrath of Almighty God and the blessed Peter and Paul his Apostles.

Given at Latera, * * May, in the second year of our Pontificate—1263."

It does not appear that the licence granted by this bull was ever exercised. The "*Monasticon*" describes Dunscroft, one of the Abbey granges near Doncaster, as a cell of Roche, but *Mr. Hunter* is most decided in his opinion that such was not the case.

In the "*Placitorum Abbreviatio*,"[b] we find the following suggestive fragments :—

Henry III. "The abbot of Roche offered himself on the 4th

---

[a] Lambeth Library: No. 643, f. 8. [This bull is partially damaged.]   [b] Page 130, 136.

day against Richard de Barneby, Hugh and Alexander his brothers, on the plea why they had *beaten, enormously wounded and illtreated* against the peace &c., Alan de Smetheton and Nicholas de Rypun his monks and brother Thomas the Granger.

And they did not come &c. And the Sheriff commanded that Richard should be attached by Alexander de Stubbes and Robert Carzon; and Hugh by Thomas, son of Hugh de Barnby and Nicholas de Bramwith; and Alexander by Thomas Thoc and Thomas de Sandal. Thereupon they give sufficient pledges that they will on the Octave &c.

Henry III. The abbot of Roche by his attorney &c. Against Richard de Barneby, Hugh and Alexander his brother, on the plea (aforesaid.) And they did not come &c. Thereupon they were all in mercy. And let the Sheriff distrain upon their lands &c. So that he should have their bodies &c."

What the cause of this quarrel was does not appear, but it was most likely about game. Barnby Grange was one of the first possessions of the monks, and remained in their hands as long as their house stood. It was given them by Gervis de Barnby.

In December, 1264, certain Bishops, sundry Barons, an unheard of crowd of Priors and Abbots (among whom was Walter, abbot of Roche,) and from each county two most loyal, upright and discreet Knights, and from each borough two of the more discreet, loyal and upright of their citizens and burgesses were called together by the following mandate, to consult with Simon de Montfort, who " in all but name a king," having defeated the Royal army at Lewes held King Henry captive at the time this summons was issued:—

Summons to Parliament.

"HENRY, by the grace of God, King of England, Lord of Ireland and Duke of Aquitaine, to the venerable father in Christ, Walter by the same grace, Abbot of Roche, greeting! Forasmuch as after serious contests and disturbances which had long been taking place in our realm, our dearest son Edward was given up and detained as a hostage in order to secure and confirm peace in our realm, and now, blessed be God! that the aforesaid disturbance is quieted, it behoves us to take measures for making secure provision for the liberation of the same, and for confirming and completing full security and tranquillity of peace, the honour of God and the benefit of our whole realm, and about certain other affairs of our realm which we are unwilling to dispatch without your advice and that of our other prelates and magnates; we therefore send this our mandate, desiring you by that fidelity and love in which you are bound to us, to postpone every pressing matter and lay aside all other affairs, and be with us at London on the Octave of St. Hilary next to come, to discuss with us and the aforesaid prelates and magnates whom we have caused to be summoned to the same place, and to give your advice, and this as you love us and our honour and yours, and the common tranquillity of our realm, by no means omit.

Witness the King at Worcester, December 14th."

Prior to this time parliament had consisted of only eleven prelates and twenty-three peers. Now more than one hundred of the inferior dignified clergy, two knights from each county and two representatives from each borough were summoned, an innovation which proved too popular to be laid aside when the King regained his liberty.

This parliament assembled on January 28th, 1265.

On the 28th of May of the same year, Prince Edward escaped from his guards and joined Mortimer. On August 4th he took the field against Simon de Montfort at Evesham, defeated and killed him and set his father the King at liberty, notwithstanding that parliament had enacted that neither the King nor Prince Edward should aggrieve Montfort or his associates for their past conduct.

Whatever may be said against Simon de Montfort it should always be remembered that to him we owe the three estates of parliament, king, lords and commons.

Besides attending parliament Walter would have to attend a general chapter now and then in France. In 1256 all the English Cistercian abbots were invited to attend on St. Michael's day, to consider whether they should grant an aid to the Pope and King Henry III., which they declined.

We may judge what a confused and turbulent state the country was in at this time, by an Inquisition which was taken this same year (1265)—" Whether Walter had intruded himself into the manor of Sandbec by occasion of the troubles late in England, and the jury found that he had not, but that he had been in possession before the troubles, in the troubles and after the troubles."

Walter the eight abbot of Roche and the first to sit in parliament died in 1268.

Alan, Jordan and Philip.

1268—1286.

ALL that we know of these three abbots is that they reigned between the above dates. Alan may have been the Alan de Smetheton, who in the last abbot's time was one of the monks "beaten and wounded."

In 1275 we find from the "*Hundred Rolls,*" that two other monks got into trouble at Armthorpe. A complaint is made against Richard de Heydon, seneschall to Earl Warenn who sent William de Counhal, Alan Fitz Chapel and many others, "To the grange of the Abbot of Roche at Armthorpe, beyond the liberties of the said Earl, and took brother Richard the granger, and John the forester of the said Abbot, because the said John had shot a certain animal in the aforesaid wood of the said abbot, and had pursued it into the warren of the said Earl, and he (Richard de Heydon) imprisoned them at Coningsbro, and detained them until the said Abbot came and paid a fine of 40*l.* for the said brother,—which he fully paid; but the said John he would not let go on any account, but kept him in prison for a whole entire year." This was indeed very hard upon John the forester, especially if he were kept in that damp circular pit which is now to be seen in the keep of the Castle of Coningsbro'. This same Richard is also accused of having practised "diabolical and innumerable oppressions."

The affairs of the Abbey seem to have glided quietly on about this time, the only other thing worthy of notice is that the abbot's right to free warren in Roche, Armthorpe and Brancliffe was disputed, which as we have already seen was given them in Abbot Richard's time by Henry III. The abbot came in answer to the summons "And said that he claimed free warren in Roche &c., by charter of Lord Henry the King, father of our Lord the King that now is, granted in the 35th year of his reign, which he produced and which testified that the said Lord the King granted to a certain abbot and convent of Roche, predecessors of that abbot, that they and their successors for ever should have free warren in all their demesne lands of Roche, Armthorpe and Brancliffe in the county of York, &c."

Considerable possessions still continued to fall into the hands of the monks of Roche, notwithstanding the restrictions of Mortmain Act which was passed at this time, and provided that no person religious or other should buy or sell or receive under pretences of a gift or term of years, or any other title whatsoever, nor should by any art or ingenuity appropriate to himself any lands or tenements in mortmain *(in mortua manu)* upon pain that the immediate lord of the fee, or, on his default for one year, the lords paramount, and in default of all of them, the King might enter thereon as a forfeiture. This however was soon got over by the religious houses setting up a fictitious title to the land which it was intended they should have, and then bringing an action to recover it against the tenant, who by fraud and collusion made no defence, and thereby judgment was given for the religious house, which then recovered the land by a sentence of law upon a supposed prior title.

Philip ceased to be abbot in 1286.

Thomas.

1286—1287.

THOMAS profeſſed canonical obedience to John Romaine, Archbiſhop of York, on the 7th non. Nov., 1286, and held his abbacy a year all but a few days, but beyond that, nothing is known of the life of this abbot.

In the liſt of the abbots of Roche given by Dr. Burton in his "*Monaſticon Eboracense*," no mention is made of this abbot, and the preſidency of Stephen the next abbot is made to commence a year earlier than it really did. Thomas terminated his ſhort rule in 1287.

Stephen.

1287—1300.

STEPHEN profeffed canonical obedience as abbot of Roche, to John Romaine, Archbifhop of York, in 1287. The following is his form of profeffion:—"I brother Stephen, abbot of Roche promife that I will perpetually fhow fubjection, reverence and obedience as appointed by the Holy Fathers, according to the rule of the order of St. Benedict, to thee Father John, Archbifhop of York, and to thy fucceffors canonically to be fubftituted, and to the Holy See of York, fave my order, and this with my own hand I fubfcribe. Given at Thorpe, 3 non. November." •

Stephen held his abbacy during ftormy times and muft have lived any thing but a peaceful and fecluded life. When Durandus poor and unknown firft fheltered himfelf in a fecluded valley beneath fome rocks, a life of fimplicity feemed poffible, but now—with poffeffions innumerable and fcattered, with courts to prefide over and law fuits to anfwer and with chapters and parliaments to attend;—peace muft have been impoffible. However alluring it may appear in the abftract to live in undifturbed repofe, it can never be the lot of man; and Stephen perhaps was none the lefs happy in having to perform in addition to his duties as a religious fuperior, thofe of a temporal and patriotic lord.

In 1293 a Norman and an Englifh veffel met off the coaft near Bayonne and landed for water. Both crews arriving at the well at the fame time, a quarrel enfued which ended in one of the Normans being killed. To revenge this the Normans feized an Englifh fhip and having hanged at the yard-arm together with fome dogs feveral of the crew, they again abandoned the veffel. The Englifh retaliated in a like barbarous manner on all French fhips without diftinction,

• Reg. John Romaine, page 12.

and the French revenged themselves again in return on the English and Saxons, until the sea became a scene of piracy and murder. At length a fleet of two hundred Norman vessels sailing south for wine, and committing the usual barbarities on all the English ships they met with, so roused the ire of the English in the sea ports that they sent out sixty armed vessels to meet them on their return. An obstinate battle was the result, in which the English were victorious, and it is said that the loss of the French was 15,000 men. In consequence of this defeat, Philip the French King, demanded reparation and restitution, and cited Edward as Duke of Guienne to appear before his court in Paris, to answer for these offences. To prevent a national war, King Edward sent over to Paris his brother Edmund, to arrange matters and prevent further hostilities. But Philip would be appeased only on one condition. Edward must give him seizin and possession of the province of Guienne; he would then feel his honour satisfied, and promised to restore it immediately. Edward who was engrossed with the Scots agreed, and Philip as might have been expected, finding himself so easily in possession, again cited Edward, and for non-appearance condemned him, and Guienne by a formal sentence was declared forfeited and annexed to the crown of France. King Edward enraged and ashamed at being so over-reached determined at once to invade France, and recover his lost territories. To do this effectively he invoked the aid of every one, and even went so far as to empty the jails and make soldiers of thousands of the prisoners. Of course the abbot of Roche having interest and money had to do his share, and he received the following summons to attend a council of the clergy.

"THE King to his beloved in Christ, the abbot of Roche, greeting! In what manner the King of France has maliciously cheated us of our territory of Guienne, and has thence by fraud ejected us, unjustly detaining the same, we believe is not unknown to your fraternity. With a view therefore to recovering that territory from the hands of the said King, we rely upon your counsel and aid, as well as that of the rest of the prelates and clergy of our realm, whom this business touches equally with ourselves, being forthcoming. Therefore, we have arranged (God willing) to be in person at Westminster on the feast of St. Matthew the Apostle and Evangelist, next coming, to treat together with you and the rest of the prelates and clergy of the said realm, towards applying a remedy against this sort of malice. We command you, firmly enjoining you by the faith and love in which you are bound to us, that you be present in person at the said day and place &c.

Witness the King, at Portsmouth, August 19, 1294."

The King opened the assembly in person. After stating the necessities of the war in Guienne, he requested both their prayers and their aid. "Because, my good Lords," he continued "You see that the Earls, Barons, and Knights not only contribute their goods, but expose their lives in your defence; and as to you therefore, who cannot venture your bodies, it is fitting that you should afford some aid from your purses." After many debates the clergy voted two tenths, but the King was not satisfied with this, and at length after much threatening they consented to give what the King demanded, a moiety.

The army which Edward sent at first, met with many successes, but the advantages obtained were lost by the Governor of Podensac, who, when that small fortress was besieged by the French Commander, capitulated, and agreed to articles, which though favourable to the English, left the Gascons prisoners at discretion. The French Commander immediately hanged fifty of them, and the consequence was that the Gascons enraged at their comrades being delivered up so easily, joined the French, and the English were obliged to capitulate and return. Not content with the advantage thus obtained, Philip threatened an invasion of England, and even made a sudden attempt on Dover which he burnt.

Edward in trouble at this and fearing for the safety of his kingdom, was again in need, and asked for parliamentary supplies. Stephen therefore with others received a summons to parliament.

"THE King to his beloved in Christ, the Abbot of Roche, greeting! In what manner the King of France has fraudulently and craftily cheated us of our territory of Guienne, by unjustly detaining it from us is known to you. Now however, not content with the aforesaid fraud and malice, having got together a very large fleet and a great multitude of warriors, with which he has now in a hostile manner invaded our realm and the inhabitants of the said realm, and purposes to blot out entirely from the land the English tongue, (which God avert!) if his power correspond to the detestable intent of his iniquitous conception. Inasmuch then as foreseen darts are less injurious, and your interest as well as that of the rest of the citizens of the said realm is at stake in this matter, we command and enjoin you by the faith and love with which you are firmly bound to us, to be present on the Sunday next after the feast of St. Martin in the winter next to come, at Westminster in person." November 13, 23 Edward I.

But Edward's fears were groundless. England did not fall into the hands of the French, nor was the English language blotted out. After making an attempt upon Dover the French forces were compelled to retire.

The differences with France still remained unsettled. Abbot Stephen was summoned again to appear in person at Bury St. Edmunds on the morrow of All Souls, (November 3, 1296) for the purpose of confirming the grant of a subsidy stated to have been promised in case the King of France should refuse to conclude a truce of peace.*

A fifth was demanded from the clergy, but they refused to grant it, saying that both themselves and the King would be excommunicated if they did so, as it would be contrary to the constitution lately published by Pope Boniface VIII., forbidding the clergy to contribute anything belonging to the Church to a secular Prince. The King was pleased for the time to receive this answer, and the business was adjourned to another parliament to be held at London in the beginning of the ensuing month of January.

When the clergy reassembled pursuant to this adjournment, they again deliberated whether they could comply with the King's demands and after much discussion came to the conclusion that they could not. The King became extremely indignant at their answer and put the whole of them out of the protection of the law. " If they went abroad, in quest of maintenance, they were dismounted, robbed of their horses and clothes, abused by every ruffian, and no redress could be obtained by them for the most violent injury." The clergy were soon compelled by these vexations to yield, and the Archbishop elect of York with many others compounded. The clergy in the north yielded sooner than those in the south, as the former were in daily dread of the Scots, and were glad to pay anything for their protection.

But besides having to give money the abbot of Roche was expected to find men with horses and arms. In 1297 Edward to increase his army which he intended to direct against France, required the attendance of every proprietor of land, possessed of twenty pounds a year; and Stephen consequently received a command similar to the following from the Sheriffs of Yorkshire, Nottinghamshire and Derbyshire, in all of which counties he had property.

" ON the part of our Lord the King I have especially summoned required and firmly enjoined on all my bailly, possessing twenty pounds

---

* This summons was repeated.

of land and rent per annum and more, to be at London on the Sunday next after the Octave of St. John Baptist; with horses and arms ready with the King in person to cross over to foreign parts."

Soon after this the Sheriff received another brief, and he continues,

"AFTERWARDS by another mandate which came to me afterwards, all the aforesaid are premonished to be at Nottingham at the aforesaid day and in form aforesaid, before William de Ormesby the assignee of the Earl Warrenne, to cross over into the parts of Scotland and to do there what the said William on the part of our Lord the King may enjoin upon them. To the Abbot of Roche."

From the above documents it would seem that Stephen in his time must have been a busy and an important personage. But he had yet another duty to perform.

When a royal person died the clergy were required to celebrate his or her exequies. The following is a copy of the order received by Stephen to celebrate those of Edmund, brother of King Edward; and who, as the reader has seen, was sent by the King to France, to make peace with Philip.

"KING Edward to his beloved in Christ, the abbot of Roche. The most High Creator of all things, has created human nature after his own image and similitude and has placed it, being constituted of soul and body, in this miserable world for this end, that having at his will and pleasure finished the course of this life as of some journey, that of which it is composed should be resolved into its elements, and on the return of the body to the earth from which it proceeds the spirit should return to the Lord by whom it was given. And this journey no one can perform without coming in contact with many defilements, just as the feet of travellers cannot pass along without the adhesion of dust. Wherefore those who are passing from the present world greatly stand in need of being assisted by the prayers of the living. Inasmuch therefore as that illustrious man Edmund, our most dear and only brother, who was always ready, devoted and faithful in our interests and the interest of our realm, and in whom manifold virtuous and gracious gifts shone forth, has been withdrawn from this light, as seemed good to the Creator, (on account of which withdrawal we reckon ourselves and the said realm to be rendered most desolate) which we announce to you not without grievous bitterness of soul: we earnestly require and ask your friendship now that we are solemnly and with devotion celebrating the exequies of our said brother, that you commend his soul to the most High God, with singing of masses and other aids of devout prayers, specially enjoining the same upon all and singular the religious under your charge. Witness the King at Aberdeen, * * * * 1296."

Almost the last act which Stephen performed must have been that of attending the parliament held two months before the election of the next abbot, John.

This parliament was held in London on the 6th of March, 1300, "for the safety of the crown and the welfare of the people," and the abbot of Roche was commanded to be there in person, "to advise with the other 'magnates' and 'proceres' on the affairs of the King and the kingdom."

John.

1300.

JOHN'S abbacy was of shorter continuance than that of any other abbot of Roche. He professed canonical obedience to Thos. Corbridge, Archbishop of York, on May 30th, 1300, and resigned or died before December 18th of the same year.* This profession was made in the Chapel of Lautun (Laughton), in the presence of the Prior of Workfop and other Priors, W. de Wentworth, S. de Rotherham and many others.

John was summoned to attend parliament at Lincoln on September 25th, or January 20th, 1301. This summons had to be answered by the next abbot Robert. The only recorded act which it is probable was performed by John, was that of celebrating, on 25th September, by command of the King, the exequies of "that noble man Edmund, formerly Earl of Cornwall, our most dear cousin who was always ready, devoted and faithful to our interests and the interests of our realm &c."

* Reg. Thomas Corbridge, page 5.

Robert.

1300—1324.

ROBERT profeſſed canonical obedience as abbot of Roche at Scroby, on December 18th, 1300, and held his abbacy twenty-four years. He led a life of great activity, and the troubles he had to contend with, as we ſhall preſently ſee, were not a few. He was in conſtant attendance at parliament.

In 1301 he had to attend the parliament to which the former abbot John had been ſummoned, and which was held at Lincoln, on the Octave of St. Hilary, 20th January. "Great debates aroſe at this parliament reſpecting the perambulation of the foreſts."

In 1302 Robert was ſummoned to parliament at Weſtminſter, on the Octave of the Nativity of St. John the Baptiſt, 1ſt July, in order to treat and adviſe on certain arduous affairs with the other prelates and nobles.

Again in 1302 he was ſummoned to parliament at Weſtminſter, at Michaelmas—prorogued to the morrow of St. Edward, 14th October. The Scots were once more troubleſome, and abbot Robert had again to furniſh men and arms.

In 1305 he was ſummoned to parliament at Weſtminſter, on Tueſday, the fifteenth day after the Purification, 16th February—prorogued to the Sunday next after the Feaſt of St. Matthias the Apoſtle, 28th February, to conſult "on certain affairs which ſpecially concern the kingdom of England, and alſo the ſettlement of Scotland."

In 1307 Robert was ſummoned to the celebrated Parliament held at Carliſle, on the Octave of St. Hilary, 20th January. At this parliament was paſſed the "Statute of Carliſle," in which all religious perſons were forbidden to ſend any tax beyond the ſea. "Alien ſuperiors having ſet divers unwonted and heavy payments, and impoſitions on the monaſteries in ſubjection to them in England, the King can no longer ſuffer ſuch loſſes and injuries to be winked at, and provides a ſufficient remedy &c."

But besides this (which must have been a great relief to many monasteries,) very important alterations were made in the use of seals in religious houses.

"AND further, our Lord the King hath ordained and established that the abbots of the orders, Cistercianses and Premonstranses, and other religious orders, whose seal hath heretofore been used to remain only in the custody of the abbot, and not of the convent, shall hereafter have a common seal, and shall deposit the same in the custody of the prior of the monastery or house, and four of the most worthy and discreet men of the convent of the same house, to be laid up in safe-keeping under the private seal of the abbot of the same house; so that the abbot, or superior of the house which he doth govern, shall by no means be able of himself to establish any contract or obligations as heretofore he hath used to do. And if it fortune hereafter that writings of obligations, donations, purchases, sales, alienations, or of any other contracts, be found sealed with any other seal than such a common seal kept as is aforesaid, they shall be adjudged void and of no force in law."

This statute was sent with the King's letters patent to the abbots of the undermentioned places:—Eglifton, St. Agatha, Jeroval, Byland, Fountains, Roche, Welbeck, Rufford, Gerwedon, and Spalding.

Why this statute was sent to so few abbots does not appear, nor why the abbot of Roche was singled out as one of the few. It however was a step of great importance, for hitherto the monks had had very little control over the management of the possessions of the monastery to which they belonged. It was to them an enfranchisement similar to the introduction of the commons into parliament.

At a council held in St. Paul's Church, at London, in 1237, before the Pope's Legate, it was decreed: "that in order to prevent the issuing of false instruments, all archbishops, bishops, abbots, priors, deans, &c., should hold seals; in the granting of the use of which, faithful and circumspect caution was to be observed; faithful, that it might be easily granted, to those who required it, and circumspect, that it might be denied to false and fraudulent persons,"

Fig. 1, Plate X. is the secretum, or private seal of the abbot of Roche. Bishops and abbots usually had oval seals. The former held the pastoral staff in the left hand, abbots in the right. Symbols were also sometimes introduced, indicating the worth and character of the abbot, In this seal the *star* is the symbol of the Epiphany.

The *crescent* signifies the increase of the gospel.

The *flowers* denote purity of life.

At the death of an abbot his seal was sometimes broken by a hammer, upon one of the steps before the altar.

Fig. 2, Plate X. is a sketch of the matrix of the private seal of the abbot of Roche, now in the possession of G. S. Foljambe, Esq., of Osberton Hall, near Worksop, in whose family it has been for several generations.

The earliest common seals which were cut directly after the passing of the statute of Carlisle, bore the representation of the patron saint of the Abbey; but in later seals the abbot took the place of the saint, to whom he is represented praying. Before the reign of Edward the III. these saints and abbots were seated upon thrones, but after this time they are represented standing beneath canopies and arches.

Fig. 3, Plate X. is a representation of the earliest common seal of Roche, which has yet been found. It is appended to a deed made in 1385, which is now in the possession of Mr. Mitchell, of Sheffield. This seal has never before been published.

Fig. 4, Plate X. is the last common seal of Roche. It was with this that the deed surrendering the Abbey to King Henry VIII. at the dissolution was sealed.

Besides the parliament held at Carlisle, abbot Robert was summoned in the same year, 1307, to attend a parliament at Northampton, on the 15th day after St. Michael, 13th October, in order to treat and advise concerning the celebration of the funeral of the late King, and also, about the solemnization of the espousals and coronation of the present king, Edward II.

In 1309 he was again summoned to parliament at Westminster, one month after Easter, 27th April, to consult with the King on "certain arduous affairs."

In 1311 he was summoned to parliament at London, on Sunday next before the feast of St. Laurence, 8th August. Robert is commanded to lay all other matters aside, and to appear in person before the king at the said day and place, to treat and advise with the prelates and nobles. At this parliament Piers Gaveston the king's favourite, was banished the king's dominions.

In 1312, Robert was summoned twice to attend parliament, on the 23rd of July, and on the 20th of August. The King was in trouble at home and abroad, and needed the help of all at that time. His favourite Gaveston was murdered and his enemy Robert Bruce under arms.

From this laſt parliament, held Auguſt 20th, Robert muſt have gone over to a general chapter of his order, as the following document ſhews:—

"THE King to the guardians of the paſſage of the port of Dover, health! We command you, that you freely permit our beloved in Chriſt, the abbot of Roche, of the Ciſtercian order, who is about to ſet out to his general chapter to be held immediately at Ciſteaux, to paſs in the harbour of the aforeſaid to foreign parts, and to pay him for his expenſes twenty marks at this time. Witneſs the King at Canterbury, Auguſt 21ſt, 1312."

In 1313 abbot Robert was ſummoned to attend parliament three times: on the 18th of March, the 8th of July, and the 22nd of September, "to treat on the affairs of the kingdom and the war againſt the Scots." He was required alſo to do more than give his advice on this laſt ſubject.

"THE King to his beloved in Chriſt, the Abbot and Convent of Roche, greeting! Inaſmuch as for the purpoſe of making reſiſtance to Robert de Bruce, a rebel and enemy to us, and his accomplices and adherents, who propoſe ſhortly to invade with hoſtile intent our Scottiſh Marches—as we think has already come to your notice—we have ordered certain nobles of our kingdom, with a fixed number of armed men to take their deſtination to the ſaid parts, for doing which it behoves us neceſſarily to have a large ſum of money, and ſince certain prelates of the province of Canterbury in our parliament convoked on the 8th of July, one by one liberally, on loan yielded and granted certain ſums of money in aid of the buſineſs aforeſaid, to be allowed to them at their next payments to us, whether from tenths or from military ſervice due from them in Scotland, or otherwiſe; we, equally confiding in you alſo to exhibit your zeal for our defence, earneſtly require and aſk you to be willing to lend us to the extent of *fifty marks* for the exigent purpoſe aforeſaid, according as our beloved clerk William de Melton ſhall deem fit to require of you on our behalf. And this by all means do, as ye love us, our honour and your own, and the preſervation of the realm, receiving from the ſaid William letters patent witneſſing the receipt of the ſaid money. Witneſs the King at Wyndſor, Auguſt 13th."

Beſides theſe fifty marks he had to ſend horſes and arms, to muſter at Berwick-on-Tweed, on the 10th of June.

The King determining to put an end to the conſtant wars which were being carried on againſt Scotland aſſembled at this time an enormous army from Gaſcony, Flanders, Wales and Ireland, and with which and his Engliſh ſoldiers he marched into Scotland, to the fatal field of Bannockburn, where on the 25th of June, 1314, was fought "the great and decisive battle of Bannockburn, which secured the independence of Scotland, fixed Bruce on the throne of that kingdom, and may be deemed the greatest overthrow that the English nation (since the conquest) has ever received."

What was the fate of the men, horses and arms which Robert sent from the quiet valley of Roche?

But the valley of Roche was anything but peaceful a few years after this, for we find in 1322, John de Mowbray and others, with 80 men at arms and 400 footmen, adherents of Thomas, Earl of Lancaster, ravaging the whole country about Roche Abbey. They besieged the castle of Tickhill, which was successfully defended by the king's constable, William de Anne, and despoiled the town and church of Laughton, carrying away all their cattle and goods. Abbot Robert must have had a very difficult part to act during these disturbances, for while it was evidently to his interest to remain on friendly terms with the rebels that his Abbey and property might escape spoilation, at the same time the king demanded "that he should raise as many men at arms and foot as he could to march against the rebels and adherents of the Earl of Lancaster, who are destroying our people and besieging with an armed force our castle of Tickhill."

Robert received this mandate on the 16th of February, and the muster was to take place at Coventry, on February 28th, "where he proposed to be, (the Lord willing) with horses and arms, as decently and powerfully as he could." On the 16th of the next month, the battle of Boroughbridge put an end to our good abbot's troubles, and on the 23rd of March, the turbulent Earl of Lancaster was also no more.

Robert held his abbacy only two years after this period.

William.

1324—1330.

WILLIAM, the fifteenth abbot of Roche, profeſſed canonical obedience to William Melton, Archbiſhop of York, on the 9th of December, 1324.

In 1327, William received the following order to ſtay at home, and take care of his abbey, which was in danger, in conſequence of the Scots having entered England, Robert Bruce hoping to take advantage of the weak ſtate of the government:—

"THE KING to his beloved in Chriſt, the abbot of Roche greeting! How the Scotch, our enemies and rebels have entered our kingdom with hoſtile intent, inhumanely perpetrating homicides, depredations, fires and other ills innumerable, and as we (Edward III) are in our own perſon with our army poſted in the parts of the march of Scotland, to reſtrain their malicious deſign, your foreſight well knows; and inaſmuch as it ſtands ordered by ourſelves and our councils that no nobles, prelates or others, nor any perſon of note ſhould go out of the ſame kingdom, and eſpecially from the parts on this ſide Trent, ſo long as the ſaid enemies thus ſtay within our realm, and it is given us to underſtand that you propoſe to betake yourſelf in perſon to our general chapter, to be held at Ciſteaux, we, wiſhing the aforeſaid order to be inviolably obſerved, prohibit you under penalty of a heavy forfeiture to us, to betake yourſelf to any ſtrange places beyond your own bounds, ſo long as the ſaid enemies thus remain in our realm, under pretence of any licence by us to you previouſly granted, until we ſhall have thought right to order otherwiſe thereupon, but that you attend more carefully than uſual to the cuſtody of your Abbey, and to all other the premiſes. Witneſs, the King at Stanhop, Auguſt 3rd, 1327."

Twelve other abbots whoſe monaſteries were in the north of England, received the ſame command.

William ceaſed to be abbot of Roche in 1330.

Adam de Giggleswick.

1330—1349.

GIGGLESWICK is a place famous for its Well, which is said to rise and fall about eighteen inches several times a day.

> " At Giggleswick where I a fountain can you show
> That eight times in a day is said to ebb and flow."
> *Drayton's Polyolbion.*

An Adam, son of Adam de Gigglefwick is mentioned in *Burton*, as having given to the Monks of Fountains Abbey "3*s*. 4*d*. per annum, to find veils for the * * * * * who came to the abbey gate to be cured." ·It is not impossible that Abbot Adam may have been connected with this family. It is not however necessary that an abbot should be of high origin. Monks, according to *Chaucer*, " Cominly comen of pore peple," and " Ther farthirs ride but on ther fete." But, however high or low may have been the birth of Adam de Gigglefwick, he had sufficient interest with the Monks of Roche to induce them to elect him as their abbot in 1330.

The intense religious feeling which had in the few previous centuries induced men to give up so much of their property to the church was already beginning fast to wane; and it doubtless was not without reason that complaint was made at this time to the Pope, that "The alms and devotion of all men were diminished." Religious communities would be ill able to bear any loss of income, at a time when the King, for the purpose of carrying on his wars with France, was ever demanding heavy subsidies and loans, both in wool and money.

For fifteen years Adam struggled on with these difficulties until 1345, when there came a bright and happy day for the monks of Roche. John, the last Earl of Warren, beholding the poverty of the Monastery of Roche, and admiring the beauty of its buildings, gave the monks that year "*in loco penitentiæ*," says *Mr. Hunter*, the Church of Hatfield, valued at that time at seventy marks per annum; having previously obtained a licence from the King to enable him to do so.

An imperfect copy of the charter which conveyed this gift to the monks of Roche is among *Dodsworth's MS.*, of which, as far as it could be made out, the following is a translation:—

Charter of John de Warren, Earl of Surrey.

"KNOW all men as well present as future, by these presents that we, John de Warren Earl of Surrey, beholding the scarcity of fruits, rents and possessions generally pertaining to the religious men, the Abbot and Convent of Roche, in the diocese of York, and to their monastery; also nobly grieving for the paucity of monks serving God there; and being most deeply anxious for the augmentation of divine worship, and also for increasing (by the help of God), the number of brothers in the same; have given and granted in form and manner underwritten for the causes aforesaid, and other devotions moving us thereto, as far as in us lies, and we can rightly do so, the right of the patronage or advowson of the Parish Church of Hatfield in the said diocese of York, belonging to us by hereditary right, with all rights, fruits, rents, possessions and appurtenances whatever to the said church in any way pertaining from ancient time, to the said abbot and convent and their monastery by the will, consent and assent of our Lord Edward the third, the illustrious King of England, requested by us on this behalf from the Lord King himself, and obtained, and by special licence as by letters royal, composed on occasion of the aforesaid remaining in the possession of the Abbot and Convent, evidently appears. To have and to hold the said right of patronage or advowson of the Church aforesaid, for all times to the aforesaid Abbot and Convent and their monastery aforesaid, in such manner, namely, that from the time of the appropriation of the said Church to the said religious and their monastery, being sufficiently, lawfully and strictly made, according to the requirements of the law, and in which they shall enjoy peaceable possession of the right of receiving and holding for the greater part, the fruits and rents of the tithes to the said Church belonging, free from impediment or calumny of any kind, then incontinently thereafter, with all diligence, without delay, they shall take and assume into their habit and vows beyond the number constituted in the said monastery at the time of its foundation, thirteen honest men and competently skilled in literature; and the said number thirteen beyond the said monks constituted at the time of the said foundation, the said Abbot and Convent and their successors in the said monastery shall, by immediately supplying new ones in the place of those who die or otherwise fail of the said thirteen, acknowledge, sustain and for ever find and have patiently to serve Almighty God unto their live's end * * * * all the aforesaid monks for ever, from that time in which the said number * * * shall have been (God granting) beyond * * the foundation * * * daily XIII * * * monks * * * according as * * * * was for the time, VIII. masses a day with collects * * * * for the souls of the said Lord Edward the King, and the most excellent Lady Philippa, the Queen, his consort, and William, their son, who * * * * of the said King and Queen, and also for our good state and soul, and for the souls of all our relations, and all the faithful dead, so long as * * * * other masses and the said obsequies in the said monastery * * * * shall make and pay, and shall make our death * * * * on the day of our anniversary, as well in largesses, alms, * * * * in saying masses and other customary devotions, and as for death * * * * in other monasteries * * * * in divine and other offices aforesaid is wont solemnly to be performed * * * and if they shall cease in their service (which God forbid!) the said Abbot and Convent, the said burdens interposed in the manner in which it is permitted * * * * either in part or three times, publicly admonished about performing and observing the premises by us, our heirs or executors, shall have corrected or and thenceforth * * * * the Church of Hatfield aforesaid which we our heirs or successors who for the time being shall be * * * * the aforesaid John Earl of Surrey, and our heirs will warrant and defend for ever against all people, the said right of patronage or advowson of the Church aforesaid, with all its rights and appurtenances, to the said Abbot and Convent and their monastery aforesaid, in manner and form aforesaid. In testimony whereof to this writing indented, my seal together with the common seal of the said Abbot and Convent are alternately appended. Witness, &c., given at Lewis, on the first day of December, in the tenth year of the reign of King Edward, the third since the Conquest."

The appropriation of this magnificent gift was effected by William la Zouch, Archbishop of York, reserving out of the profits an annual pension of ten marks to himself, and five for the Dean and Chapter, and ordering a proper house to be built by the Abbot of Roche, for the vicar, who was to be paid fifteen pounds a year at Easter, Michaelmas and Christmas by equal portions.

When John, Earl of Warren, died, all his lands north of the Trent went to the crown and were settled upon Edmund of Langley, a younger son of the King. But as he was only six years old, his mother, Queen Philippa, was allowed to receive the profits for the education of her children. The fecond fon of Edward the third was born at Hatfield, and in confequence took the name of William de Hatfield. "Upon this occafion," fays *Thorefby*, Queen Philippa gave five marks per annum to the Abbey of Roche, and five nobles to the monks there. This fum, however, when the Prince died, was tranfferred to the Church of York, where he was buried, to pray for his foul!*

Adam de Gigglefwick ceafed to be Abbot of Roche in 1349, and it is not improbable that he may have fallen a victim to the peftilence which raged that year, and which, *Stowe* fays, " Was fo vehement and fharpe that there remained not the tenth perfon alive throughout the realm."

* Ducatus Leodienfis pref. p. xv.

Simon de Baukewell.

1349—1358.

SIMON DE BAUKEWELL, or Bakewell, profeſſed canonical obedience on the 25th October, 1349, and on the ſame day received the benediction of William de la Zouch, Archbiſhop of York, in the chapel of his Manor of Cawood.[a]

Already monachiſm was upon the decline, and bitter ſarcaſms were in circulation. *Walter Mapes*, who had a ſtrong hatred of the clergy, and of the Ciſtercians in particular, wrote about this time ſuch ſentences as the following[b]:—

"I saw the warkes and trade of abbots there eche one,
    Of whom their flock to leade to hell not one doth miſſe."

"Worse than a monke there is no fende nor sprite in hell,
    Nothing so covetuose nor more strange to be knowen,
For if you give him ought, he maie poſſeſſe it well,
    But if you aſke him ought, then nothinge is his owne."

Simon ceaſed to be abbot of Roche in 1358.

[a] Reg. William de la Zouche, p. 41.   [b] Walter Mapes, Cam. Soc., p. 279, 280.

John de Aston.

1358—1396.

JOHN DE ASTON, like several of the preceding abbots, seems to have come originally from a place not far distant from Roche. He professed canonical obedience as abbot of Roche, to John Thoresby, Archbishop of York, on 23rd of November, 1358.[a]

During the abbacy of John de Aston, the advowson of Roche Abbey changed hands from John Levet to Richard Barry, citizen and merchant of London.

In 1362, monachism received a severe blow from the author of "*Peirs Ploughman's Vision and Creed.*" In it the monks are accused of having falsified religion, and of being actuated solely by pride, covetousness, and self-love. A most remarkable prophecy may be found in the *Vision*, commencing at line 6239.

> " Ac ther shal come a Kyng,
> And confesse you religiouses,
> And beat you as the bible telleth
> For brekynge of your rule.
>
> * * * * *
>
> And thane shall the abbot of Abyngdone,[b]
> And all his issue for ever,
> Have a knok of a Kyng,
> And incurable the wounde."

John de Aston ceased to be abbot of Roche in 1396.

---

[a] Reg. John Thoresby, p. 202.
[b] Abingdon in Berkshire was the house into which monks, strictly so called, were first introduced in England, and is, therefore, very properly brought forward as the representative of English monachism.

Robert.

1396—1438.

THE name of this abbot is given on the authority of *Dr. Burton*, who, however, does not give the fource from whence he derived his information.

Although the Abbeys of England had yet a hundred years to ftand, many prophecies of their ultimate fall were made about this time, the moft interefting of which is perhaps the following prophetic parable:—

"WHEN on a certayne time a byrde was brought into the worlde all bear and without fethers, the other byrdes hearing thereof, came to vifite her: and for that they fawe her to be a merveilous fayre byrde, they counfailed together how they might beft do her good, fith by no meanes without fethers, might fhe either flee or live commodioufly. They all wifhed her to live for her excellent forme and beauteis fake, in fo much that among them all there was not one, that would not graunt fome part of her own fethers to deck this byrd withall: yea, and the more true they fawe her to be, the more fethers ftill they gave unto her, fo that by this means fhe was paffing well penned and fethered and began to flee. The other byrdes that thus had adorned her with goodly fethers, beholding her to flee abroad, were merveiloufly delighted therewith. In the end, this byrde feeing herfelf fo gorgeoufly fethered, and of all the reft to be had in honour, began to wax proud and hawty, in fo much that fhe had no regard at all unto them by whom fhe was advanced: yea, fhe punged (pierced) them with her beak, plucked them by the fkinne and fethers, and in all places hurted them. Whereupon, the byrdes fitting in councell agayne, called the matter in queftion, demanding one of another what was beft to be done touching this unkinde byrde, who they fo lovingly with their own fethers had decked and adourned: affirming, that they gave not their fethers to the intent that fhe thereby, puft up with pride, fhould contemptuoufly defpife them all. The peacocke therefore anfwereth firft: 'Truly,' faid he, 'for that fhe is bravely fet forth with my painted fethers, I will again take them from her.' Then, faith the falcon, 'And I, alfo, will have mine againe.' This fentence at length took place among them all, fo that every one plucked from her thofe fethers which before they had given, challenging to them their own againe. Even fo, oh you Cardinals, fhall it happen unto you; for kings, potentates and princes have beftowed upon you goods, lands and riches, that fhould ferve God; but you have poured it out and confumed it upon pride, all kinde of wickednefs, ryot and wantonnes."[a]

The painful forefhadowings of future trouble, feem however, not to have materially affected the health of abbot Robert. He held his abbacy forty-two years, during which time the crown of England three times changed hands.

Robert ceafed to be abbot of Roche in 1438.

[a] Foxe.

John Wakefield.

1438—1465.

JOHN WAKEFIELD was elected abbot of Roche and received the benediction of Archbishop John Kemp, on June 7th, 1438.*

During his time, Roche Abbey obtained a new benefactor and founder in Matilda of York, Countess of Cambridge, who lived in the neighbouring castle of Coningsborough. The following is a translation of the part of her will referring to Roche:—

Will of the Countess of Cambridge.

"IN the name of God, Amen. On the feast of the assumption of the Blessed Virgin Mary, in the year of our Lord 1440, I, Matilda, of York, Countess of Cambridge, being of right mind and sound memory, make my will in this manner:

First, I leave and commend my soul to God and the Blessed Mary and all His saints, and my body to be buried in the monastery of Roche, in the chapel of the Blessed Mary, before her image, situate in the southern part of the church of the said monastery.

Also, I will that there lie over my grave a stone of alabaster, raised aloft after the manner of a tomb, with an effigy, after the manner which I will tell to my executors.

Also, I leave to each chaplain present at my funeral two-pence, and to each parochial clergyman, six-pence.

Also, that my executors appoint wax to be burnt about my body at the time of my funeral, according to their discretion.

Also, I will that twelve poor persons be clad in white gowns, each of whom shall bear one twisted wax taper, of the larger size, in honour of our Lord Jesus Christ and the Blessed Mary, and all

* Reg. John Kemp, p. 393.

His saints; and that these be held by them at the time of my funeral and of my mass, and that each of them have twelve-pence.[b]

Also, I leave to three chaplains of honest conversation, forty-two marks, that they may celebrate and pray for my soul, and for the soul of my lord, and for the souls of my parents; and that one keep a school, if he will.

Also, I will that every year each of them say onet rental of the blessed Gregory, and daily say in their masses this prayer:—"*Deus qui est summa nostræ Redemptionis, &c.*," when they can conveniently do so.

Also, I leave to the monastery of Roche one white vestment, to the intent that one monk of the same place may celebrate for my soul for a week, and have daily one penny; and another monk for another week, and so each in turn may separately celebrate and pray for my soul in the said monastery, for the space of seven years complete.

Also, I leave to the abbot of Roche six shillings and eight-pence, and to each monk there, twenty-pence, on the day of my burial.

Also, I leave to the abbot and convent of the same place, forty marks, on condition that if they are willing sufficiently to show their obligation to their *founder*, they shall, once in each year, for ever, for my soul's health, celebrate my obit in funeral services, and a mass with two wax candles burning over my body during the same time.

Also, I will that my whole vestment of red colour, worked with gold, with one chalice and two crewets, two best silver candlesticks and one silver bell, remain with my body, for the perpetual use of the said church, * * * * * In witness whereof, I have to this present writing affixed my seal. Given in the monastery of Roche, on the day and place aforesaid."[c]

Matilda, Countess of Cambridge, was the daughter of Thomas Lord Clifford, and the second wife of Richard Plantaganet, ordinarily known as Richard of Coningsborough, Earl of Cambridge. She did not long survive the making of her will. It is dated 15th August, 1446, and she died on the 26th of the same month. Her successors were held *founders* of Roche up to the time of the dissolution.

John Wakefield died in the middle of the year 1465, and was buried at Roche with all the honours due to his station.[d]

---

[b] Thomas Duke of Exeter, who died in 1426, ordered something similar to this. "I will that there be as many poor men as I may have lived years at my funeral, each carrying a torch, and habited in a gown and hood of white cloth, and each receiving as many pence as I have lived years; and that there be the same number of poor women, of good character, clothed in a gown and hood of white cloth, and each receiving a penny."—"Testamenta Vetusta," vol. i. p. 208.

[c] "Testamenta Eboracensia," Surtees Society, vol. ii. p. 118.

[d] Reg Geo. Nevil., part i. p. 11.

John Gray.

1465—1479.

CONCERNING the election and benediction of John Gray, we have the following letter and memorandum, which are preserved in the Archbishop's register at York:—

Letter from the Abbot of Newminster.—

"TO the most reverend father in Christ, George, by the grace of God, Archbishop of York. Your devoted son, John, abbot of Newminster, of the Cistercian order, in the diocese of Durham, father abbot and immediate visitor of the monastery of the Blessed Mary of Roche, sends all manner of reverence and honour due to so great a father. We would signify to your most reverend paternity by the tenor of these presents, that the monastery of Roche being lately vacant by the death of the venerable father in the Lord, John de Wakefield, the last abbot; and he being dead and his body buried with the exequies due to his ecclesiastical office, the prior and convent of the aforesaid monastery of Roche, proceeding to the election of a future pastor, elected the religious man, brother John Gray, whose election, after due enquiry made into his fitness, we have confirmed. Wherefore, we pray your Lordship's pre-eminence to grant him your holy benediction. In testimony of which, our seal and the seal of the venerable father in the Lord, the abbot of Rufford, our coassessor is appended. Given in the monastery of Roche, the seventh day of August, 1465.

"Memorandum. That, on the sixth day of September, 1464, the Lord Archbishhop received the aforesaid letter, at Scrooby, and commanded Lord William Bifhop of Dromore, his fuffragan, to confer benediction upon brother John Gray, the aforefaid abbot elect."

It will be noticed that an interval of a month took place between the election and the benediction of this abbot.

John Gray vacated his abbacy, not by death as *Dr. Burton* has it, but by refignation, on the 5th of June, 1479.[a]

[a] Reg. Geo. Nevil, pt. i. p. 11.

William Tikil.

1479—1486.

THE letter of the abbot of Newminster to the Archbishop of York, concerning this abbot, is also preserved, and is even more interesting than the one relating to abbot John Gray.

Letter from the Abbot of Newminster.

"TO the most reverend father and lord in Christ, Lord Laurence, by the grace of God, Archbishop of York, Primate of England, the lord abbot of Newminster, of the Cistercian order, Father abbot and immediate Visitor of the monastery of the Blessed Mary of Roche, of the order aforesaid, and the aforesaid diocese, sends all manner of reverence with the honour and deference due to so great a father, to the utmost gratification of his wish. We humbly thought right to explain to your lordship's preeminence, by the tenor of these presents, that our filial monastery of Roche aforesaid, lately becoming vacant by the voluntary cession and free resignation of the religious man, Master John Gray, late abbot of the said monastery, and so resigning, we, by our paternal authority, which we exercise on this behalf, on the 5th of June, 1479, absolved and exonerated him from all jurisdiction and rule over the said monastery, and from his place and state in the chapter of the monastery; and the venerable father of Rufford, acting as our coassessor in the calling of a new pastor, in due form, according to the rules of the order there was presented, and elected the discrete man, brother William Tikil, one in morals, knowledge of temporals and experience of age, sufficiently furnished. Whom thus canonically presented and elected, we confirmed and led him into the church and installed him, and brought him back into the chapter house, and bound him by an oath, in the customary form of the order, and did all other things which are, or were requisite by the right of our order. Wherefore, we pray your lordship's pre-eminence to be graciously pleased to confer the boon of your sacred benediction upon the said person so elected and instituted. Whom, may God, the giver of all good gifts, prosper with felicity in this present vale of tears, and lead at last to the infinite joys of His heavenly kingdom. In witness whereof, we have caused to be placed to these present writings the seal of our office, together with that of our coassessor aforesaid. Given in our chapter-house of Roche aforesaid, in the month and year above expressed.*

William, Tikil, (Tickhill,) was elected abbot of Roche June 5th, 1479, and he held his abbacy until the latter end of 1486.

* Reg. Laurence Booth, p. 104.

Thomas Thurne.

1486—1488.

IN the register of Thomas Rotherham, Archbishop of York, there is the copy of a letter given under his seal at Scrooby, on the 19th day of December, 1486, empowering his venerable confrere and Bishop William Dromore, his suffragan, to confer benediction on brother Thomas Thurne, who had been elected and confirmed abbot of Roche.[a]

Thomas Thurne (Thorne) ceased to be abbot of Roche early in 1488, after having held his abbacy little more than a year.

[a] Reg. Thomas Rotherham, p. 234.

William Burton.

1488—1491.

WILLIAM BURTON professed canonical obedience and received benediction at the hands of Bishop William Dromore, his suffragan, on the last day of February, 1488.* He ceased to be abbot of Roche in 1491.

* Reg. Thos. Rotherham, p. 242.

John Morpeth.

1491—1503.

ON the eighteenth of August, 1491, Archbishop Thomas Rotherham granted a commission to William, by the grace of God Bishop of Dromore, to confer benediction on John Abbot of the monastery of Roche.*

We may conclude from the name of this abbot that he originally came from Newminster; Morpeth being the name of a town near that monastery.

John Morpeth ceased to be abbot of Roche in 1503.

* Reg. Thomas Rotherham, p. 251.

John Heslington—Henry Cundal.

1503—1538.

THE DISSOLUTION.

A wake, ye ghoſtly perſons! awake, awake,
B oth prieſt, pope, byſhop, and cardinall,
C onſider wiſely, what wayes that ye take,
D aungerouſly beyng like to have a fall,
E very where the miſchiefe of you all,
F arre and neare, breaketh out very faſt:
G od will needes be revenged at the laſt.
H ow long have ye the world captived
I n ſore bondage, of men's traditions?
K ings and Emperours ye have deprived,
L ewdly uſurping theyr chiefe poſſeſſions:
M uch miſery ye make in all regions.
N ow your fraudes be almoſt at their latter caſt,
O f God ſore to be revenged at the laſt.
P oore people to oppreſe, ye have no ſhame,
Q uaking for feare of your double tyranny;
R ightfull juſtice ye have put out of frame,
S eeking the luſt of your god—the belly:
T herefore, I dare you boldly certifie,
V ery little though ye be thereof agaſt,
Y et God will be revenged at the laſt.*

A. B. C. by William Thorpe.

* Foxe.

THROUGHOUT the whole of the first quarter of the sixteenth century, tremblings and commotions, every day increasing in violence, were felt, and only too well recognized by the monks as the forerunners of that relentless earthquake which was to shake their fair abbeys into ruins, and to cast them forth upon the world, homeless and despised.

Monachism received its first fatal shock when Cardinal Wolsey, in order to found a College at Oxford (now Christ's Church,) and another at Ipswich, his native place, obtained leave from Pope Clement to suppress and appropriate the revenues of what he called certain poor and small monasteries, in which he acknowledged that neither God was served, nor religion kept. The abbots, seeing the danger of such a precedent, endeavoured to induce Wolsey to abstain from seizing upon the abbey lands, by offering him instead, large sums of money. The abbot of St. Mary's, York, to save his cell of Romburgh in Suffolk, offered the Cardinal three hundred marks sterling. But all these intercessions of the abbots were in vain, the work of demolition and impropriation commenced at once, and continued steadily until the desired sum had been raised, jealous Catholics here and there expressing their disapprobation in different ways. At Beggam, in Sussex, after the brethren had been turned out of their house, "a riotous company, disguised and unknowne, with painted faces and visers, came to the same monasterie, and brought with them the chanons, and put them into their place again, and promised that whensoever they rang the bell, that they would come with a great power and defend them." But resistance was in vain, the enthusiastic defenders of the religious men of Beggam and elsewhere were soon silenced and punished, and the monastic system had to carry on its existence with its foundations sapped, and its superstructure propped as well as might be. There however, is nothing which so urgently tempts interference as a prop! In the first place, one despises anything which is so dilapidated as to require such assistance, and then one immediately begins to speculate as to the probable consequences of removing it: and lastly, to prove the accuracy of these speculations, the required blow is given. We need not be surprised then, to find that there existed a party whose aim was to knock away the props which upheld monachism without themselves being at the same time buried in the ruins. King Henry VIII., after having read the Beggar's Supplication against the monks, is reported to have said "If a man should pull downe an old stone wall and begin at the lower part, the upper part thereof might chance to fall upon his head." If this be true, it would appear that the Defender of the Faith himself was of the iconoclastic party.

Volumes might be written shewing the numerous causes which had rendered the monks so unpopular, but the two following descriptions of a monastery and a monk will satisfy the reader:—

MONASTERY.—"A house of ill-fame, where men are seduced from their public duties, and fall naturally into guilt from attempting to preserve an unnatural innocence."*

MONK.—Treated after the Linnæan system.

"*Definitio.*—An animal, anthropomorphic, hooded, howling by night, thirsting.

"*Descriptio.*—Body erect, biped, back curved, head depressed, always hooded, and clothed in every part, covetous, fœtid, filthy, drunken, lazy, more patient of want than labour; at the rising and setting of the sun, and especially at night, they congregate, and when one cries out, all cry; run together at the sound of a bell, walk always in couples, are clothed in wool, live by rapine and plunder, assert that the world was made for them alone, carry on their amours clandestinely, do not marry, expose their young, fight with their own species, and attack their enemies unawares from ambushes.

"The female differs little from the male, except in having her head always veiled, is cleaner, less drunken, and never leaves home, which she keeps clean. When young she grasps at all sorts of play things, stares about her on all sides, and salutes the males by nodding. When older, she becomes spiteful and malignant, and when angry, agitates her jaw bones incessantly with open mouth. When called, they answer "Ave." When allowed, they chatter promiscuously, and if a bell rings are suddenly mute.

"*Differentia.*—Man speaks, reasons, wills; the *monk* is often mute, has no reason or will, is governed solely by the orders of his superiors. The head of *man* is erect, the head of a *monk* is depressed with eyes turned to the ground. *Man* seeks his bread by the sweat of his brow, the *monk* growes fat by laziness. *Man* dwells among men, the *monk* seeks solitude and hides himself, avoiding the light. Whence it follows, that the *monk* is a genus of mammalia distinct

* "The Tin Trumpet."

from *man*, intermediary between him and the ape, approaching nearest to the latter, from which it differs very little in voice or manner of living.

"*Usus.*—An useless burthen on the earth."[*]

The worst enemies of the monks could not wish more to be said than is contained in the foregoing lines. They contain doubtless a great amount of exaggeration, but if even a quarter of the accusations in them be true, it is not surprising that the enemies of the monks were numerous.

In 1534, the king, having been pronounced by Parliament supreme Head on earth of the Church of England, determined to exercise his right of visiting every religious community, for the purpose of finding out their real condition. He accordingly commanded his secretary, Thomas Cromwell, to issue a commission to that effect. Thomas Cromwell, was the descendent of a Lincolnshire family, and was well fitted for this work, having been employed by Wolsey in the suppression of the monasteries already referred to. He appointed three visitors, Doctors Legh, Layton, and Ap Rice; and probably towards the end of the year 1535, the two former appeared before the gate of Roche Abbey, for we find them about that time at Fountains, the abbot of which place they wrote to Cromwell was "a vara fole and a miserable ideote."

The manner in which the visitors approached an abbey, was to come upon it suddenly, summoning the brethren immediately before them. An amusing illustration of this may be found in *Dr. Layton's* letter to Cromwell, describing what he did on arriving at the Abbey of Langdon.

"Immediately discending from my horse, I sent Bartlett, your servant, with all my servants to circumcept the abbay, and surely to kepe alle bake dorres and starting hoills, etc. I my self went alone to the abbot's lodging, joynyng upon the feldes and wode, evyn lyke a cony clapper full of startyng hoilles, a goode space knokkyng at thabbottes dore, *nec vox nec sensus apparuit*, saveyng thabbottes litle doge that, within his dore faste lokked, bayede and barkede. I found a short polax standing behynde the dore, and with yt I dasshhede thabbottes dore in peisses, *ictu oculi*, and set one of my men to kepe that dore, and aboute house I go with that polax in my hande, *ne forte*, for thabbot is a daingerouse desperate knave and hardy. But for a conclusion, his gentle woman beystrrede her stumpis towards her startyng hoilles, and ther Bartlett

[*] Specimen Monachologiæ.

wachying the purfuet towke the tendre damoifel, and after I had examined hir, to Dover ther to the maire to fett hir in fum cage or prifon for viii dayes, and I brought holy father abbot to Canterbury and here in Chriftes church I will leve hym in prifon. In this foden doying *ex tempore* to circumcept the houfe and to ferche, your fervant John Antonie his men mervelede what fellow I was, and fo dyde the refte of thabby, for I was unknowyn ther of alle men. At laft, I founde her apparel in thabbottes cofer. To tell howe all this commodie, but for thabbot a tragedie, hit were to long. How hit fh'alle appere to gentilmen of this contrey, and other comons, that ye fhalle not deprive or vifite but upon fubftanciall groundes. Surely I fuppos Gode him felf put hit in my mynde thus fodenly to make a ferche at the begynnyng, bycaufe no chanon appered in my fyght; I fuppofede rather to have founde a woman emongifte them than in thabbottes chambre. The refte off alle this knaverie I fhall differ tyll my cumyng unto you, whiche fhalbe with as muche fpede as I can poffible, doyng my affured deligence in the refte. Scribulled this Satterday, and written with the hafty hand of your affured fervant

RICHARD LAYTON.

When the vifitors had affembled the brethren together, they gave leave to every one under twenty-four years of age to go where he pleafed, and if any chofe to quit their monafteries they had a fecular drefs given them and forty fhillings, and were reftored to the full privileges of the laity.

Gifted with fuch unbounded power, it is not to be wondered at that the vifitors performed their tafks fometimes in an unfeeling manner. Dr. Ap Rice complained to Cromwell of the overbearing manner of Dr. Leigh in his vifitations,—that he was too infolent and pompatique, and handled the fathers too roughly for not meeting him at the door when they had no warning of his coming —that he had twelve men waiting on him in livery, befides his brother, which were a great tax upon the fmall monafteries,—and that he took too much money in the filling up of the vacancies which he found in abbeys.

After the King's fupremacy was eftablifhed, all thofe abbots that had formerly received confirmation of the Archbifhop, were now confirmed by him, through his Lord Vicegerent Cromwell; fo that when a vacancy occured, care was taken to allow no one to become the head of a religious houfe, unlefs he was favourable to the king. Leave to elect was given, but the name of the perfon to be chofen was first declared. It is not unlikely that HENRY CUNDAL, the last abbot of Roche, was instituted in this manner, for no record of his confirmation and benediction can be found in the Regifters of the Archbifhops of York.

What treatment the brethren of Roche experienced at the hands of Doctors Legh and Layton is not known, nor has the document defcribing the moral condition in which the monaftery was then found been preferved.

The queftions which the vifitors demanded of them were eighty-fix in number, and have been epitomized by *Burnet* as follows:—

Whether divine fervice was kept up day and night, in the right hours? and how many were commonly prefent, and who were frequently abfent?

Whether the full number, according to the foundation, was in every houfe? Who were the founders? What additions have been made fince the foundation? and what were their revenues? Whether it was ever changed from one order to another? By whom? and for what caufe?

What mortmains they had? And whether their founders were fufficiently authorized to make fuch donations?

Upon what fuggeftions and for what caufes they were exempted from their diocefans? Their local ftatutes were alfo to be feen and examined.

The election of their head was to be inquired into. The rule of every houfe was to be confidered. How many profeffed? And how many novices were in it? And at what time the novices profeffed?

Whether they knew their rule, and obferved it? Chiefly the the three vows of poverty, chaftity, and obedience? Whether any of them kept any money without the Mafter's knowledge? Whether they kept company with women within or without the monaftery? Or if there were any back-doors by which women came within the precincts? Whether they had any boys lying by them?

Whether they obferved the rules of filence, fafting, abftinence, and hair fhirts? Or by what warrant they were difpenfed with in any of thefe?

Whether they did eat, fleep, wear their habit, and ftay within the monaftery, according to their rules?

Whether the Mafter was too cruel or too remifs? And whether he ufed the brethren without partiality or malice?

Whether any of the brethren were incorrigible? Whether the Mafter made his accompts faithfully once a year?

Whether all the other officers made their accompts truly? And whether the whole revenues of the houfe were employed according to the intention of the founders?

Whether the fabric was kept up, and the plate and furniture were carefully preferved?

Whether the convent feal and the writings of the houfe, were well kept? And whether leafes were made by the mafter to his kindred and friends, to the damage of the houfe? Whether hofpitality was kept? And whether at the receiving of novices, any money or reward was demanded or promifed? What care was taken to inftruct the novices?

Whether any had entered into the houfe, in hope to be once the mafter of it?

Whether in giving prefentations to livings, the Mafter had referved a penfion out of them? Or what fort of bargains he made concerning them?

An account was to be taken of all the parfonages and vicarages belonging to every houfe, and how thefe benefices were difpofed of, and how the cure was ferved.

Having obtained anfwers to the eighty-fix queftions, the Vifitors were ordered to give before departing feveral injunctions to the following effect:—

"That they fhould endeavour, all that in them lay, that the act of the King's fucceffion fhould be obferved;" (where it is faid that they had under their hands and feals confirmed it. This fhows that all the religious houfes of England had acknowledged it:) "and they fhould teach the people, that the King's power was fupreme on earth, under God; and that the Bifhop of Rome's power was ufurped by craft and policy, and by his ill canons and decretals, which had been long tolerated by the Prince, but was now juftly taken away.

The abbot and brethren were declared to be abfolved from any oath they had fworn to the Pope, or to any foreign potentate; and the ftatutes of any order, that did bind them to a foreign fubjection, were abrogated, and ordered to be razed out of their books.

That no monk fhould go out of the precinct, nor any woman enter within it without leave from the King or the Vifitor; and that there fhould be no entry to it but one.*

Some rules were given about their meals; and a chapter of the Old or New Teftament was ordered to be read at every one. The Abbot's table was to be ferved with common meats, and not with

---

* The ftrictnefs of this injunction was intolerable, and was the caufe of many giving up the monaftic life.

delicate and strange dishes; and either he or one of the seniors, was to be always there to entertain strangers.

Some other rules follow about the distribution of their alms, their accommodation in health and sickness. One or two of every house were to be kept at the university, that, when they were all instructed, they might come and teach others: and every day there was to be a lecture of divinity for a whole hour: the brethren must all be well employed.

The Abbot or head was every day to explain some part of the rule, and apply it to Christ's law; and to show them that their ceremonies were but elements introductory to true Christianity; and that religion consisted not in habits, or in such like rites, but in cleanness of heart, pureness of living, unfeigned faith, brotherly charity, and true honouring of God in spirit and in truth: that therefore they must not rest in their ceremonies, but ascend by them to true religion.

Other rules are added about the revenues of the house, and against wastes; and that none be entered into their house, nor admitted under twenty-four years of age.

Every priest in the house was to say mass daily; and in it to pray for the King and Queen.

If any broke any of these injunctions, he was to be denounced to the King, or his Visitor General.

The Visitor had also authority to punish any whom he should find guilty of any crime, and to bring the Visitor General such of their books and writings as he thought fit.

Cromwell's Visitors having ascertained the condition of every religious house, at length returned and laid upon the table of the House of Commons the famous "Black Book" of the Monasteries which stated that two thirds of the monks of England were living a life so drunken, so profligate, and so iniquitous that the details of it may not be entered into. This parliament assembled on the 4th of February, 1536, and be it remembered it was a Catholic one. When the contents of the "Black Book" were read out in the Parliament House, the indignation produced was so great that the cry arose of "Down with them!"[a] and under the influence of this strong feeling the Act for the dissolution of the smaller monasteries having a yearly income less than two hundred pounds, was passed, "by the consent of the great and fatte abbottes" says *Grafton*,[b] "in hope that their great monasterys should have continued still. But even at that

---

[a] Latimer's Sermons, p. 123. [b] p. 445.

tyme one fayde in parliament houfe, that thefe were as thornes, but the great abbottes were putrifyed old okes, and they muft needs followe."

The preamble of this act runs as follows:—

"FORASMOCH as manifeft fynne, vicious, carnall and abomynable lyvyng, is dayly ufed and commytted amonges the lytell and fmal eabbeys, pryoryes, and other relygyous houfes of monkes, chanons, and nounes, where the congregacion of fuch relygyous perfones is under the nombre of XII perfones, whereby the gouvernours of fuch relygyous houfes and thir convent, fpoyle, deftroye, confume and utterly wafte, afwell their churches, monafteyres, pryoryes, principall houfes, fermes, granges, landes, tenementes, and heredytamentes, as the ornaments of ther churches and ther goodes and cattalle, to the high dyfpleafour of Almyghty God, flaunder of good relygyon, and to the greate infamy of the kynges highnes and the realm, if redres fhuld not be hadde therof; and albeit that many contynuall vyfytacions hath bene hertofore had by the fpace of two hundreth years and more, for an honeft and charytable reformacion of fuch unthrifty, carnall and abhomynable lyvyng, yett neverthelefle, lytell or none amendement ys hytherto hadde, but ther vycyous lyvigng fhamelefly encreaffeth and augmentith, and by a curfed cuftome is fo rooted and enfefted that a greate multytude of the relygyous perfones in fuch fmale houfes doo rather chofe to rove abrode in apoftafy than to conforme them to the obfervacions of good relygyon; foe that without fuche fmall houfes be utterly fuppreffed, and the relygyous perfons therein commytted to greate and honorable monafteries of relygyon in this realme where thei maye be compelled to lyve relygyoufly for the reformacion of their lyves, ther canne elles be noo reformacion in this behalf. In conclufion whereof the Kynge's moft Royall Majefty beyng fupreme hede on erthe under God of the church of England, dayly findyng and devyfyng the increafe advauncement and exaltation of true doctryne and vertue in the feid churche, to the onelye glorye and honor of God and the totall extirpyng and dyftruccion of vyce and fynne, havyng knowledge that the premyfes be true, as well by the comptes of his late vyfytacions as by fundry credyble informacions, confyderyng alfo that dyverce greate folempne monafteryes of this realme, wherein, thankes be to God, relygyon is right well kept and obferved, be deftytute of fuch full noumbers of relygyous perfons as they ought and maye kepe, hath thought good that a playne declaracion fhould be made of the premyfes afwell to the lordes fpirituall and temporall as to other his lovyng fubjectes the commons in this prefent parliament affembled; whereupon the feid lordes and commons by a greate deliberacion fynally be refolved, that yt ys and fhalbe moche more to the pleafour of Almyghty God and for the honor of this his realme that the poffeffions of fuch fpiritual relygyous houfes, nowe beyng fpent, fpoyled, and wafted for increafe and mayntenance of fynne, fhould be ufed and converted to better ufes, and the unthrifty relygyous perfons foo fpendyng the fame to be compellyd to reforme their lyves. And therupon moft humbly defire the kynge's highnes that yt may be enacted by auctoryte of this prefent parliament, that his majeftie fhall have and enjoy to hym and his heirs for ever all and fynguler fuche monafteryes pryoryes and other relygyous houfes of monkes, chanons, and nonnes, of what kyndes or dyverfyties of habyttes, rules, or orders foo ever ther be called or named, which have not in landes and tenements, rentes, tythes, porcions and other heredytamentes, above the clere yerely value of two hundreth pounds; and in lyke maner fhall have and enjoy all the fcytes and circuytes of every fuche relygyous houfes, and all and fynguler the manors, granges, meafes, londes, tenements, revercions, rents, fervyces, tythes, pencions, portions, churches, chapelles, advowfons, patronages, annuyties, rightes, entres, condycions, and other heredytamentes apperteynyng or belongyng to every fuche monafterye, pryory, or other relygyous houfe, not havyng as ys aforefeid above the feid clere yearly value of two hundreth poundes, in as large and ample maner as the abbottes, pryours, abbeffes, pryoreffes, or other governers, of fuche monafteryes, pryoryes, and other relygyous houfes now have or ought to have the fame in the right of ther houfes. And that alfo his highnefs fhall have to hym and to hys heires all and fynguler fuch monafteryes, abbeis, and pryoryes whiche at eny tyme, within one yere next aftre the makyng of this acte, hath be gevyn and graunted to His Majefty by any abbot, pryor, abbes or pryores, under the covent feals, or that otherwyfe hath be fuppreffed or dyfolved. And all and fynguler the manors, londes, tenementes, rentes, fervyces, revercions, tythes, pencions, portions, churches, chappelles, advowfons, patronages, rightes, entrees, condicions, and all other intereftes and hereditaments to the fame monafteryes, abbeys, and pryoryes, or to any of them, apperteynyng or belongyn. To have and to holde all and fynguler the premyffes with all ther rightes, profyttes, juryfdiccions, and commodytyes, unto the Kyng's Majeftye and to his heires and affigns for ever, to doo and ufe therwyth his and ther owen wylles to the pleafor of Almyghty God and to the honor and profytte of thys realme."[a]

[a] 27 Hen. VIII. cap. 28.

Provision is then made to render void any alienations of land or property which any abbot may have made, fearing the diffolution of his monaftery. All ornaments and goods are given to the King as well as the monafteries themfelves and their lands. The greater monafteries are ordered to admit the members turned out of the leffer.

The yearly income of Roche Abbey having been returned as more than two hundred pounds,* it was not affected by this act. It however had a very narrow efcape, as the furplus income which preferved it was only twenty-two pounds.

To carry out the act of Suppreffion, Doctors Legh and Layton again made their unwelcome appearance in Yorkfhire, and, as might be anticipated, were not more popular than they had been during their former vifit. In fact it was impoffible that men whofe employment was one of facrilege and deftruction, could be looked upon by any but a few Puritans, with anything but diffatiffaction. Their fervants alfo treated the monks with an infolent contempt; taking from the churches and chapels of the diffolved houfes, their relics and fpoils, and difplaying them as they travelled from one place to another. Some made faddle-cloths of the church veftments, or wore them as garments; and fome hammered the filver relic cafes into fheaths for their daggers. The people feeing thefe things going on, began to wonder what would be the end, and a rumour foon fpread that all religion was to be done away with, and that the parifh churches would foon fhare the fate of the monafteries, or that only one for every feven or eight miles would be left, the plate of which would be confifcated, and chalices of tin fupplied inftead. They alfo thought from the enquiries which Cromwell was making about births, deaths, and marriages, that they would foon have to pay a fine to the King for every chriftening, burial and wedding, whereas that fagacious ftatefman had only the admirable intention, which he two years afterwards carried out, of inftituting parifh regifters. In all thefe fufpicions, the people were encouraged by the great abbots, who were now forely taxed by the crowds of monks who arrived from the fuppreffed houfes, and who knew well that their turn was foon coming.

At Louth, in Lincolnfhire, the feeling of the priefts and people had grown fo ftrong, that it at length broke out into a formidable infurrection. Beginning on the firft of October, 1536, with a few inhabitants gathered together in a knot on the green of the town, and headed by a cobbler, they in a few days numbered thoufands,

---

* See "Valor Ecclefiafticus."

there being among them priefts, and monks to the number of feven or eight hundred, whofe words of peace were "Kill the gentlemen, if they will not join us they fhall be hanged."*

On the third of October they drew up fix demands which were to be made of the King. The firft was that the religious houfes fhould be reftored; and the others required that they fhould be relieved from obnoxious taxes and perfons, one of the latter of courfe being Cromwell. Two meffengers were fent to London with thefe demands, and while they were detained there, fixty thoufand rebels had found their way to Lincoln, but for want of provifions, could not remain there. The royal army feeing them rapidly difperfing, began to fear there would be no battle.

After fome time the anfwers to the demands of the rebels arrived and were read in the chapter houfe of the Cathedral. Thefe being more or lefs fatiffactory, the rebel army being much demoralized, broke up, the whole rifing and difperfion having occupied lefs than a fortnight. But the fire of infurrection only fmouldered!

The Pilgrimage of Grace.

THE rebellion in Lincolnfhire was immediately followed by a ftill more formidable rifing in Yorkfhire, called the "Pilgrimage of Grace." One Robert Afke, a Yorkfhire gentleman and a barrifter in good practice at Weftminfter, and who had been fpending the law vacation in his native country, on his way back to his bufinefs, met with a party of the Lincolnfhire rebels who demanded his name, and offered him the popular oath to be "faithful to the King, the Commonwealth, and to Holy Church." Thefe rebels having thus "taken" him, as Afke afterwards called it, became his body-guard, and with ftrange rapidity, the name of Afke became the rallying cry of the rebels.

Upon the failure of the infurgents in Lincolnfhire, Robert Afke left that country and returned into Yorkfhire, and there he grew ftill more famous. The fire of infurrection re-kindled, and the ftuff of the Yorkfhire rebels proved to be even more inflammable than that of the Lincolnfhire. Bells and beacon-fires were clanging and burning all over the country, and addreffes bearing the name of Robert Afke, which he afterwards declared to be forgeries, were handed about and pofted on every church door, requefting the people to affemble "to preferve the Churche of God frome fpoylyng &c."

* Froude, vol. iii., p. 114.

Upon hearing of the infurrection, the King wrote to Lord Darcy to fupprefs it, but that nobleman fhut himfelf up in his Caftle of Pomfret, and would not mufter his men.

On the 14th of October, the rebel force collected on Weighton Common, where Afke was chofen commander-in-chief. This army appears to have been a very formidable one, as the men were ftrong and well armed. They were grouped, according to their parifhes, in companies, the priefts bearing the croffes of their churches before them. On their banners they had a crucifix with the five wounds and a chalice; and every one wore on his fleeve as the badge of the party an emblem of the five wounds of Chrift, with the name Jefus wrought in the midft.[a]

Before this force, Hull, Pomfret, and York foon furrendered, and in all the places where they were victorious, the monks were reinftated in their monafteries, and "though it were never fo late when they returned," writes the Earl of Oxford to Cromwell, "the friars fang matins the fame night."

On the 21ft of October, the rebel army had its head quarters at Pomfret, in the caftle of which place "the great captain" Afke fat at the head of the rebel council, together with the Archbifhop of York, Lord Darcy, and others. Here he received "with a cruel and ineftimable proud countenance," the Lancafter Herald, who had been fent with a royal proclamation, and which proclamation, in fpite of the entreaties of the Herald, he would on no account allow to be read.

On the 24th of October, the royal army under the Duke of Norfolk and Lord Shrewfbury, was at Doncafter, to which place the rebels alfo marched from Pomfret, thirty thoufand ftrong, the royalift army numbering no more than eight thoufand.

Having arrived, they deployed along the banks of the river, which was much fwollen, from Ferribridge to Doncafter; and thus with the river dividing them, the two armies lay watching each other for two days; the heads of each party, in the meanwhile endeavouring to come to fome arrangement which might prevent bloodfhed.

At length, on the 26th of October, it was agreed that a conference fhould be held upon the bridge, when nine gentlemen from either fide met, and Sir Thomas Hilton, on behalf of the rebels, explained their demands. Thefe were arranged into twenty-four articles.[b] The portions of thefe articles which more particularly relate to our fubject, were that "the abbeys fuppreffed be reftored—

[a] Burnet, vol. i. p. 416.   [b] Froude, vol. iii., p. 136.

houses lands and goods." "That the Lord Cromwell have condign punishment as a subverter of the good laws of the realm." "That Dr. Legh and Dr. Layton have condign punishment for their extortions in the time of their visitation of the religious houses, and other their abominable acts by them committed and done."

This conference lasted the whole day, and in the darkness of night it was agreed that Sir Robert Bowes and Sir Ralph Ellercar, accompanied by the Duke of Norfolk, as an intercessor, should carry the articles to the King. It was also arranged that there should be an armistice, and that the mustered on both sides should be disbanded.

On the 29th of October, the King received the messengers graciously, and in order to gain time, detained them a fortnight; in the meanwhile sending messengers north to endeavour to combat the delusions of the people.

On the 14th of November, Bowes and Ellercar were dismissed "with general instructions of comfort," and a promise that a final reply should be given in a month. But when at length this answer arrived, it did not suit the insurgents, and after a hasty council, held at York, Aske again collected his army. The royal army also reoccupied the line of the Don, and had its head-quarters at Rotherham. And yet only one thing kept up the insurrection. The King would not grant a complete pardon to the rebels. He would have five or six of the worst offenders.

This obstacle at length, however, was removed, the King granting, by the advice of his privy-council, a general pardon; and on the 2nd of November, an agreement was come to at Doncaster, the rebels believing that their entire petition had been granted. At the close of this meeting, Aske knelt down in the presence of the Lords, and having desired that he should no more be called "captain," with others, pulled off their badges crossed with the five wounds, all of them saying "we will wear no badge or figure but the badge of our sovereign Lord."

It had been well if the "Pilgrimage of Grace" had thus ended, but the people growing suspicious that the King's promises would not all be fulfilled, again rose under Sir Francis Bigod. George the eldest son of Lord Lumley, tried to take Scarborough and failed. Hallam attempted Hull with the same result. Bigod succeeded in taking Beverley, but was soon obliged to fly.

The King enraged at this new rebellion, sent down orders to execute a large number of the insurgents in every town and village, and make such a "fearful spectacle" as shall be a warning to others, and "Finally, forasmuch as all their troubles have ensued by the solicitation and traitorous conspiracies of the monks and canons of those parts, we desire you at such places as they have conspired or kept their houses with force since the appointment at Doncaster, you shall, without pity or circumstance, cause all the monks and canons that be in any wise faulty, to be tied up without further delay or ceremony. "The Duke of Norfolk obeyed this order and hanged seventy-four persons. The Abbot of Kirkstead, the Abbot of Barlings, and seventeen others were also hanged at Lincoln. The Abbot of Fountains, the Abbot of Jervaulx, the Abbot of Rievaulx, the Prior of Bridlington, Bigod and others were hanged at Tyburn. Lord Darcy and Aske were also arrested and accused of having been concerned in this fresh attack. On the arrest of Aske, " his servant, Robert Wall, did cast himself upon his bed and cried 'Oh, my master! Oh, my master! they will draw him, and hang him, and and quarter him;' and therewith he did die for sorrow." The prophecy of this faithful one was only too true. In July, 1537, Robert Aske was drawn through the streets of York on a hurdle, and afterwards hanged, from the top of a high tower, his last request being granted "Let me be full dead or that I be dismembered, that I may piously give my spirit to God, without more pain." Lord Darcy was executed on Tower Hill. And thus, at last, drowned in its own blood, rebellion died!

The demolition of the religious houses which had been checked for awhile by the rebellion, again commenced, and went on rapidly. And the King knowing that he had nothing now to fear, began to make arrangements for the suppression of the greater monasteries.

In the summer of 1537, a new visitation of the religious houses was ordered. Dr. Legh and Dr. Layton being again appointed Visitors for the North of England. They were ordered to examine the monks strictly in all things that related either to their affection to the King and the supremacy, or to their superstition, in their several houses; to discover what cheats and impostures there were either in their images, relics or other miraculous things, by which they had drawn people to their houses on pilgrimages, and gotten from them any great presents. Also to try how they were affected during the late commotions; and to discover every thing that was amiss in them, and report it to the Lord Vicegerent.[a]

In answer to these questions we have the following document relating to Roche, two copies of which exist. One in the Rolls

[a] Burnet.

House, "*Historical and other documents*, No. 761, p. 8." and the other in the British Museum, "*Lansdowne MSS.*, 988 fol. 4."

"The compendium of the discoveries made by Dr. Legh and Dr. Layton in the visitation of the royal province of York in the Bishoprics of Coventry, Lichfield and others, in the time of Henry VIII.

𝕽𝖚𝖕𝖆 𝖆𝖑𝖎𝖆𝖘 𝕽𝖔𝖈𝖍𝖊.

Sodomites. { William Hela
John Wheland
Robert Reine
Henry Wilson
John Doddesworth.

Suspected of Treason. { John Robinson, suspected of the crime of treason and imprisoned at York.

Superstition. { Pilgrimage is made hither to an Image of the Crucifix, found (as it is believed) on a rock, and is held in veneration.

Founder. { The Earl of Cumberland.

The annual account, 170*l*.
The House owes 20*l*."ᵃ

There are many points of interest in the foregoing writing. Of the five monks who are said to have been guilty of an unnatural crime, two, John Wheland and Robert Rein had left the monastery before the dissolution, which took place a year afterwards.

John Robinson, who at the time of the visitation was confined in York Castle, suspected of treason, was probably not guilty, as we find him liberated and receiving his pension in the reign of Queen Mary.

The search for objects of superstition seem not to have been very successful at Roche, as only the Image of the Crucifix on a Rockᵇ is recorded; but at other Houses most extraordinary objects were found. Relics innumerable. The parings of St. Edmund's toes;

ᵃ Memorandum (in a modern hand) "This filthy Book of Calumnies was invented by the Commissioners for the purpose of justifying the suppression of the religious houses, and the robbery of the Church. It is referred to in 'Burton's Anatomy of Melancholy,' Part 3, Sec. 2, number 1."
Another memorandum says "The whole of the visitation is of this description."

ᵇ I have sought in vain for any traces of this curious object. The Visitors had instructions to deface and utterly destroy everything of an useless or superstitious character, and they seem to have done their work thoroughly here.

the pen-knife and boots of St. Thomas a Becket; pieces of the true crofs, enough to build a fhip; a piece of St. Andrew's finger, in pledge for 40*l*, but which the Vifitor will not redeem at the price. In fact every reliquary feems to have been

"Icrammed ful of cloutes and bones"

each one fuppofed to have its own peculiar power. There were relics againft bad weather, againft weeds, againft difeafe and pain, and there were relics which would bring you every blefling,

"So that he offer pense or elles grotes."

But what brought the monks into ill favour more than thefe relics was their images. The moft popular of thefe was the Crucifix of Boxley Abbey, in Kent, which went by the name of "*the rood of grace.*" The eyes of this Image on fit occafions "did ftir like a lively thing," the body bowed, the forehead frowned, and the lower lip dropped as if about to fpeak. The people of Kent believed in this rood above all others, and the offerings to it were enormous. At length, however, a fceptical commiflioner arrived, and nothing awed, examined the figure clofely. The refult of this infpection was the difcovery of a fufficient amount of mechanifm to produce the forementioned actions. The Image was immediately taken down and publicly exhibited. It was fhewn at Maidftone. It performed before the court at Whitehall, and finally, it went through its motions at Paul's Crofs, where the Bifhop of Rochefter lectured upon it, and when the indignation of the people was at its higheft, it was given to them, and in a few moments it was torn in pieces. Celebrated Images from Walfingham, Ipfwich, Doncafter, and Penrice, were alfo brought to Smithfield, and burnt together.

When the people faw how they had for centuries been deceived and tricked out of their money, a ftrong reaction took place, and inftead of the feeling of fear and devotion which had fo long chained them, a recklefs and barbarous inconoclafm now poffeffed their minds; and they were ready when a religious houfe was fuppreffed, to pull down, fpoil and pilfer, and to defecrate even the churches in which only a few days before they had worfhipped!

But to recur to the difcoveries of Dr. Legh and Dr. Layton at Roche. The Earl of Cumberland is returned as the Founder. This was Henry Clifford, the firft earl and the defcendant of Thomas de Clifford, the fixth lord, whofe daughter, Matilda, Countefs of Cambridge, became founder of Roche in 1446. (See page 59.)

It will alfo be feen that the yearly income had fallen in a year from 222*l* to 170*l*, and that the Houfe had run into debt 20*l*. This falling off in the yearly value, laid Roche Abbey under the power of the act for the suppression of the lesser monasteries, and looks as if Henry Cundal, the last abbot, like the abbots of other Houses, had made away with the property to enrich himself before being driven out.

A year after this second visitation of the monasteries, Roche Abbey was surrendered to the Crown.

Surrender Deed of Roche Abbey.

"TO all the faithful in Christ, to whom the present writing may come, Henry (Cundal) Abbot of the Monastery or Abbey of the Blessed Mary the Virgin, of Roche, in the diocese of York, of the Cistercian order, and the Convent of the same place, eternal salvation in the Lord!

KNOW YE that We, the aforesaid Abbot and Convent by unanimous assent and consent, after due deliberation in our minds, of our certain knowledge, and by our own pure act, for certain just and reasonable causes specially moving our minds and consciences thereto of our own accord and will, have given and granted and by these presents do give and grant, yield and consign to our Most Illustrious Prince and Lord, Henry VIII, by the grace of God, of England and France, King, Defender of the Faith, Lord of Ireland, and on Earth Supreme Head of the English Church, the whole of our said Monastery or Abbey of Roche and all the site, groundplot, circuit and precinct of the said Monastery of Roche aforesaid. Also all and singular manors, demesnes, messuages, gardens, backyards, tofts, lands and tenements, meadows, pastures, woods, rents, reversions and services, mills, transit fees, military fees, wards, marriage fees, born villeins with their belongings, commons, liberties, frankpledges, jurisdictions, offices, courtleets, hundreds, views of frankpledge, fairs, markets, parks, warrens, vineyards, waters, fisheries, ways, paths, empty homesteads, advowsons, nominations, appointments, donations of churches, vicarages, chapels, chantries, hospitals and other ecclesiastical benefices whatever, rectories, vicarages, chantries, pensions, portions, annuities, tithes, oblations, and all and singular our emoluments, profits, possessions, hereditaments, and rights whatever, as well within the said County of York as within the Counties of Lincoln, Derby and Nottingham or elsewhere within the realm of England, Wales and the marches thereof, whatever way belonging, regarding, appending or devolving upon the same Monastery or

Abbey of Roche aforesaid; and all our charters, evidences, writings, and muniments of every kind in any way regarding or concerning the said Monastery or Abbey, its manors, lands and tenements and the rest of the premises with the appurtenances, or any parcel thereof; TO HAVE, hold and enjoy the said Monastery or Abbey, its site, groundplot, circuit, and precinct of Roche aforesaid; also all and singular domains, manors, lands, tenements, rectories, pensions and the rest of the premises with all and singular their appurtenances, to the aforesaid our most Invincible Prince and Lord King Henry, his heirs and assigns, to whom for all effect of law in this behalf which may or can follow therefrom, we subject and submit as in duty bound, ourselves and the said Monastery or Abbey of Roche aforesaid, and all rights in whatever way by us acquired, giving and granting, as by these presents we do give and grant to the said Royal Majesty, his heirs and assigns, all and every manner of full and free faculty, authority and power to dispose of us and all the Monasteries of Roche aforesaid, together with all and singular manors, tenements, lands, rents, pensions, services and singular the aforesaid, with their rights and appurtenances, and at his Royal pleasure and will to alienate, give, convert and transfer to any uses whatever, according to his Majesty's pleasure, and such disposals, alienations, donations, conversions and translations by his said Majesty in what manner soever to be made, we promise by these presents that we will consider that they ought from that time forth to be ratified, and will hold them ratified, granted and for ever confirmed. And that all and singular the premises may have due effect, we have moreover of our own free choice, for ourselves and our successors, openly, publicly, expressly, with sure knowledge and willing minds, renounced and ceased from all quarrels, provocations, appeals, actions, litigations and instances whatever on our part which in any way seek or may hereafter seek for remedies and benefits for us and our successors in that behalf under pretext of disposal, alienation, translation and conversion aforesaid and the rest of the premises, all mistakes arising from fraud, fear, ignorance, or any other matter having without dispute, exception, objection or allegation, been entirely removed and laid aside, as by these presents we do renounce and cease from, and in this writing give up our interest in the same. AND WE the aforesaid Abbot and Convent and our successors will warrant against all people by these presents, the said Monastery, precinct, site, mansion and Church of Roche aforesaid, and all and singular the manors, demesnes, messuages, gardens, backyards, tofts, meadows, feedings, pastures, woods, underwoods, lands, tenements and all and singular the rest of the premises with the appurtenances to the said Lord the King his heirs and assigns for ever. In testimony whereof We the aforesaid Abbot and Convent have caused to be placed to this writing our common Seal.[a] Given in our Chapter House on the 23rd day of the month of June, in the 30th year of the reign of King Henry aforesaid."[b] (1538.)

Henry, Abbot
Thomas Twell, Subprior
Richard Drax

J. Happa

Nicholas Collys

Thomas Wells

J. Dodsworth

Thomas Cundall

Richard Fyshburn

Thomas Medyltun

Thomas Acworth

Henry Wylson

Christopher Hyrste

William Carter

William Helay

John Robynsone

Richard Moslay

Thomas Smythe

[a] See Plate X., Fig. 4.   [b] From the Augmentation Office.

This Deed was executed before Doctor William Petre, a Clerk of Chancery, (afterwards Secretary of State) at the time* and place above mentioned.

The fignatures of the Abbot and Monks, fac-fimiles of which are here given, are written upon the margin of the deed and are becoming very obfcure.

Of the after hiftory of the monks who figned the Surrender Deed little is known beyond what may be gathered from the contents of the following document:

Roche.

"The Abbot (Henry Cundal) for penfion XXXIII li VIs. VIIId.
The Sub-prior (Thomas Twell) VI li XIIIs. IIIId.[b]
The Bourfer (John Dodfworth) VI li [c]
XI prefts Monks every V li——LV li.
IIII Novices every LXVIs. VIIId.——XIII li VIs. VIIId.
The Abbot to have his books and the IIIIth parte of the plate the Cattal the houfehold ftuf a Challis and Veftment and XXX li in money at his departure with a contentment porcion of Corn att difcreation.

Every Monk to have at his departure his haulf years porcion by waye of Rewarde and XXs. befides towardes his apparail.

Every to have his porcion feparite and free.

Every fervaunt by waye of Reward his haulf yeres wages.

The Kynges Majeftie to pay the debts of the Houfe."[d]

From the handfome provifion made for the Abbot, it may be taken for granted that he refigned his abbacy with a good grace, and gave the commiffioners very little trouble.

In 1553, fifteen years after the diffolution, twelve of the eighteen who figned the Surrender, ftill enjoyed their penfions.[e]

---

[a] The date of the furrender of Roche Abbey, has by all who have written on the fubject hitherto, been given as 1539. The 30th year of Henry VIII begins April 22nd, 1538, and ends April 21ft, 1539. The 23rd of June, 30 Henry VIII muft therefore be in 1538.

[b] Thomas Twell feems to have remained in the neighbourhood of Roche after the diffolution. Mr. Hunter's keen eye which omits nothing, firft difcovered this interefting fact, from the two following entries in the accounts of the Sheffield Church Burgeffes.—"Hallamfhire," p. 140.

ITEM. P^d to the ryngers y^t dyd ryng for Sr. Thomas Twell, at the recevynge of certen ftuf gevyn by hym to the Church, wth p^d to the preftes and clerk for dyrge XVId.

ITEM. P^d for the cofts and charges for feching Sr. Thomas Twell will from Blythe IIs.

[c] The Burfar was the treafurer of the Houfe. He received the rents, paid the wages, and difcharged all the debts of the Abbey.

[d] Chapter Houfe Ebor. Bag. 25.   [e] Bibl. Bodl. 8° D. 50. 51. Jur.

	£	s.	d.		£	s.	d.
Henry Cundal	33	6	8	Thomas Medyltun	5	0	0
Thomas Twell	6	13	4	Henry Wilfun	5	0	0
John Dodefworth	6	0	0	William Carter	5	0	0
Richard Fyfhburn	5	0	0	Thomas Welles	5	0	0
Thomas Harryfonne (?)	5	0	0	John Robynfone	3	6	8
Nicholas Collys	5	0	0	Richard Moflay	3	6	8

The following is an account of the plate, cattle, corn, &c., which the the Abbey had at the diffolution. The quantity of plate is fufpicioufly fmall. Had Henry Cundal, like other abbots, provided for the future, by felling part of it?[a] The fact of a tabernacle being in pledge for 40*l* does not allay the doubt.

The Inventory.

"This is the inventorye of all the lands and gudes perteyneing to the Monafterye of Roche by eftimacion.

Imprimes, Landes and tenementes perteyneing to the fame Monafterye in divers plafis fome CCXXII li or thereaboutes by eftimacion.

Item. Plate in the fame Monafterye.
A croffe w^t a fhanke parcell gilte.
Item. VII Chalice where of one lentt.
Item. One croche[b] parcel gilte.
Item. A tabarnacle wyche lyes in plege for XL li.
Item. II faltes gilte w^t one covering.
Item. One ftandinge Cupe w^t cover parcell gilte.
Item. One whitt bolle.
Item. A Alte Cupe parcell gilte.
Item. Mafers[c] VI.
Item. Spoones XXXII.[d]
Item. Catle perteneing to the fame.
Item. *Imprimis.* IIII fcore oxen kyen and yonge beftis.
Item. V cartte horse.

---

[a] The Abbot of Fountains at midnight caufed his chaplain to steel the fexton's keys, and took out a jewell and a crofs of gold with ftones. One Warren, a Goldfmith of the Chepe, made the Abbot believe a ruby was a garnet, and otherwife cheated the venerable Father, he being "a vara fole, and a miferable ideote." "Suppreffion of Monasteries p. 100."

[b] Crofier [c] Wooden Bowls or Goblets. These masers are called "Anasers" in the Mon. Ang.

[d] The Vifitors were commanded to take away with them all fuperfluous plate. It would appear from the above fuspicioufly small lift that the Abbot of Roche, like the Abbot of Fountains had become aware of the fact, and had made a timely difpofal of part of it.

THE DISSOLUTION.

Item. II mears one folte and one ftagge.[a]
Item. VI fcore fhepe yonge and olde.
Item. XL fwyne yonge and olde.
Item. XI feder bedes w^t all other thenges belonging.
Item. In Whitt and Malte IIII fcore quarter.

(In the oppofite column.)

Ffeis payed of the fame lands and tenementes as after foluis:—
The Corrody of John Keeper and his wife Cs.
Item, imprimis to my lord of Hampton for the Stewardfhipe of Armthorpe fomme XXVs VIIId.
Item. To Thomas Greene for kepeing of the courtes pertening to the fame Monafterii, fomme XXXs.
Item. To the balye of Rokeby, fomme XIIIs. IIIId. w^t a lyverye cotte.
Item. To the balye of Armthorpe fomme XIIIs. IIIId., with a liverye cotte.
Item. To James Bankes for Receiving of Rents at Sannbeke and Hawton, and other plaifes fomme XXs.[b]

Thefe be the detts y^t ys owing to the fame Monafterye:—
Imprimis. Mafter Roberd * * * fomme XVIII li.

Thefe be the detts that the faid monafterye doth owe :—
Imprimis. To Mafter Robert Stelle fomme XL li.
Item. To William Hellingworth fomme XX li.
Item. To Willyam Halle of the newe mylne fomme VI li XIIIs. IIIId.[c]"

It is rather a fingular fact that the following interefting letter fhould have efcaped the notice of all previous writers on Roche. It is fuppofed to have been written by Cuthbert Shirebrook, a dignified ecclefiaftic, who was born near Roche Abbey, and educated at the free fchool of Rotherham, and whofe uncle was prefent at the fuppreffion of Roche.

Letter on the Suppression of Roche Abbey.

"IN the plucking down of religious houfes for the moft part this order was taken: that the vifitors fhould come fuddenly upon every houfe and unawares, to the end to take them napping, as

---

[a] A Horfe under three years old.
[b] This is not a complete lift of the officers employed by the Abbot of Roche. There was befides thefe a fteward and a bailiff at Thurftonland, a bailiff at Streetthorpe, a fteward at Roxby, and a receiver at Barnby.
[c] Chapter Houfe, Ebor. Bag. 25.

the proverb is, left if they should have had so much as any inkling of their coming, they would have made conveyance of some part of their own goods to help themselves withal, when they were turned forth of their houses, and both reason and nature might well have moved them so to have done, although it will be said all was given to the King before by Act of Parliament; and so they had neither goods, houses, nor possessions. And then they had to give the King great thanks, yea pray for him upon their black beads, that he was so gracious a prince to them, to suffer them to stay so long after that all was given from them. And therefore if the visitors being the King's officers and commissioners in that behalf, took their dinner with them, and then turned them forth to seek their lodging at night, or at the furthest the next day in the morning, where they could find it (as it was done indeed,) they did no wrong; nor truly no great right : for so soon as the visitors were entered within the gates, they called the abbot and other officers of the house, and caused them to deliver up to them all their keys and took an inventory of all their goods, both within doors and without : for all such beasts, horses, sheep, and such cattle as were abroad in pastures or grange places, the visitors caused to be brought into their presence : and when they had so done, turned the abbot with all his convent and household forth of the doors.

"Which thing was not a little grief to the convent, and all the servants of the house departing one from another, and especially such as with their conscience could not break their profession : for it would have made an heart of flint to have melted and wept to have seen the breaking up of the house and their sorrowful departing; and the sudden spoil that fell the same day of their departure from the house. And every person had every thing good cheap; except the poor monks, friars, and nuns, that had no money to bestow of any thing : as it appeared by the suppression of an abbey, hard by me, called the ROCHE ABBEY; a house of white monks : a very fair builded house, all of freestone; and every house vaulted with freestone, and covered with lead (as the abbeys was in England, as well as the churches be.) At the breaking up whereof an uncle of mine was present, being well acquainted with certain of the monks there; and when they were put forth of the house, one of the monks, his friend, told him that every one of the convent had given to him his cell* wherein he lied : wherein was not anything of price, but his bed and apparel, which was but simple and of small price : which

---

* Dr. London on suppressing the Charter House gave " to every brodor his celle."—Sir Hy. Ellis', "Orig. Letters," 3rd Series, vol. iii. page 183.

monk willed my uncle to buy something of him; who said, I see nothing that is worth money to my use: No, said he; give me ijd. for my cell door, which was never made with Vs. No, said my uncle, I know not what to do with it. (For he was a young man unmarried, and then neither stood in need of houses nor doors.)* But such persons as afterwards brought their corn and hay or such like, found all the doors either open, or the locks and shackles plucked away, or the floor itself taken away, went in and took what what they found, filched it away.

"Some took the service books (of parchment?) that lied in the church, and laid them upon their waine coppes (waggon copes) to piece the same: some took windows of the Hayleith and hid them in their hay; and likewise they did of many other things: for some pulled forth the iron hooks out of the walls that bought none, when the yeomen and gentlemen of the country had bought the timber of the church. For the church was the first thing that was put to the spoil; and then the abbot's lodging, dortor, (dormitory) and frater (refectory) with the cloister and all the buildings thereabout, within the abbey walls; for nothing was spared but the ox-houses and swinecoats, and such other houses of office, that stood without the walls;[b] which had more favour showed them than the very church itself; which was done by the advice of Cromwell, as Fox reporteth in his book of "*Acts and Monuments.*" It would have pitied any heart to see what tearing up of the lead there was, and plucking up of boards, and throwing down of the sparres; and when the lead was torn off and cast down into the church, and the tombs in the church all broken (for in most abbeys were divers noble men and women, yea and in some abbeys kings, whose tombs were regarded no more than the tombs of all other inferior persons: for to what end should they stand, when the church over them

---

* The monks seem to have been very anxious to make the most of the occasion to realize as much as possible. Dr. Layton, writing from Bisham Abbey, says.—"When we were makyng salle of the olde vestments within the chapitre house, the monks cryede a newe marte in the cloister, every man bringing his cowle caste upon his nec to be solde, and folde them indede.—" Ellis, 3rd Series, vol. iii., page 267."

I am indebted to the Rev. J. Eastwood for the following interesting entry from the Churchwardens accounts at Ecclesfield, which shews that the vestments were sold at Roche :

"1542 Sir Robert Cobcroft, ten shillings, which he paid for vestments at Roche."

[b] John Freeman writing to the Lord Privy Seal about the razing of the Abbeys in Lincolnshire says,—"The King's Commission commandeth me to pull down to the grounde all the walls of the Churches, stepulls, cloysters, frraterys, dorters, chapter howfys, with all other howfys, saveyng them that be necessary for a farmer," the charge of doing this would be so great he continues that he thinks it would be best to take down the bells and lead and pull down the roofs and batilments and stairs, and "lete the wallis stande, and charge som with them as a quarre of ston to make falys of as they that hathe nede will fetche."—Sir Hy. Ellis' "Orig. Letters," 3rd Series, vol. iii., page 269.

was not spared for their cause,) and all things of price either spoiled, carped away, or defaced to the uttermost.[a]

"The persons that cast the lead into fodders, plucked up all the seats in the choir, wherein the monks sat when they said service; which were like to the seats in minsters, and burned them, and melted the lead there withall: although there was wood plenty within a flight shot of them[b] for the abbey stood among the woods and the rocks of stone: in which rocks was pewter vessels found that was conveyed away and there hid: so that it seemeth that every person bent himself to filch and spoil what he could: yea even such persons were content to spoil them, that seemed not two days before to allow their religion, and do great worship and reverence at their mattins, masses and other service, and all other their doings: which is a strange thing to say, that they could this day think it to be the house of God, and the next day the house of the devil: or else they would not have been so ready to have it spoiled.

"For the better proof of this my saying, I demanded of my father, thirty years after the suppression, which had bought part of the timber of the church, and all the timber in the steeple, with the bell-frame, with others his partners therein, (in the which steeple hung viij. yea ix. bells; whereof the least but one could not be bought at this day for XXli., which bells I did see hang there myself more than a year after the suppression,) whether he thought well of the religious persons and of the religion then used? And he told me, yea: for, said he, I did see no cause to the contrary. Well, said I, then how came it to pass you was so ready to destroy and spoil the thing that you thought well of? What should I do? said he. Might I not as well as others have some profit of the spoil of the abbey? for I did see all would away; and therefore I did as others did.[c]

"Thus you may see that as well they that thought well of the religion then used, as they which thought otherwise could agree

---

[a] The Commissioners seem to have taken their workmen with them. John Portman writing to Cromwell, from Lewes, in Sussex, (the monks of which place had their part with the monks of Roche of the eels caught in the fisheries belonging to Earl Warren, at Hatfield, &c.,) says,—"We brought from London xvii persons, 3 carpentars, 2 smyths, 2 plummars, and one that kepith the fornace (for melting the lead.) Every of these attendith to hys own office: x of them hewed the walles abowte, among the whych ther wer 3 carpentars, thiere made proctes (props) to undersette wher the other cutte away, thother brake and cutte the waules."—"Suppression of Monasteries," page 181.

[b] At Fountains Abbey heaps of ashes were found when the nave was excavated, which Mr. Walbran thinks must be the remains of the stalls and screens of that abbey, but we know that all the wood work of the monasteries had not this fate.

[c] Dr. London writing from Warwick, says,—"The power people thorowly in every place be so gredy upon thee Howtys when they be suppressed that by night and daye, nott only of the townys, but also of the country, they do contynually resorte as long as any dore, wyndor, yren, or glass, or lowse ledde remaynythe in any of them. In every place I kepe wacche as longe as I tary and prison those that do thus abuse them selvys, and yet other will not refrayne."—Sir Hy. Ellis' "Orig. Letters," 3rd Series, vol. iii., page 139.

well enough, and too well, to spoil them. Such a devil is covetousness and mammon! and such is the providence of God to punish sinners, in making themselves instruments to punish themselves, and all their posterity from generation to generation! For no doubt there hath been millions that have repented the thing since; but all too late. And thus much upon my own knowledge touching the fall of the said Roche Abbey."[a]

The following verses give in a few words the rise and fall of monachism. They are entitled "A Tale of Robin Hoode dialoguewise, between Watt and Jeffry;[b]" and, like the foregoing letter, they describe the eagerness and greed with which the people seized upon the property of the monks when the abbeys were dissolved:—

> "Adam Bell[c] was ware and wise
> When hee first began to rise,
> As the bee in summer's prime
> Sucks the marigold and thyme,
> Sucks the rose and daffodill,
> Leaving, taking what she will,
> And from flower to flower doth glide,
> Sweetly by the river side;
> Where chrystal streams delightfull runninge,
> Are ever sweetened with his cumminge.
> Such was Adam in his prime,
> In the flower of his time,
> Soe he tastes every sweete
> Till with fatt he fell asleepe;
> As he slumbered in the dale,
> Spread upon the gentle vale,
> A famished Lion[d] came that way,
> Hungry, panting for his pray,
> In his grasping pawes he bent him,
> And in pieces all to rent him;
> Yet his cabin doth remaine
> Beaten with the winds and raine,
> Spoyled of all the passers by
> Whose huge frame doth terrify;
> All that wondrous monument
> All the world's astonishment.
> When the wolves[e] and foxes[f] saw
> Adam in the Lion's paw;
> Ours is Robin's strength they cried,
> And sett him round on every side."

[a] MS. Cole. vol. xli. p. 1—49.   [b] MS. Harl. 367 f. 150.   [c] Monachism.   [d] King Henry VIII.   [e] Puritans.   [f] Politicians.

But although Cundal had surrendered his Abbey to the King, the Commissioners, on surveying the lands, found their value to be over 200*l* per annum. It did not therefore yet come under the power of the Act. And this being the case with many other abbeys, a new Act was called for, and passed in 1539, for the suppression of the greater monasteries. By it all the religious houses of whatever value, which had been or should be suppressed, were given to the King and his successors for ever. A sweeping sentence! Almost enough to make Richard de Busli and Richard Fitz Turgis, who had given their lands to the monks "*for ever,*" rise from their graves in remonstrance!

But the money of the peaceful monks was required for other and far different purposes. The introduction of artillery had rendered all our ports and harbours liable to attack and destruction; every exposed position therefore, had to be guarded by earthworks, and forts, and numerous batteries had to be erected. To accomplish this the spoils of the Church were used. The clear yearly value of all the suppressed houses is stated to have been 131,607*l*. 6*s*. 4*d*., but the true value was at least *ten times* as much,[a] 18,000*l* of this money the King designed to convert into a revenue for eighteen[b] Bishopricks but this number dwindled down to six.

Of the inmates of Roche there is little more to say. A monk of Roche compiled a history of the Manor of Todwick, from the Conquest to the reign of Henry III. It is printed in the "*Monasticon.*" Another of the monks shortly before the dissolution went about making notes of the churches in Yorkshire.[c] It is to be regretted that that both his name and MS. are lost, and that all attempts to recover them have been fruitless. Extracts from the MS. were made by Mr. de la Pryme, which are now in the British Museum with the rest of that gentleman's collection. When he saw it it was bound up with other manuscript matter, and in the possession of Mr. Canby, of Thorne.

In judging of the value of the monastic institution, the dissolution of which has now been described, it is not fair to give undue prominence to that period when decay was fast approaching, lest gazing on the decrepitude of age, we may chance to forget that the healthy vigour of manhood ever existed. It is easy to join the popular cry,

---

[a] Burnet, Vol. i., p. 488

[b] Worksop was to have been one of the eighteen.—"Suppression of Monasteries, p. 264.

[c] Mr. Hunter has used these notes in his "Deanery of Doncaster," Vol. i. p.p. 41, 188.

> "O aye, the monks, the monks, they did the mischief
> Theirs all the grossness, all the superstition
> Of a most gross and superstitious age!"

But there doubtless was a time when the monks did good service in England, and

> "We will as soon believe with kind Sir Roger
> That old Moll White took wing with cat and broomstick
> And raised the last night's thunder,"

as that the inmates of the monasteries were the cheating pestilent knaves which some historians have represented them to have been.

Let us remember that for centuries they were the sole keepers of the records of religion philosophy and antiquity; that to them we are indebted for a great portion of the early history of this country; and that they were the promoters of science and art. They were lawyers, doctors, architects, chemists, artists, poets and practical farmers. The good they did by settling down in waste places and reducing them to a state of cultivation must have been very great. In wild and solitary places they made roads, cut drains, and otherwise rendered them habitable.

> "Be courteous, Commerce—there are bridges high,
> Ranging their salient angles o'er the strand,
> Which the monks reared; where some proud dwellings lie,
> A fane exorcised agues from the land."

There can be no doubt also that the monks spent a large sum of money in entertaining strangers and way-farers, and in alms to the poor. A sufficient proof of this may be found in the draft of an Act of Parliament, prepared after the dissolution of some of the monasteries for the purpose of enforcing the practice of hospitality upon those who bought the abbey lands. In the MS. the following passage is underlined:—

"NEVERTHELESS, the experience which we have had by those houses that are already suppressed, sheweth plainly unto us that a great hurt and decay is thereby come, and hereafter shall come, to this realm, and great impoverishing of many the poor subjects thereof, for lack of hospitality and good householding that were wont in them to be kept, to the great relief of the poor people of all the counties adjoining the said monasteries beside the maintaining of many smiths, husbandmen and labourers that were kept in the said houses.

It should therefore be enacted that all persons taking the lands of the suppressed houses must duly reside upon the said lands, and must keep hospitality; and that it be so ordered in the leases.[a]

Besides the hospitality which the monasteries offered they were also the refuge and the sanctuary of those victims of ceaseless tyranny which in the vicinity of a baronial castle were ever to be found.

Let us not then condemn monachism, because when it had accomplished its work, it became the parent of ignorance, bigotry, and licentiousness; but let us rather recall the period when it was " the guardian of learning, the author of civilization and the propagator of humble and peaceful religion."

> " The sacred taper's light is gone,
>   Grey moss has clad the altar-stone,
>   The holy image is overthrown,
>   The bell has ceased to toll.
>
>   The long ribbed aisles are burst and shrunk;
>   The holy shrine to ruin sunk,
>   Departed is the pious monk,
>   God's blessing on his soul!"

[a] Rolls House MSS., 1st Series, p. 900.

The Possessions.

THE POSSESSIONS.

HE landed possessions of Roche Abbey were for the most part situated in the West Riding of Yorkshire, and within a few miles of the spot on which the Abbey was built; but other lands of importance were in the neighbouring counties of Nottingham, Lincoln, Derby, and Lancaster. In the descriptions of the following places, when no County is mentioned, it must be understood that they were situated in Yorkshire.

Abby.—The Abbot of Roche had property in this hamlet, which is situated five miles north of Rotherham, but what it was or who gave it is not known. It probably came into the hands of the monks after the year 1232, and could not have been of great value, as, in 1535, it and three other places were together estimated at only 33s. 9d. per annum.

Aggcroft.—The grange of this place was, with its appurtenances, given by the Founders, and confirmed to the monks by Alice, Countess of Eu, in 1219.[a]

Alverley.—Whatever property the monks had here could not long have continued in their possession, for it is not named in the list of the places mentioned in the confirmation of Henry III. 1232, and between the years 1238 and 1254 it was exchanged for some lands in Slade Hooton, belonging to Robert de Ripariis. *(See Loversal.)*

In 1277, William, son of John Vavasor, quitclaimed all right in wards, escheats, &c., in this place.

Anes see **Oneash.**

Anston.—Nicholas de Saint Paul gave an oxgang[b] of land with

---

[a] See page 17.
[b] As much land as an ox can plough in a year, varying in quantity from six to forty acres.

a toft* and croft here, and confirmed to the monks what had been given to them by Leo de Manvers, and Michael, his fon. He alfo gave them all the woods and rents which he had recovered from the faid Leo and his fon. *(See Brancliffe.)*

The monks held land in Lumby and Afton in 1535, for which they paid 1½d. to the heirs of Weftnis (Wafteneys.)

Armthorpe.—This place, which in old charters is written Arneldthorpe and Arnethorpe, was a moft important part of the poffeffions of the monks. The grange was given them by Thomas de Arnethorpe before 1186.

Roger, fon of Hugh Fitz Walter, gave two oxgangs of land with a toft and croft here, and a culture called Gunhale, with the North-wood in this territory, which Agnes, daughter of Robert de Brunington, quitclaimed.

William, fon of Henry de Marifco, in 1246 quitclaimed all his rights in the inclofures here.

Adam, fon of Ralph de Armthorpe, gave one oxgang of land here.

Henry de Armthorpe of Pollington, fon and heir of Adam de Armthorpe, quitclaimed all his rights in the manor of Armthorpe in 1330.

Jeremiah, the parfon of Roffington, with his corpfe, gave all his meadow in the fouth part of the wood here, called South-wood.

It appears by "*Kirby's Inqueft*" that the monks held Armthorpe as one Knight's fee[b] of the King *in capite* in pure and perpetual alms the gift of Richard I.

In 35 Henry III. the Abbot of Roche had a grant of free warren here. This grant was difputed in the time of Edward I., and the abbot was fummoned to fhow by what warrant he claimed free warren. In anfwer the abbot produced the charter of Henry III., which fhewed his right.[c]

In 9 Edward II. the Abbot of Roche was returned Lord of Armthorpe. He had in his employ a Steward, a Bailiff,[d] a Forefter, and a Granger, who was a monk.[e]

---

[a] A houfe, or rather a place where a houfe ftood, which is decayed.

[b] A Knight's fee is fo much inheritance as is fufficient to maintain a Knight, which in Henry the Third's time was fifteen pounds, or two hundred acres.—Bailey.

[c] In 1535, Sir William Fitz William was fteward of Armthorpe, and Miles Wyn bailiff; the former receiving 40s. and the latter 20s. per annum.

[d] See page 89.   [e] See page 34.

The yearly income derived from Armthorpe is given in the "*Valor*" as £23 10*s.*, this sum being made up of rents, falls of wood, profits of court, rents of assize, &c.

At the Dissolution all the property which the monks had here went to the crown, and in 33 Henry VIII., the King, wishing to extend the limits of Hatfield chase, added Armthorpe to it. Not so much, however, with the intention of increasing the space for his deer as to ensure their safe keeping by placing it under the authority of the officers of the chase; for we find that the manor of Armthorpe was granted in 1551 to the Duke of Northumberland. It had been let from the dissolution until the date of this grant in two portions, one at £2 16*s.* 4¼*d.* and the other at £21 19*s.* 2*d.* per annum, out of which 13*s.* 4*d.* was paid to the collector of the rents, making the clear yearly value £24 2*s.* 2¾d.*

Arncliffe.—It would appear from *Tanner's* references that the monks held a tenement in this place, but the reference given is incorrect, as it has been found to refer to property formerly belonging to the Abbot of Westminster. It is certain, however, that the monks of Roche had possessions in the neighbourhood of Arncliffe, and it is not unlikely that they also had the tenement referred to by *Tanner*.

Ashenbeech see **Rochdale.**

Ashover.—Property in this place, which is also called Aexoure, in Derbyshire, was given to the monks before the year 1186, by Simon de Plesley. It was still in their hands in 1232, but seems to have been disposed of before the dissolution.

Askern.—In the Confirmation of Henry III. the monks are returned as having property in this place. At the dissolution it still remained in their hands.

Balne.—Henry, son of Maurice de Askern, gave one oxgang of land here, but it does not seem to have remained long in the hands of the monks.

Barnby.—The grange of this place was given to the monks before the year 1186, by Gervas de Barnby; and in 1245, Benedict, the Rector of Barnby, gave them the tithe of the grange also.

In 10 John, there was a fine between William Fitz Thomas and Alice his wife, and Osmund the Abbot of Roche, in which a verdict

---

* Particulars for grants 5 Ed. VI. sect. e.

was returned for the abbot of one bovate of land with the appurtenances in Barnby.

In 13 Henry III., there was a fine between the Abbot of Roche and William, son of Richard de Barnby, in which the said William acknowledged and granted for himself and his heirs that the aforesaid abbot and his successors should, as is fitting, have common right of pasture for the whole year, for every kind of beasts from the grange of the said abbot, except goats, everywhere in the wood of the said William de Barnby; and that they should have pigs of the actual breeding of the said grange in the same wood, free from pannage* for ever. And, moreover, the said William granted for himself and his heirs, that the aforesaid abbot and his successors should have and receive every year from the aforesaid wood, six cartloads of wood for ever, to wit, two cartloads of good building timber, of oaks not shaped, and two cartloads of wood for burning, and other two for fencing. And in like manner the said William granted for himself and his heirs that whenever it should happen that he pared sods or dug turfs with one or more of his men in the said wood, it should be quite lawful for the said abbot and his successors to pare sods or dig turfs in the same place, to the extent of half the number of the same men, without impediment.

The Abbot of Roche rented land in Barnby of the Lord of Sprotburgh.

At the dissolution the yearly value of Barnby grange was given as £7 10s. 8d. The monks had also a rent-charge of £1 10s. 1d. and rent and a farm valued at 13s. 9d., and perquisites of court, 1s. 4d., in all £9 15s. 10d. John Green, bailiff and receiver of Barnby,[b] had 10s. per annum at the dissolution.

In 36 Henry VIII., the manor of Barnby, late parcel of the possessions of Roche, was granted to Richard Turke, citizen of London. The quantity and value of the timber growing upon the manor of Barnby and Bramwith at this time may be learnt from the following entry:—"There be growing aboute the scytuation of the sayd mannor and V tenementes there, and in the hedges inclosyng the landes apperteyning to the same, CXL. okes and ashes of LX. and LXXX. yeres growth, most parte usually cropped and shred, whereof LX. reserved for tymber for housboote to repayre the houses standing uppon the scyte and for stakes for hedgeboote to repayre and maynteyne the said hedges and fences and LXX. resydue valued at VId. the tree whiche is in the holl XLs."[c]

---

[a] Money paid for licence to feed swine upon mast (l. e. the fruit of wild trees) in the woods.
[b] Brother Thomas was granger at Barnby in the time of Henry III., and in trouble. See page 32.
[c] Particulars for grants. Miscellaneous No. 61, Rolls House.

Barnoldswick.—The grange here is mentioned in King Henry's "*Valor*" as one of the poſſeſſions of the monks of Roche, and is valued at £8 per annum. It does not ſeem to have belonged to them in 1232, as no mention is made of it in the confirmation of Henry III. It was here that the monks of Kirkſtall firſt ſettled in 1147.

Bawtry.—The Abbot of Roche had property here in 1232, but of what it confiſted and who gave it is not known. It had been diſpoſed of before the diſſolution.

Bilham.—In the reign of King John, William de Barvile gave to the monks of Roche four oxgangs in this place and quitclaimed his right in four other oxgangs, which Henry de Worthley unjuſtly detained. *Dodſworth* ſays that he gave the monks *all* his lands in Bilham.

Blitheſhaw see **Thirnſcoe.**

Blyth.—John de Kyveton, parſon of the church of Radcliffe-on-Trent, made a fine with the King of twenty ſhillings for licenſe to aſſign one meſſuage, thirty-ſix acres of land, three acres and twenty-four ſhillings of rent, with the appurtenances in Blythe and Torworth, to the Abbot of Roche and the convent of the ſaid place. *(See Kiveton.)*

In the time of Edward III., the Abbot of Roche was ſummoned to anſwer to the King "by what warrant" he claimed to hold certain lands and tenements in Blyth in perpetual alms, free and quit from all taxes, &c., in anſwer to which the abbot produced the charter of Henry III.,* which he ſaid the preſent King had confirmed at Clipſton in his ſecond year. In anſwer as to how the abbot and his predeceſſors had uſed their liberties, twelve jurors on their oath ſaid that they had uſed them well. That they were always amerced with others in the country, and as to pontage, they ſaid that the abbot ought not to be quit from making and repairing the bridge of Nottingham, called the "Town Bridge."

In the Regiſter of Blyth Priory, fol. 103, there is a compoſition between the prior and convent of that place, and the prior of Roche, acting for the abbot, concerning tithes here.

In Edward II. the Prior of Blyth held of the Honour of Tick-hill the whole town of Blyth in demeſne in pure alms, except 40s. which the Abbot of Roche held in that town in exchange for the mill of Serlby in Nottinghamſhire.

* See page 20.

Botildewellewang see **Todwick.**

Braithwell.—The monks seem to have had no property here until the beginning of the thirteenth century. An oxgang of land with pasture for eighty sheep was granted them by Thomas, son of Artrop de Braithwell, who also confirmed all that his ancestors had given, and Richard, his brother, confirmed the same.

William, son of Gerbode gave ten acres of land in the fields of this town, with pasture for sixty sheep, and Robert, his brother, gave twenty acres of land in the same fields, with pasture for six score sheep.

The monks of Roche had therefore the right of pasture here for two hundred and eighty sheep.

Before the dissolution the monks paid one quarter of corn yearly at the mill of Coningsborough from the land which they held in Braithwell. After the dissolution the house and land of the abbot, together with some property called Bellstring Lands, were let to W. Wilson at £1 6s. 2d. per annum, paying thence to the crown 24s., and to Lord Hundesdon at his manor of Coningsborough one quarter of wheat. In 1563 all this property was granted to Charles Jackson, of Firbeck, Co. Notts., gent., at thirty-two years' purchase (£16 17s. 4d.). The moiety of the money to be paid in hand and the rest within fourteen days. The wood and underwood were sold the next year to Charles Jackson and Wm. Mason, for forty marks.*

Bramley.—Mabilia, the widow of Ote de Tilli, the seneschal of Coningsborough, gave two oxgangs of land with a toft and croft here, of her own patrimony, or according to *Dodsworth*, "her lordship of Bramley," but the monks were not to have common of pasture for more than a hundred sheep. She also confirmed three oxgangs in the same place.

The monks first had property here about the year 1190.

The abbot paid seven-pence rent to Roger Fretwell for land in Bramley.

Mr. *Hunter* says, that the grange of the Abbot of Roche here, after the dissolution, became the seat of a family of Spencer, who acquired much of the property that had been in the hands of the *religious*.

Bramwith.—Gervis de Barnby gave the grange here, before the year 1186.

William, son of William de Bladesworth, gave and confirmed

* Particulars for grants.

what he had here, and what the monks held of the fee of Allen de Hooton in this place.

In 3 King John, there was a fine between William de Infula and Ofmund, Abbot of Roche, tenant of two carucates of land with the appurtenances in Bramwith. Verdict to William. And William granted to the aforefaid Abbot and his succeffors all the aforefaid land with the appurtenances, to hold of him and his heirs at the fervice of two marks per annum, fave foreign fervice.

In 10 Henry III., there was a fine between Adam of Halyhton and Jane his wife, Robert, fon of Richard, and Sufanna his wife, plaintiffs; and Richard (? Reginald) Abbot of Roche, tenant of one bovate of land and half a fishery, with the appurtenances in Bramwith.

The rents of affize and cuftomary tenements here were valued in 34 Henry VIII. at £3 15s. 9½d.

The manor of Bramwith at the diffolution was granted to Richard Turke, citizen of London.

Brancliffe.—This grange was given to the monks before 1186 by Leo de Manvers. In 35 Henry III. they had a charter of free warren here.

At the diffolution, the Abbot's land here, which is called "The farm of the grange," was valued at £20. In 36 Henry VIII. it was granted to William Butler and others.

In the lane leading from this grange to the Sheffield and Workfop road, there is still a bridge which goes by the name of the "monks' bridge."

Bridlington.—The property of the monks feems to have extended to this well-known place, which is fituated in the Eaft Riding. Odenell, fon of Nicholas d'Aubeney, gave one mark per annum out of his mill at Bridlington. There is no mention of this gift in the lift of the poffeffions of Roche at the diffolution; it had probably therefore been difpofed of before that time.

Brookhouse.—This place is fituated in the parish of Laughton, and appears in the "*Valor Ecclefiafticus*" of Henry VIII. as one of the places belonging to Roche.

Broom Riddings.—This place lies about a mile and a half on the road from Rotherham to Roche Abbey. Robert de Herthwic, for the good of the foul of Beatrix his wife, gave two acres of land here, abutting upon Gofeker, with the meadow lying at the head of the faid acres. The monks feem to have difpofed of this property before the diffolution.

Bugthorpe.—This place is situated in the East Riding, near Pocklington. Idonea, wife of Nicholas de Bugthorpe, gave two acres of land here. No mention is made of it at the dissolution.

Brathmere see **Hatfield**.

Callinglow.—This place is near Oneash grange, and formed part of the property which the monks had in Derbyshire at the dissolution.

From the "*Particulars for Grants*" we learn that "the farm of the grange in the Peak, called Calengelawe, with all lands, meadows, pastures, &c., parcel of the possessions of the late monastery of Roche, freely resigned, were in 1540 demised to John Leke, Esq., at 40*s*. per annum."*

Campsal.—The monks had something here at the dissolution.

Carlton.—From the "*Hundred Rolls*" we find the following history of the manner in which this place came into the hands of the monks.

The ancestors of the King (4 Edward I.) had one manor in Carlton, belonging to the Crown, which was wont to yield £10 per annum, of which, King John gave to one Eustachius de Ludham and his heirs 30*s*. yearly. And King Henry III. gave the residue of the said rent, to one Algret, the Cross-bow man by his charter, and the said Algret gave that rent to the Abbot of Roche, who then held it, and paid the King 6*d*. yearly.

From the same source we learn that the Abbot had here twenty acres of meadow of the fee of Tickhill.

Sarah, relict of Richard de Bawtry, quitclaimed all her right in one oxgang of land here.

In 31 Henry III., the Abbot of Roche obtained a charter of confirmation of liberties and privileges in the manor of Carlton-in-Lindric, in Nottinghamshire, which was some time the King's demesne.

The monks did not hold this property long, as we find from the following charter :—

Royal Charter.

"The King to all whom, &c., greeting. Inasmuch as we have learnt by an inquisition which we have caused to be made by Hugo de Rodmerchewyet, in the county of Notts., that it is not to the

---

* Rolls House. Miscellaneous, No. 24.

injury or prejudice of ourself or others if we grant to our beloved in Christ, the Abbot and Convent of Roche, power for them to give and grant ten librates[a] of land and rents with the appurtenances in Carlton-in-Lindrik, which the said Abbot and Convent hold of us by the service of a pair of gilt spurs or sixpence per annum for all service, to our beloved and faithful Richard de Furneys to have and to hold to the said Richard and his heirs of us and our heirs by the service aforesaid for ever, we wishing to do the said Abbot and Convent a special favour in this behalf have given licenfe as far as in us lies for them to be able to give and grant the aforesaid ten librates of land and rents with the appurtenances to the said Richard, to have and to hold to him and his heirs of us and our heirs as aforesaid, and to the same Richard we in like manner grant as a special favour by these presents power to receive the said ten librates of land and rents from the aforesaid Abbot and Convent, being unwilling that the said Abbot and Convent or their successors by reason of the donation and grant of the said ten librates of land and rent, or the aforesaid Richard or his heirs by reason of the reception of the same should by us or any of our heirs whatever be disturbed, molested, or in any way aggrieved. Tested at Canterbury the first day of October, 1295."[b]

Carr.—At the dissolution the yearly rents of Slade Hooton and Carr were valued at £9 8s. 1d.

Castleshaw see **Rochdale.**

Catwick.—William, son of Gilbert de Catwick gave in 1263 one essart of land with a toft in this place.

Chatsworth.—Adam de Edinsor gave twenty acres of land upon Stanhege, in the territory of Chatsworth in Derbyshire, with pasture for two hundred sheep and sixty cattle, forty hogs and six saddle horses, with their produce of two years of age.

Coningsborough.—Although many of the benefactors of Roche lived here, the monks never seem to have had large possessions in Coningsborough.

Robert, son of Glai, gave the land and wood of this place as far as White Well, between the road and the river. The grant was confirmed by Pope Urban in 1186. It was in their hands in 1232, but had been disposed of before the dissolution, at which time, however, they paid 2s. 6d. rent for the mill of Coningsborough.

---
[a] A librate of land is, according to Cowel, four oxgangs of fifteen acres each. Bailey says fifty-two acres.
[b] Pat. Rot. 23 Edw. I. M. 5.

Cudworth.—About the middle of the thirteenth century, Thomas, son of Robert, of Ecclesfield, quitclaimed to the Abbot and Convent of Roche, for ever, all right and claim that ever he had in four bovates of land with the appurtenances in Cudworth, which Henry of Selesai gave them; the Abbot for the quitclaim paying two marks of silver. The monks had no property here at the dissolution.

Cumberworth.—From the following charter we find that the monks had property here at a very early period:—

Charter of William Earl Warren.

"To all the faithful in Christ whom this present charter may come, William Earl Warren, greeting in the Lord. Know that I have granted, and by this my present charter confirmed to God and the Blessed Mary and the monks of the Rock, for the welfare of my soul and those of my ancestors, all the land of "Cumbrewode," with the messuages and all the appurtenances which Matthew de Shepley gave and confirmed to them by his charters, to hold in perpetual alms according to the tenor of the charter of Matthew. These being witnesses: William son of William, Malveisin de Hersy, Richard de Memers, Baldwin de Hersy, Robert de Brettvile, Ralph de Eccleshale, John de Wakling, *clerk;* John Wakefield, *clerk;* Reginald Coc.'"

The property which the monks had in this place is now called Upper Cumberworth Half.

Deepcar.—This place, with Rawmarsh, Abdy, and Haugh, was valued at the dissolution at 33s. 9d.

Denshaw see **Rochdale.**

Doncaster.—The two following charters give a distinct account of the property of the monks in this town:—

Charter of William de Rossington.

"KNOWE YE that I, William, son of Wulfagh, of Rossington, have granted and given, and by this my charter confirmed to God, the Blessed Mary, and the Monks of Roche, for the welfare of my soul and that of Leuusa, my wife, my toft in Doncaster, with the appurtenances in which I abode, which I held of Ralph, son of William Albus, near the church of St. George, to have and to

---

* Morehouse's History of Kirkburton.

hold for ever, freely and quietly. Paying thrice yearly to the said Ralph, son of William Albus, and his heirs, two shillings for all service and demand, at the four stated terms (of the year) in Doncaster. Moreover, I have granted and given to the said monks that land which I held of Walter, son of Leon, to have and to hold for ever, freely and quietly, paying thrice yearly to the said Walter or his assigns four-pence for all service and demand, at the four statute terms in Doncaster. Moreover, I have granted and given to the said monks four-pence in my lifetime, yearly, to be paid at the four statute terms in Doncaster. Witnesses: Jeremiah de Rossington, William, his brother, Hugh de Langethwait, Peter de Waddeworth, Reginald, the bailiff, Henry de Marsh, John, son of Eudo de Bruntot."

Charter of Amabill de Brampton.

"KNOW &c., that I, Amabill, daughter of Robert de Brampton, formerly wife of Roger, son of William Strie, in my widowhood and free power have granted and quitclaimed of me and my heirs for ever to Michael de Brampton, my brother, and his heirs, to give and assign to whomsoever and at whatever time he may please, all the right and claim which I had or might have had under the name of dowry, or in any manner or occasion, in all that land with the buildings and the appurtenances in the town of Doncaster, which William de Warmsworth, chaplain, conferred upon the Abbot and Convent of Roche, to wit, that which lies between the land which Gena de Castello held, and the lane which extends from Francis street towards the Church of St. George, in length and breadth, as William Albus, my grandfather, held it, without any reservation. In such manner, to wit, as that neither I nor any of my heirs shall be able henceforth to place or require any right, or claim, or challenge in the said land, nor in the buildings, nor in the appurtenances; and that this my grant and quitclaim may remain ratified and firm, I have confirmed this present charter with my seal. Witnesses: Peter de Waddeworth, Reginald de Ketelbergh, Peter de Rosington, Richard, son of Hugh, Adam de Scawsby, John Bruntat, (?) Robert, his brother, Reginald, the tailor, Reginald, son of Reginald, and others."[*]

The Abbot of Roche had property here at the dissolution, at which time they paid elevenpence three farthings rent to the provost of the Lord the King of Coningsborough, issuing from the land in Doncaster with its members.

---

[*] For these charters I am indebted to Dr. Sykes, of Doncaster, who possesses the originals.

William de Warmſworth, chaplain of this place, alſo gave the monks a piece of land with certain buildings here.

Dunſcroft.—The Abbot of Roche erected a grange here for the management of his poſſeſſions at Hatfield, from which place it is about half a mile diſtant.

The "*Monaſticon Anglicanum*" gives Dunſcroft as a Cell to Roche Abbey, and refers to a ſeal publiſhed by Edward Rowe Mores, Eſq., as the ſeal of the Cell.

Mr. Hunter ſays, the legend of this ſeal is not Dunſcroft, and that no Cell ever exiſted here.[a]

Pope Alexander IV. granted permiſſion in 1263, to the Abbot of Roche, to celebrate ſacred offices in his granges, &c.; but there ſeems no reaſon to believe that Dunſcroft grange ever held a higher poſition than any other of the abbey granges.[b]

Eilrichthorpe.—This place, which adjoined the abbey grounds, was given to the monks ſoon after the foundation, by Richard de Buſli, the ſon of the Founder.[c]

Ewes.—Walter, ſon of John de Wolvethwait, gave all his land here. This place is called Ehus by *Dr. Burton*. From a charter before me, it appears that the property of the monks at Ewes, called Holtheng, was given at the diſſolution to Robert Thornhill, of Walkeringham, and Hugo his brother, who in 1547 granted it to John Sanderſon.

Ernuſe.—In 1248, the Abbot of Roche gave the King Henry III. five marks for having ſeizen of the mill of Ernuſe in the county of Nottingham.[d]

Farworth see **Harworth**.

---

[a] South Yorkſhire, vol. i. page 187.

Through the kindneſs of Dr. Hunter I have learnt that the opinion of the venerable hiſtorian of South Yorkſhire reſpecting this queſtion remained unaltered. In anſwer to my inquiries he wrote:—"I had been long ſuſpicious that there was ſome miſtake about Dunſcroft, when I met with Rowe Mores' engraving of the ſeal. The legend is imperfect, but there is enough to ſhew that the name of the place is not Dunſcroft, to which he erroneouſly, as I believe, aſcribed it.

If there had been really any Cell there, I muſt have met with ſomething more deciſive than the report of the Antiquarian of the time of Torr,—ſome deed or document of the time when it was in exiſtence, or at leaſt, ſome mention of it in ſuch Surveys as the "Valor" of King Henry VIII.

I have ſeen nothing to diſtruſt the opinion expreſſed in the S. Y. that it was the grange at which reſided the perſon who attended to the intereſt of the monaſtery at Armthorpe, and in the Level, a ſuperior one, as the officer was probably a perſon of a ſuperior claſs to the ordinary grangiarii.

I ſhould not have expreſſed myſelf ſo ſtrongly had I had the leaſt doubt about the miſreading of the legend on the ſeal."—M.S. letter, April 13th, 1860.

[b] See page 31.   [c] See page 9.

[d] I can find no place of this name. My information is derived from the "Abbreviatio Rotulorum Originalium."

Firbeck.—Walter, son and heir of John de Wolvethwaite, gave an annuity of sixpence out of a toft in this place. The monks had property here at the diffolution.

Fishlake.—William, Earl of Warren, gave the tithe of the eels caught in his fisheries at this place.[a]

Flixburgh.—William, son of Henry de Arcy gave the monks a sufficient carriage road between North and South Stather, near the bank of the Trent, in Lincolnshire, with a convenient place at which to load and unload ships or vessels in this place.

In the survey of the lands of Roche after the diffolution, the meadow in Flixburgh is valued at 10s. per annum.

Gildingwells.—In this place which is situated in the parish of Laughton, the monks possessed something at the diffolution.

Goderic-Riding.—This property lay between Wadworth and Wellingly, and was the gift of John de Chaworth. It is described by *Dr. Burton* as "all his demesne in this part." William Chaworth, mentioned in the following charter, was one of the lords of Wadworth in 1236.

Charter of William de Chaworth.

"To all the sons of Holy Mother Church present and future, William de Chaworth greeting. Know all of you that I have given, granted, and by this my charter confirmed to God and St. Mary and the Monks of Roche, for the welfare of my soul and that of my father and mother, and for the welfare of the soul of John my brother, and my heirs and all my relations, all that part which I had in my domain in 'Godrikeriding.' To wit, the land at West, which the aforesaid John gave to them, and I in like manner have given to the said monks all the brush which lies between the land of Eudo (de Wadworth) and the brook which runs toward the grange of Wellingly in pure and perpetual alms, free and quit from all service and from all which belongs to the land. And I and my heirs will warrant to the aforesaid monks the aforenamed land and brush, and quit it against all men. Witnesses: Ralph, priest of Wadworth, Henry de Chaworth, Robert, son of Payn, Robert, son of Gebod, William, son of Eudo, Godfrey de Wadworth, Robert, son of William."[b]

[a] See page 28.
[b] Dodsworth's M.S., vol. VIII. fol. 319 a.

Harworth.—The monks had property in this place as early as the end of the twelfth century. It is situated in the North-west corner of Nottinghamshire, about two miles East of Tickhill. Its old name was Farwath.

Gamellus de Harworth gave one oxgang of land here which he held of the fee of Robert, son of Ralph de Styrrup.

Robert de Styrrup gave one toft at the west end of the town of Harworth, with one acre of land near it, and pasture for a hundred and twenty sheep.

This property had gone out of the hands of the monks before the dissolution.

Hatfield.—William, Earl of Warren, gave the tithe of his eels here after the monks of Lewis had taken their tithe.[a]

John, Earl of Warren, "Beholding the scarcity of fruits, rents, and possessions generally pertaining to the religious men, the Abbot and Convent of Roche, in the diocese of York, and to their monastery, *and admiring the magnificence of the stone work as well in the buildings of the said Abbot and Convent as in their monastery;*[b] also, nobly grieving for the paucity of monks serving God there, gave for the support of thirteen additional monks the advowson of the Church of Hatfield, then valued at seventy marks per annum." In 1345, King Edward III. granted licence to the Earl to effect this gift.

Royal Charter.

"The King to all whom, &c., greeting. Know that inasmuch as our beloved cousin and liege, John de Warenn, Earl of Surrey, holds the manor of Haytfield with the appurtenances for his whole life, by the gift and grant of Lord Edward, lately King of England, our father, in such a manner that after the death of the said earl the said manor with the appurtenances, with remainder to Matilda de Feyrford for the term of her life, and after the death of the said Matilda, to John de Warenn, son of the said Matilda, and the heirs male of his body issuing, and after the discease of the said John, if he die without heir male of his body issuing, to Thomas, brother of the said John and the heirs male of his body issuing, and after the discease of the said Thomas, if he die without heir male of his body issuing, to the heirs of the body of the said earl issuing, and if the said earl die without heir of his body issuing, then the said manor,

---

[a] See page 28.
[b] This sentence in italics has been omitted in the charter which is printed at page 51.

with the appurtenances, to revert entirely to our said father and his heirs, as in the letters patent of our said father, thereupon executed more fully is contained; and now the said earl has besought us that (inasmuch as the said Matilda is dead, and the aforesaid John, son of Matilda, and Thomas have taken the habit of religion in the order of the brothers of the Hospital of John of Jerusalem, in England, at Clerkenwell, and in the said order are professed,) we will grant to the said earl power to give and grant the advowson belonging to the Church of Haytfeld, which he holds from us in chief, as it is said, which said church is worth seventy marks per annum, to our beloved in Christ the Abbot and Convent of Roche, to possess to them and their successors for the whole life of the said earl, we yielding graciously to the request of the said earl, have granted and given license for us and our heirs, as far as in us lies, to the said earl that he may give and grant to the Abbot and Convent to have and to hold to themselves and successors from us and our heirs for the term of the life of the said earl, and to the said Abbot and Convent by the tenor of these presents we, in like manner, have given special licence to receive the said advowson from the said earl, and to hold to them and their successors in form aforesaid, the statute enacted about not placing land and tenements in mortmain notwithstanding. We will, moreover, and of our more abundant grace, grant for us and our heirs to the said Abbot and Convent that they may have and hold the said advowson (which ought from the causes aforesaid to revert to us and our heirs after the death of the said earl) to them and their successors from us and our heirs in pure and perpetual alms for ever, and that they may have power to appropriate the said church after the said gift and grant of the advowson aforesaid by the said earl to them made, when they see expedient, and may hold it thus appropriated to their own uses to them and their successors for finding thirteen monks chaplains to celebrate for ever divine offices in the Abbey of Roche for us, Philippa Queen of England, our Consort, and our dearest children, and for the said earl, also for the soul of William our son, who *nuper humanitus contigit* in the said manor, and for the souls of our progenitors and those of the said earl and all the faithful defunct: the statute aforesaid or any right which might belong to us after the death of the said earl, if he die without heir from his body issuing, or by reason of the profession of the said John, son of Matilda, and Thomas in the aforesaid order while they are living, or after their death, without heirs male of their bodies, notwithstanding; wishing that neither the said earl nor the said Abbot and Convent, nor the successors of the said

Abbot and Convent, by reason of the premises or statute aforesaid, or because the said advowson ought to revert to us and our heirs (as parcel of the manor aforesaid which is held of us in chief, as is said) together with the said manor after the death of the said earl in form aforesaid, or from any other causes whatever, be by us or our heirs, justices, escheators, sheriffs, or other our bailiffs, or servants whatever, hindered, molested, or in any way aggrieved. Witness, the King at Westminster, November 22nd, 1345."

The appropriation was effected by William la Zouch, Archbishop of York, he reserving certain rights.[a]

In 1348, three years after they had obtained this important gift, the Abbot and Convent of Roche, parsons of the Church of Hatfield, set forth in petition to parliament that they ought to have each year an oak in the park or woods of Hatfield; and instead of tithe of herbage, sixty large beasts running in the park or wood throughout the year. And also instead of tithe of pannage, to have all their pigs which are fed in the parsonage, running in the same woods without paying anything for pannage; and further for the tithe of the fishery of Brathmere and Neuflet, a bynde[b] of eels every year to be taken as the right of the Church of Hatfield. The Earl of Warren being dead, and the manor in the hands of Queen Philippa, they prayed that certain impediments might be removed. They were referred to the chancellor, who was to call all parties together and to do justice amongst them.

In 1355, on the day of Pentecost, an indenture was made between the Abbot and Convent of Roche, on the one part, and Thomas Rillington, John Fitz Peter, Thomas Margens, Alan del Cotes, John, his brother, John del Parkes, John Fitz Peter de Stainford, parishioners of the Church of Hatfield, on the other part, that the said Abbot of Roche, having the Church of Hatfield appropriated, granted and permitted that the said parishioners, and other the inhabitants of the town of Stainford, might, by the archbishop's licence, maintain at their own cost a chaplain to celebrate divine service in the Chapel of Stainford, newly builded, for the space of three years daily, excepting on Sundays and other great festivals, whereon they were to repair to the parish church of Hatfield. This agreement was confirmed by the archbishop's vicar-general on the 17th November, 1535.

---

[a] See page 52.
[b] A Bind of Eels according to KENNETT, consisted of two hundred and fifty.

In 1535, the profits of the rectory received by the Abbot were as follows:—

	£	s.	d.
Manfion there (the Vicarage)	0	8	8
Glebe	1	13	4
Clofe and Pafture	0	5	0
Tithe of herbage of the park with pafture for 24 beafts	0	18	0
Tithe of pannage of hogs there	0	1	0
Tithe of wood, viz., one fuel tree to be delivered by the bailiff	0	1	0
Tithe of grain at Hatfield	8	0	0
Tithe of grain at Thorne	7	0	0
Tithe of grain at Stainford	5	0	0
Tithe of hay	1	10	0
Wool and lamb	2	0	0
Oblations	2	0	0
Minute and privy tithes	12	0	0
Mortuaries	0	6	8
Tithe of eels of Bràthmere	0	11	0
	£41	14	8

REPRISALS.

	£	s.	d.
To the Vicar	15	0	0
To the Archbifhop	7	10	4
To the King's bailiff	0	7	9
	22	18	1
Clear yearly value	£18	16	7

At the diffolution the intereft which the monks had in this place again reverted to the crown.

Haugh.—The monks had property at Haugh, near Rawmarfh, at the diffolution.

Hellaby.—Mauger, fon of Roger de Stokes, confirmed the grant of fix oxgangs of land here made by Geffery Fitz Payne, of Newerth. The property here and at Bramley was valued at the diffolution at £9 18s. 8d.

Hefley.—This place is fituated near Roffington, in the county of Nottingham. The monks owned property here at the diffolution.

Hestwell.—The monks had property here, the gift of William the Fleming, which was confirmed by Pope Urban III. in 1186.*

Hillbrigthorpe see **Rochdale**.

Holme.—Peter de Roffington gave the monks a wood here, now called "Holmes Carr Wood."

Holme see **Thurnscoe**.

Hooton-Levet.—In 1249, Manfelyn, of Doncafter, Manfelyn, of Brodfworth, and Elias, fon-in-law of the faid Manfelyn, releafed to the Abbot and Convent of Roche all lands, rents, and tenements which they had of Hamond de Levet, in the territory of Hooton-Levet, from the beginning of the world to the world's end. For better fecurity they had put to *their Hebrew letter* with their feal. This feems to have been an interference on the part of the monaftery between Hamond de Levet and the Jew money lenders, fimilar to that mentioned in page 13.

Hamond, fon of William Levet, gave one oxgang of land, with a toft and croft in this place.

Richard, fon of William Levet, gave half of the mill here, with the pool and free water courfe from Maltby mill to the Monk's mill, with the fuit of the faid moiety, referving a right to himfelf, his heirs and affigns, to grind all their corn that fhall grow upon four oxgangs in this territory, at a multure of the fixteenth bowl.

Jordan, fon of Jordan de Infula, and Elizabeth his wife, gave all their land at Hooton-Levet.

Adam, fon of Simon de la Roche, and Joan his wife, daughter of Robert de Wickerfly, gave one oxgang of land here, with a toft and croft, which gift Sir Robert de Wickerfley, knight, confirmed.

Henry de Lacy granted and confirmed the donation which Richard de Wickerfley, and Roger and Jordan Hooton, made to the monks of Roche of common pafture of all the territory of Hooton.

The property here was valued at the diffolution at £4 19s. 2d. per annum.

Hooton-Roberts.—The monks had a farm at this place which was valued at the diffolution at 1s. per annum. *(See Slade Hooton.)*

Hope.—*(Derbyshire.)*—The monks poffeffed fomething here at the diffolution.

* See page 16.

Ichells.—It is not known from whom the monks derived this property. It is defcribed in 1552 as "a clofe called Ichells, lying near the dyke leading from Haugh to Wentworth on the eaft, in the tenure of Thomas Wentworthe, Efq., at the will of the Lord the King from year to year, paying at the terms of St. Martin in winter and Pentecoft equally nine fhillings per annum." It was at this time granted to Admiral Lord Clinton.[a]

Ickles.—The Monks had two mills in Ickles, near Rotherham. *(See Templeborough.)*

Ingbirchworth.—From the following interefting charter we find that the monks had property here at an early date :—

Charter of Henry de Shelley.

"Know all men, prefent and future, that I, Henry de Shelley, fon of Robert, have given, granted, and by this my charter confirmed for the welfare of my foul and of all my anceftors and heirs, to the Abbot and Monks of St. Mary of Roche, the homage and fervice of John, fon of Robert del Ker (Car) which he owed to me and to my heirs or affigns for two bovates of land with the appurtenances in Bircheworth, and the homage and fervice of John, fon of Adam, which he owed to me and my heirs and affigns for one bovate of land with the appurtenances in the fame vill, and two bovates of land with the appurtenances which Richard and Joan held of me in the fame vill, and the faid Richard and Joan with all their progeny, and the faid Robert and Adam with all their progeny, and one bovate of land with the appurtenances which Gilbert, the chaplain, held of me in the fame vill, which is called Wetelay, to have and to hold in perpetual alms, free and quiet from all fervice to me and to my heirs belonging, fave foreign fervice, as far as pertains to one carucate of land, nine carucates of which make one knight's fee. And I and my heirs will warrant all the aforefaid land with the appurtenances to the aforefaid Abbot and Monks of Roche for ever againft all men. Thefe being witneffes: Dom. Henry, parfon of Rothell; Hugh de Urnethorp, then fteward of Pontefract; Robert de Stapleton, Henry Walent, Robert, fon of Adam; Thomas de Littel, Alan, fon of Robert de Smeaton; Robert, fon of Gilbert; Simon, fon of * * * Alan, fon of Alan."[b]

Inngeby.—Simon Fitz Simon, gave land in this place, which Pope Urban III. confirmed.

---

[a] Particulars for grants 6 Ed. VI. sect. 6. [b] Morehoufe's Hiftory of Kirkburton.

Kilnhurst.—In 1385, the Abbot and Convent of Roche granted in fee to John Montforth, of Kilnhurst, one messuage, four acres of meadow and six acres of land in the town and territory of Kilnhurst, four acres of which lie near the wood of Rawmarsh, on the east side, stretching north and south; one acre abutting on Walkerfall, and one acre abutting on the town of Kilnhurst, all which they had of the gift of Roger de Kilnhurst: and that * * * which extends itself to the north field of his toft aforesaid. Also one half acre of meadow which they had of the gift of Thomas de Kilnhurst, reserving therefrom thirteen shillings and four pence rent, and a double payment from every tenant at his first entry, which if not paid within forty days, should give the Abbot the right to re-enter and seize upon the tenements again.

The earliest common seal of the Abbey is appended to the deed from which the above information is obtained. See plate x., fig. 3.

The profits of this place together with those of Ickles and Hooton-Roberts, were at the dissolution £1 7s. 8d.

Kiveton.—No remains of "the Chapel of the Holy Trinity of Kyveton," mentioned in the following charter, are now to be found.

Royal Charter.

"The King, to all to whom, &c., greeting. Know that, inasmuch as Lord Edward, lately King of England, our grandfather, by his letters patent granted and gave licence for himself and his heirs to John de Kyveton, parson of the Church of Radeclyf-on-Trent, to give and assign one messuage, thirty-six acres of land, three acres of meadow, and twenty-four shillings worth of rent, with the appurtenances in Blithe and Torworth, to the Abbot and Convent of Roche, to have and to hold to them and their successors for finding a certain secular chaplain to celebrate divine offices for the soul of the said John and the souls of his father, mother, and his ancestors and all the faithful departed, in the Chapel of the Holy Trinity of Kyveton every day, and also the same our grandfather granted and gave licence for himself and his heirs to the aforesaid Abbot and Convent to give and grant to the aforesaid John for the tenements aforesaid a certain corrody, to be received from the said Abbey to him and his heirs for the sustenance of the said chaplain and his successors for ever, and to the said John having received the said corrody and being seized thereof, to give and assign the said corrody to the said chaplain to have for himself and his successors who were to celebrate in the said chapel as aforesaid for their sustenance for ever, as in the letters patent of our grandfather aforesaid, thereupon made more fully is contained ; and the aforesaid John did afterwards also give and assign, according to the force and effect of the licence of the King aforesaid, as we have learnt, to the aforesaid Abbot and Convent and their successors, the said messuage, land, meadow, and rent, with the appurtenances, and to the aforesaid chaplain and his successors the corrody which he obtained by the gift and grant of the aforesaid Abbot and Convent and their successors. We now, at the request both of our beloved in Christ the present Abbot and Convent of Roche, who hold the messuage, land, meadow, and rent aforesaid, and of the present chaplain of the chapel aforesaid, who receives the said corrody from the Abbey aforesaid, and for two marks which the said Abbot and Convent have paid to us, have granted and given licence for us and our heirs, as far as in us lies, to the said Abbot and Convent to give and assign the messuage, land, meadow, and rent aforesaid with the appurtenances to the said present chaplain, to have and to hold for himself and his successors in exchange for the corrody aforesaid being given, assigned, surrendered, and released for ever to the said Abbot and Convent and their successors by the said chaplain, and to the same chaplain both to receive the said messuages, land, meadow, and rent with the appurtenances to hold to himself and his successors for ever from the said Abbot and Convent, and to give, assign, surrender, and release the said corrody to the said Abbot and Convent and their successors in exchange aforesaid for ever; by the tenour of these presents we have in like manner given special licence, the statute passed about not putting lands and tenements into mortmain notwithstanding, willing that neither the said Abbot and Convent or their successors, nor the said chaplain or his successors, by reason of the statute aforesaid, therein be hindered or in any way aggrieved by us or our heirs or servants, save however the services due and accustomed from the said messuage, land, meadow, and rent. Witness, the King, at Westminster, July 8th, 1401."

Lambcote Grange.—This place is situated in the parish of Stainton. Its original name was Lambcroft, as it is so written in the *Confirmation of Pope Urban III.* in 1186, from which document we also learn that it was given the monks by Richard de Busli and Hugh de Drigwrt.

In 1563 "Lamcottes," which had formerly been in the tenure of Robert and Agnes Hewet, was let by indenture under the common seal of the late monastery of Roche to John Wilkynson, at 60s. per annum at the terms of St. Martin in the Winter and Pentecost equally. It was at this time granted by the crown to Charles Jackson.[a]

Laughton.—Nicholas, the Clerk of this place, gave a toft lying on the south side of St. John's Church, with six acres of land, now called Throapham, and which the monks held at the dissolution.

In the time of Abbot Osmund, Cardinal Stephen gave the monks the prebend of Laughton.

From the "*Hundred Rolls*" we learn that the Abbot of Roche held thirty bovates of land in the barony of Laughton in 1276.

In 1558 the possessions in this place, lately belonging to the monastery of Roche, were on the 20th of October rated to Thomas Stephenson.

Lincoln.—In 1275 the Abbot of Roche held a mansion in this city, which was then valued at 10s. per annum. At the dissolution its annual value was only 4s.

Lindrick.—King Henry II. gave one hundred acres in Lindrick near the abbey, now called King's Wood. Many have thought from the name Lindrick that this property must have been in Nottinghamshire, but erroneously, for Lindrick, near Tickhill, and Lindrick Common, Lindrick Dale, and Lindrick Brook, near South Anston, are all in Yorkshire.

Alice, Countess of Eu, confirmed to the monks the wood of Lindrick in 1219.[b]

At the dissolution the annual falls of wood and underwood were valued *communibus annis* at 40s.

Loversall.—Reginald Gurvy quitclaimed to the monks the mill in this place.

About the middle of the thirteenth century the monks of Roche gave what they had here, at Wadworth and at Alverley, to Robert de Ripariis, in exchange for his lands at Slade Hooton, two pieces of meadow in Walkeringham, and £100 in money.

Lumby.—The monks had land, &c., in this place, which they demised to Richard Burton, Esq., and Catherine his wife, on the 20th of October, 20 Henry VI. (1441.)

Maltby.—Besides what Richard de Busli (one of the founders) gave,[c] Alan, the parson of Maltby, gave his right of common in two

---
[a] Particulars for grants.
[b] See page 17. [c] See page 4.

THE POSSESSIONS.

acres of land lying in Summer-road, in this territory. The ruins of the Abbey stand upon the southern border of this parish. *(See Roche.)*

Marr.—Jordan, son of Philip de Marr, gave all his wood in this place with four tofts, two oxgangs of land and the fourth part of an oxgang in this town and fields. By a charter dated at Woodhall, on the vigil of St. Nicholas, 1253, Thomas Fitz William confirmed to the monks all lands in Marr, of his fee, which they had of the gift of Jordan, son of Philip de Marr, and his ancestors.

John, son of Jordan de Marr, gave to the monks of Roche nine acres of land here with their capital messuage in the town, and homage and service of free men, rendering ten shillings annually and scutage. This was also confirmed by Thomas Fitz William in a charter dated at Sprotborough, Nonas Martii, 1260.

Richard, son of Hugh de Langethwaite, gave an annuity of six shillings out of a toft, and twelve acres of land in this place.

In "*Kirby's Inquest*" the Abbot of Roche is said to have held eleven bovates of the fee of Thomas Fitz William, who held the Castle of Tickhill.

The possessions at Marr and Bilham were valued at the dissolution at £8 18s. 6d.

Marr Grange was granted in 1544 to John Bere.

Micklebring.—Eugenia, relict of Gilbert de Micklebring, with the consent of Peter de Rhodes, his lord, gave four acres in this place.

Monk Bretton.—In 1285 the Abbot and Convent of Roche sold their claim to the manor and advowson of the Church of Monk Bretton to the Prior and Convent of this place for 20s. sterling.

Monyash.—John, son of Matthew de Eston, *for the support of a light at the high altar,* gave the multure* of twelve oxgangs of land in Monyash, Derbyshire, the tenants of which were to grind at the mills of the Monk's Grange, at Oneash, paying the twentieth bowl.

Morley.—This place is situated near Greasborough. William Bacon with his corpse gave nine acres of land here. The Prior of Nostel held four bovates of land in Morley.

---

* The toll or fee which a miller takes for grinding corn.

Charter of Abbot Walter.

"Know, &c., that we, Walter Abbot and the Convent of Roche, have granted and by our present charter have confirmed to Lord Thomas de Bellew and his heirs or assigns all the service which Robert Barker, of Swinton, and his heirs have been accustomed to do for us for the land of Morley, with all things that can accrue to us from the said land for ever, at an annual rent therefrom to us and our successors of sixteen pence at Pentecost, and to the House of St. Oswald in our name eight pence at the feast of St. Martin in the Winter for the said land of Morley. And we and our successors will warrant to the said Thomas and his heirs or assigns all the aforesaid service with all its appurtenances, so long as our donors shall have warranted it to us. Witness, the Lords Ralph de Horbiry, Ralph de Normanville, John de Staynton, knights; Ralph Haket, Robert Brinton, Roger de Bergh, James de Lyvet, Richard his brother, Raynder de Swinton, William de Roche, William de Swinton."

Newhall.—On November 28th, 1552, the farm of one close lying in Newhall, containing six acres of pasture, in the occupation of Joane Cousen, widow, by indenture, as it is said, for a term of years, yielding therefrom at the feasts of Pentecost and St. Martin in the Winter equally per annum 13s. 4d., and lately in the possession of the monasteries of Roche, was granted for divers considerations to the Right Honourable Lord Clinton, High Admiral of England.[a]

Newland.—This bill made the 20th of September in the 37th year of Henry VIII. witnesseth that we John Bellewe, Esq., and John Bloxolme, gent., have paid to Sir John Williams, knight, treasurer of the Augmentation of the Revenues of the King's Crown, the sum of * * * due to the King for the gift, grant, and clear purchase of "one mansion or tenemente in the parishe of St. Stephen in Newland, late parcell of Roche, togither with all and singular the woodes and underwode growinge in and upon the premises."[b]

Newsome.—Robert de Scalcebi, Adam de Newmarch, and Roger de Marr gave the monks the grange at this place. The two first of these were witnesses to the Foundation Charter of the Abbey.

Nottingham.—Philip de Oldcotes gave the monks a toft in this town and the service of another toft.

---

[a] Particulars for Grants. Sect. 8.   [b] Monasticon Ang. Appendix, p. 1643.

THE POSSESSIONS.

Oldcotes.—This place is situated in Nottinghamshire, about two miles from the Abbey. The monks had property here in the time of King Richard I.

Oneash.—*(Derbyshire.)*—The grange at this place was given to the monks soon after the foundation of the Abbey by William Avenal, Lord of Haddon. .

Richard de Vernun, with the consent of Avice, his wife, and of William his son and heir, confirmed all the land and pasture of his fee in this place, which William Avenal gave; and William Bassett, grandson of William Avenal, confirmed the same.

Richard, son of William de Verum, confirmed the above, and also what the monks had in Sterndale, with the minerals, they paying to him and his heirs 15*s.* per annum, at his manor of Haddon. He also confirmed the tenement here which William Avenal gave. Pope Urban III. also confirmed what the monks held here.

William, Earl of Ferrars, with the consent of Agnes his wife, before 1229 confirmed to the monks that way for their sheep and cattle going from their grange here, over the moor of Hartington and Heathcote, which William his father had granted to them, with some meadow; they paying to him one mark per annum.

We learn from the Taxation of Pope Nicholas, about 1291, that the possessions of the monks here, consisting of four bovates of land, a mill, mines, &c., were valued at £8 8*s.* 8*d.* per annum.

We learn from the following document that at the time of the dissolution this grange was let to Thomas Sheldon.

"In the 32nd year of the reign of the most excellent Prince Henry VIII. the farm of the grange of Oneash, parcel of the possessions of the late monastery of Roche, freely resigned, with all lands, meadows, feedings, pastures, moors, &c., from old time belonging, is thus demised to Edw. Beresford, of the County of Derby, gent., by indenture under the common seal of the late monastery at 113*s.* 4*d.* per annum, to be paid at the terms of St. Martin and Pentecost equally, viz., for the farm of the said grange £4 6*s.* 8*d.*, and for tithes thereto belonging 26*s.* 8*d.*, besides 6*s.* paid to the cathedral church of Lichfield for an ancient pension for tithes of all kind of the said grange; also 30*s.* paid to the manor of Haddon always at the feast of St. Martin in the Winter yearly, until it shall be adjudged by law that half the sum ought to suffice; also 13*s.* 4*d.* for having common of pasture in the moor of Middleton. And that the said farmer at the end of the term aforesaid or whenever he shall quit it shall leave four sextaries and twenty-four quarters of good and well cleaned oats behind him for the use of the aforesaid lord the King and his successors. Now on the same terms in the tenure of Thomas Sheldon.[a]

Oustrop.—William, son of William de Bladsworth, confirmed all the fishery in this place.

Overste.—William, son of John de Vavasor, quitclaimed all his right in ward, escheat, &c.

Ravenfield.—The monks had property here, the gift of Simon, son of Ralph de Tickhill. At the dissolution they paid 2s. per annum to the Hostle of St. Leonard at York, from land here.

Rawmarsh.—Adam de Sancta Maria with his corpse gave the monks free common in this place with a toft in Haugh, also a toft and croft, two acres of land, and his wood lying between the road to Abdy and Fildingale, leading to the fields of Swinton, with liberty to enclose the same.

Charter of John and Hugh Brun.[b]

"Know all present and future that we, John and Hugh, sons of Adam Brun, have remised and quitclaimed to God and the Blessed Mary and the Monks of Roche for the welfare of our souls and those of all our ancestors and heirs all right and claim which we had or might have had in all the land of Etheles, some of which Adam Brun our father held of Adam de Sancta Maria in the territory of Rawmarsh, with homages, wards, reliefs, escheats, and with all other profits which can in any way accrue to us or our heirs or assigns. Also, that neither we nor any other in our name can demand hereafter any right or claim in the said land with its appurtenances. In testimony of which we have to this writing placed our seals. Witness, Robert de Wath, clerk; Hugh de Brome, Thomas de Haby, Thomas de Lindric, Adam Depeker, Hugh de Wikesop, and many others."

The property which the monks had in Rawmarsh, Deepcar, Abdy, and Haugh was valued at the dissolution at £1 13s. 9d. per annum.

Risby.—*(Lincolnshire.)*—Walter de Falcunbridge confirmed the grant of two oxgangs of land in this place made by Walter de Kadburne. The monks held this property as early as the year 1198.

---

[a] Particulars for Grants. No. 24.   [b] Dodsworth's M.S, vol. VIII. fol. 80, 81.

Roche.—Some have thought that Roche Abbey derived its name from St. Roche, the Lombardy saint, others have traced its origin to the roach fish, but from the original title ("monachi de rupe") which the monks adopted, we learn without doubt the true source. It should be noticed that the monks of Roche did not use the plural as the monks of Fountains did; they simply styled themselves "Monks of the Rock." What the particular rock was has already been pointed out.[a] "De rupe" was soon changed into "De la Roche," and when the French word Roche became anglicized the monastery began to be called Roche Abbey. Had it lasted till now it would in all probability ere this have been called Rock Abbey. The actual precincts of Roche Abbey enclosed a space of thirty-one acres. It was of a triangular shape, and was surrounded by a high substantial wall, the greater part of which may still be traced in a more or less ruined condition.[b] This land was the gift of Richard de Busli and Richard Fitz Turgis.[c] It was confirmed to the monks by John de Busli[d], by Alice Countess of Eu[e], by Pope Urban III[f]., and by many of the Kings of England. Henry III. granted the monks free warren here.

In the time of Edward I. we find the Abbot of Roche summoned to answer to our Lord the King on a plea by what warrant he claimed to have free warren in all his demesne lands of Roche, Brantcliffe, Armthorpe, and Hillbrigtthorpe, without the licenſe and will of the King and his progenitors, &c. And the Abbot appeared and ſaid that he claimed free warren in Roche, Armthorpe, and Brantcliffe by charter of the Lord Henry the King, granted in the 35th year (1250) of his reign, which he produced and which teſtified that the ſaid Lord the King granted to a certain Abbot and Convent of Roche, predeceſſors of that Abbot, that they and their ſucceſſors for ever ſhould have free warren in all their demeſne lands of Roche, Armthorpe, and Brantcliffe, in the county of York, &c.[g]

Charter of Adam Fitz Burnell.[h]

"To all the faithful in Chriſt to whom the preſent writing may come, Adam Fitz Burnell, of Elmiſhall, greeting. Know all that the Abbot and Convent of Roche are quit towards me and my heirs of five marks which they owed to my father in his charter, which is in ſafe cuſtody with the holy men of Hampol, and of all debts

---

[a] See page 82. [b] See Plan of the Abbey Grounds. [c] See Charters, pages 4 and 5. [d] See page 11.
[e] See page 17. [f] See page 15.
[g] Roll. 5. D. [h] Dodſworth's MS., vol. VIII. fol. 245 D.

which they ever owed to the said Burnell my father, in such sort, however, that I Adam and my heirs shall be able to demand hereafter nothing from the said Abbot and monks by reason of any debt which they at any time owed to my father. But if any one shall bring forward in the name of my father any charter to demand any debt from the said Abbot and monks, I and my heirs with all our might will faithfully aid them. Witness, Jeremia, Parson of Rossington; William and John his brothers, Hugh de Langethwaite, Thomas de Sandal, Hugh de Bilham, John de Skellew, Reginald, Presbyter de Doncaster."

(Seal, a Lion passant.)

Elmsall lies not far distant from the property which the monks held at Thurnscoe, Bilham, Skellow, Campsall, &c. It is not unlikely that the monks bought some part of one of these of the Burnell family.

Advowson.

The advowson of Roche Abbey belonged for some time alternately to the two founders Richard de Busli and Richard Fitz Turgis or de Wickersley and their successors, and the value of it appears by one of the Clifford Inquisitions, to have been £40 each vacancy.

The right of presentation held by Richard Fitz Turgis went at his death to his son Roger de Wickersley, and from him it passed to Constantia his daughter, who married William de Levet. It then continued in the Levet family until 1377, when John Levet granted it to Richard Barry by the following charter.

Charter of John Levet.

"Be it known to all men present and future that I, John Levet, son and heir of William Levet, of Hooton Levet, have given, granted, and by this my present charter confirmed to Richard Barry, citizen and merchant of London, the whole of my estate which I have or my ancestors have ever had in the foundation of the Abbey of Roche, in the county of York, together with the patronage and advowson of the same Abbey when it may have become vacant, and with the whole of my lordship which I have or which my aforesaid ancestors ever had in the aforesaid Abbey by reason of the foundation of the same or of any other title. I also give and grant to the same Richard a certain rent of two shillings and sixpence proceeding from all those lands and tenements with their appurtenances which were given by my aforesaid ancestors for the foundation of the abbey aforesaid, along with a half-penny of rent with the appurtenances proceeding from a certain

THE POSSESSIONS.   127

fulling mill situated in the aforesaid Abbey, granted as parcell of the foundation of the same abbey, which said rent had been reserved, by my anceftors aforesaid and their heirs for ever, from the lands and tenements aforesaid and from the mill aforesaid with their appurtenances over and above the donation of these lands along with the tenements and mill aforesaid for the foundation of the abbey aforesaid. I also give and grant to the same Richard all other my services with all temporal and spiritual advantages, with all profits and appurtenances which I have or in any way ought to have of the aforesaid abbey on account of any refervation respecting the foundation of the abbey aforesaid. To have and to hold all the aforesaid, to wit, my eftate in the foundation aforesaid along with the patronage and advowson aforesaid, and with all my lordship aforesaid, and rent aforesaid, with all other things aforenamed and all their appurtenances by the aforesaid Richard and his heirs and assigns as freely, entirely, and quietly as I or any of my anceftors ever had any eftate in the same or may have had for ever. To receive the aforesaid rents in the form aforesaid, to wit, the aforesaid two shillings and sixpence from all the lands and tenements aforesaid, except from the mill aforesaid and the half-penny rent from the same mill at the usual terms: and I the aforesaid John and my heirs will warrant and for ever defend my whole eftate in the foundation aforesaid, together with the patronage and advowson aforesaid and with all my lordship above mentioned and payments aforesaid with all other services and temporal and spiritual profits above mentioned and all their appurtenances and all other things aforenamed contained in this my present gift to the aforesaid Richard and his heirs and assigns in the form aforesaid againft all people. In teftimony of which I have affixed to this my present charter my seal. Witneffes: Lord John Fitzwilliam, William de Meleton, Thomas de Meteham, knights; Henry de Grendon, Henry de Haloghby, Robert de Mersfh, and others. Given at Hooton on the twentieth day of February in the fifty-firft year of the reign of King Edward, the third after the conqueft.

In 1420 there was a fine between William Garth, John Multhorpe, and Thomas Stokes, plaintiffs; and William Levet of Hooton Levet, and Elizabeth his wife, deforciants, of the advowson of the Abbey of Roche. The right to William, John, and Thomas. Soon after this the moiety of the Fitz Turgis family seems to have become united with that of the De Busli, for in 1446 we find Maud, Countess of Cambridge, ftyling herself "founder" of Roche, and at the diffolution only one founder is returned, Henry Clifford, Earl of Cumberland. At the diffolution the fite of the Abbey and the demesne lands seem to have been let to the Earl of Cumberland, in whose hands they remained until they were sold.

Of what these consisted, their value, &c., may be learnt from the following "*Particulars for Grants,*" supplied to William Ramsden and Henry Tyrrell:—

Particulars for Grants, 37 Hen. VIII. sect. 2. Memb. 53.
William Ramsden, Grantee.
Parcel of the Possessions of the late Monastery of Roche, freely resigned, in the County of York.

The rent of the site of the said late monastery together with all houses, buildings, dovecotes, fruit gardens, orchards, gardens, ponds, and other conveniences within the precinct of the said late monastery and with the demesne land to the same belonging underwritten, as they lately were in the tenure of the late Abbot and Convent of the said late monastery, in value, to wit:—

	S.	D.
The rent of the site of the said late monastery with one dovecote and seven orchards, two of which are on the eastern side with the cemetry and the waste of Girewood, containing by estimation 2 acres, 3s. 4d. Two orchards with two little ponds on the south side and two orchards on the west side, containing among them by estimation 5 roods of land, 20d.; and one orchard called the High Orchard, with one great pond and the waste in the same, containing by estimation 2¼ acres, 4s. 2d.	15	10
For the rent of one water mill called Barkehouse Mill .	10	0
For the rent of the grange to the same site adjacent and belonging, with three small crofts containing by estimation 3 acres	5	0
Of one pasture called Hygh Hardsall, containing 60 acres of pasture there and 50 acres of arable land, with a sheepcote there	40	0
Of one close there called Grange Wood, containing by estimation 8 acres	4	0
Of one little close called the Launde, with the waste there containing by estimation 6 acres of arable land . . .	6	0
Of one meadow called Wallehouse Meadow, with the waste there containing by estimation 4 acres . . .	6	8
Of one little common called Hellegreen, with the Waste Craggs, containing by estimation 5 acres	0	20

THE POSSESSIONS.

		S.	D.
Of one clofe called Cote Croft, containing by eftimation 3 acres of arable land		0	18
Of one field called Hellewood flat, with the wafte there, containing by eftimation 26 acres of arable land . .		13	0
Of one croft on the fouth fide of the faid field, containing by eftimation half an acre of arable land		0	6
Of one clofe called Belleflette, with the wafte ground there, containing by eftimation 6 acres		2	0
Of one field called Longfield, lying *near the high crofs leading towards Blythe*, containing by eftimation 30 acres		15	0
Of one field called Milnefield, abutting on the New Milne Dam, containing by eftimation 20 acres of arable land		13	4
Of three little crofts of meadow called Barkhoufe Meadow, abutting towards a certain houfe called the Stone, containing by eftimation 2 acres		3	4
Of a certain pafture called Oxclofe, next the Milnefield aforefaid, containing by eftimation 7 acres of pafture		2	4
Of one common called Barkehoufe Green, with the wafte ground there, by eftimation 2 acres		0	8
Of one meadow lying within the vill of Sandbeck, with the wafte, containing by eftimation 10 acres . . .		16	8
Of one little carr of wafte ground called Stirrope Car, containing by eftimation 20 acres		10	0
Of one meadow called Dooles Meadow, near the White Water next Blythe, containing by eftimation 10 acres		5	0

The whole thus demifed to Lord Hy. Clifford, Earl of Cumberland, by indenture under feal of the Court of Augmentation of the Crown, revenue of the faid lord King, as is faid, but as yet not fhewn, to be paid at the feaft of the Annunciation of St. Mary the Virgin and St. Michael the Archangel equally per annum.

No reprifals.

Upon the edge of this parchment, which is very much decayed with damp, is the following :—

£8 12s. 5d. tithe, 17s. 3d. clear. In £7 15s. 3d. at 20 years' purchafe, £155 5s. Wood, £46 17s. Total, £202 2s.—In hand, £68 15s. 4d.; at Eafter next 100 marks, at Chriftmas next 100 marks.

Memorandum. That the fame is a thing of itfelf and no parcel of any other manor, farm, or grange to the faid late Monaftery appertaining. Item. What fine or fines hath been at any time given for the same I do not know. Item. As concerning any spiritual promotions to the same appertaining I know none. Item. The same is distant from any of the King's Majesties' manors, forests, parks, or chaces reserved for his Highness by a keeper, v or vi miles as I am informed. Item. I have made former particulars of the same to the above named Lord Henry the Earl of Cumberland, by virtue of Mr. Moyle's warrant, and I know none other but the bringer desirous to purchase the same.*

Examined by Hugh Fuller, Auditor.

Particulars for Grants, 37 Hen. VIII. sect. 2. Memb. 54., for Henry Tyrrell, gent., Feb. 20.

The yerely value of the scite and demeanes of the said late Monasterie of Roche, in the countie of Yorke, is viii^{li} xii^s vi^d, whereof deducted for the tenthe xvii^s iii^d, and so remayneth clere vii^{li} xv^s iii^d, whiche rated at xx yeres purchas amounteth to the some of clv^{li} v^s.; adde therunto for the woddes xlvi^{li} xvii^s and so the hole some is ccii^{li} ii^s, whereof in hand lxviii^{li} xv^s iiii^d, at Easter nexte lxvi^{li} xiii^s iiii^d, and at Christmas then nexte lxvi^{li} xiii^s iiii^d.

The King's Majestie is pleased and contente to discharge the premises of all incumbrances except leasses and the xth before, and except such charges as the fermors are bound to beare and paie by force of their indentures.

M^d. to excepte and reserve all the leade, belles, and belle mettall being in and upon the premises, togither withe all suche superfluous buyldinges, tymbre, stone, iron, glasse, and other thinges as ben excepted oute of the fermor's leasse.

Irr. per Wm. Burnell.   Edw. North.

Countye of Yorke.

The scyte and demeans of the late monastery of Roche in the seyd countye, withe one mylne called Bakehouse Mylne, in the same countye, parcell of the possessions of the seyd late monastery.

Norwood conteyneth xx acres	
Helwood Copp. conteyneth iv acres	
Backhouse Copp. otherwise called	lx acres.
Fryth Copp. conteyneth xvi acres	
Hylclyff Copp. conteyneth xx acres	

Whereof xvi acres of viii, x, and xii yeres growthe reservid to Sr. Henrye Clyfford, Knight, Erle of Cumbrelande, for his fyre bootè and hedgeboote.

* As these particulars are partly in Latin and partly in contracted English they have been modernized.

		s.	d.	£	s.
One acre of one yeres growthe		0	6		
One acre of ii yeres growthe		0	12		
One acre of iii yeres growthe		0	18		
One acre of iiii yeres growthe		2	0		
One acre of v yeres growthe		2	6		
x acres of vii yeres growthe		35	0		
x acres of ix yeres growthe		45	0		
vii acres of xi yeres growthe		38	6		
vi acres of xiii yeres growthe		39	0		
vi acres refydue of xiiii yeres growthe		42	0		
The wood every acre aforefeyd, valued as apperyth, wych ys in the holle				10	7
The fprynge of the wood or ground of xvi acres aforefeyd, not valuyed bycaufe they be refervid, and of xliiii acres refydue, rated yerely at vi^d the acre, wych ys yerely in the holle xxii^s, and amounteth after xx yeres purchafe to				22	0
In the feyd woodes about the fcytuation of the feyd late monaftery, and in the feyd demeans be growinge dccc okes and afhes of lx and lxxx yeres growthe, parte tymbre and parte ufually cropped and fhred, wherof ccclx refervid for tymbre to repayre the houfes ftanding uppon the fcyte of the feyd late monaftery, and for ploughboote, cartboote, and ftakes for hedgeboote for the feyd fermor cxl valued at xii^d the tree, and ccc refydue at vi^d the tree, which ys in the holle				14	10
Ex^{r.} per me David Clayton.	Total			£46	17

The fite and demefne lands of Roche were firft granted to William Ramfden, in 37 Hen. VIII., but they did not continue in his poffeffion long. They changed hands rapidly from Ramfden to Tyrrell, then to Banke, Hewett, Hunt, Frankland, and finally to the family whofe noble reprefentative ftill owns them.

Rochedale.—The monks acquired confiderable property in this parifh at an early date from Lord Robert de Stapelton. His great grandfon confirmed it to them by the following charter:—

Charter of Warinus de Scargill.

"To all true Chriftian people to whom thefe prefents fhall come, Warinus de Scargill fendeth greeting in our Lord. Know that I, for the salvation of my soul and of all my ancestors and heirs, have granted and confirmed to God and the Blessed Virgin Mary and the Abbot and Convent of Roche and their successors all the gifts and grants which Lord Robert, son of William de Stapelton, my great grandfather, whose heir I am, made to them. All that land and tenements which are called Hillbrigthorpe, by these boundaries: by the way which leadeth from Stone Edge to Knot Hill and passeth the water of Tame and so upwards to the other Knot Hill, and all that Knot Hill even unto Woodward Hill, east, west, and north so far as my land reacheth, with all buildings, woods, meadows, feedings, waters, pastures, and all appurtenances and other things under the earth and above the earth, with the whole forest and all other liberties to the said forest belonging. I have also granted to the said Abbot and Convent and their successors for me and my heirs full power to enclose all the said tenements by the boundaries aforesaid altogether as walled and the walls if thrown down to make up and renew as often and when they may please, and to keep the same enclosed without hindrance or reproach of me or my heirs or assigns. And also common of pasture from the great way which leadeth from Stone Edge to the Bridgewater of Tame toward the north to the boundary aforesaid; and from Knot Hill to Woodward Hill, as the water departs towards the wood of Tame. To have and to hold all the said tenements and pastures in free and perpetual alms, safe and quiet from all secular service, claims and demands for ever, so that the said Abbot and Convent of Roche and their successors may do what they will with all that is contained within their said enclosed tenements without contradiction of me or my heirs and without plea of forest. And I, the said Warinus, and my heirs will warrant, acquit, and for ever defend all the said tenements and pastures and their appurtenances to the said Abbot and Convent and their successors against all men, in testimony of which as well my seal as the common seal of the said Abbot and Convent to this writing indented are severally affixed, these being witnesses, Lord Edmund de Wastenayes, Lord Thomas de Schofelde, Lord John de Doncastre, knights; John of the chamber of Stapelton, William my son, and others. Dated at Roche, on Sunday, in the feast of the Conversion of St. Paul, in the year of Grace one thousand three hundred and fourteen."[a]

This property was situated in the township of Quick,[b] and in the division called Friar Mere.

[a] I am indebted to G. Shaw, Esq., of Saddleworth, for this charter.
[b] In the confirmation of Hen. III., printed at page 21, "Quicke" should be read, instead of "Sonke."

In 1310 the Abbots of Roche and Whalley seem to have had some dispute about tithes.

Composition between the Abbots of Whalley and Roche.

"By the tenor of these presents it is manifest to all, that inasmuch as a controversy has arisen between the religious men, the Abbot of Whalley with his convent, rector of the Church of Rochedale, on the one part, and the Abbot of Roche on the other, upon the exaction of tithes of Hillbrigthorpe, situated within the limits of the said parish; the dispute has at length by the counsel and direction of the lords Abbots of Ryevall and Bildewas, judges assigned by a general chapter of the order in the said cause, also with the consent and free will of the said parties being settled in this manner, viz., that the said Abbot of Roche pay every year to the aforesaid Abbot of Whalley or his certified proctor at Hillbrigthorpe forty pence of silver and one pound of wax and one pound of frankincense at the two terms of the year, viz., twenty pence and one pound of wax at the feast of St. Martin in the Winter, and twenty pence and one pound of frankincense at Pentecost for all tithes of garbs of all lands cultivated and to be cultivated pertaining to the said place of Hillbrigthorpe, according to the command of the bull of Lord Boniface VIII., Pope. And because in the agreement of this convention there was a doubt whether the tithe hay ought to be reckoned with the greater tithes of garbs or with the lesser, it was agreed by the parties that the said doubt should be decided by a faithful inquisition of rectors, vicars of that country, suspected by neither party, before the ordinaries of that archdeaconry in the province of the parties, and that what should be found by the said inquisition should be held good, and the present composition about tithes of garbs with the addition of the tithe of hay, either as greater or lesser tithes, as the said inquisition shall decree to be assigned after the said inquisition be renewed and corroborated by the common seals of each chapter, to remain for all time. In witness of which the parties have placed the seals which they use to this ordinance bipartite. Given at Wakefield, Friday next after the feast of St. Barnabas the Apostle, A.D. 1310."

In 1293 the Abbot of Roche was summoned to answer by what warrant he claimed to have free warren in his lands of Hillbrigthorpe. He maintained a bailiff here at a yearly income of twenty shillings. The last person who held this office was Henry Whitehead.

The rents and farms at Hillbrigthorpe were valued at the

dissolution at £20 0s. 8d., and from the following extract from the *Manchester Guardian* we are enabled to learn more in detail of what the property consisted, and also what was its ultimate destination:—

"A copy has been brought us of a Royal grant of the 35th Henry VIII. to Arthur Assheton in consideration of £361 7s. 4d. paid by him into the Court of Augmentations of the revenues of the Crown—of estates, lands, buildings, and tenements, &c., of the late Monastery of Rupe, otherwise Roche Abbey, formerly belonging and appertaining. Amongst these there are a tenement called Ashenbeech, otherwise Thoome, in the town of Saddleworth, in the parish of Ryche Dale, otherwise Rattesdale, in the occupation of Ralph and Christopher Chetham and John Wrigley, with the houses, lands, tenements, meadows, feedings, pastures, rents, revisions, services, &c., thereto belonging; the farm of Denshaw, in Saddleworth, with the mills, houses, &c.; all the lands, &c., of the grange called Castleshaw; one fourth part of the customs or services called 'boons,' to the late monastery formerly belonging; the farm of Swaincroft, in Saddleworth; the pastures called Knott-hill; the tenement in the territory of Hilbrighthorpe (now called Grange) in Saddleworth; the pastures called the Delf; all that mine of stones called Blackstondelf, in Saddleworth; various yearly rents of 16s. 4d., &c.; common pasture, turbary, &c., in Saddleworth; and the reversions of all the premises with their appurtenances; all the rents, revenues, and other yearly profits reserved in any demises of the premises; all the woods, underwoods, and trees growing upon the premises. Arthur Assheaton, his heirs, &c., to hold and enjoy all the premises, &c., as fully and entirely and in as ample manner and form as the last Abbot and late Convent of the same late Monastery at any time before its dissolution. All the issues, rents, reversions, and profits of the said granges, farms, messuages, lands, &c., are granted to Arthur Assheaton from the feast of the Annunciation of the Blessed Virgin Mary last past. (March 25th, 1543.) And lastly the King grants these letters patent under the great seal, without fine or fee, great or small, to us in our hanaper or elsewhere, to our use in anywise to be rendered, paid, or done. Witness the King at Westminster, the 5th of June. By writ of privy seal, &c."

Norby.—The Abbot of Roche derived a large portion of his revenue from the property which he held in this place. It is situated in the northern part of Lincolnshire. There exists a ready mode of communication between it and Roche by the rivers Trent and Idle, which the monks made use of, for we have already seen that they had a convenient place at which to load and unload ships on the banks of the Trent at Flixburgh, a place only a few miles off. They also had a landing place at York; so by water carriage they could easily get the produce of their land here into a good market.

About the year 1180 Hugh de Wadworth, the fourth Abbot of Roche, bought the grange of Roxby, having borrowed money from the Jews of York for that purpose.

Before the year 1186 the Abbot obtained a magnificent gift from Walter de Scoteni, called in the confirmation of Pope Urban III. "Roxby, with its appurtenances."

About the year 1200 the Abbot of Roche, in consequence of this gift, claimed the advowson of the Church of St. Mary, of Roxby. We find the following entries relating to this subject on the Roll of Pleas in the Easter term of the second year of King John :—

"*Lincolnshire.*—The Abbot of Roche sues against the Prior of the Holy Trinity of York and the Convent of the same place, that they permit him to present a fit person to the Church of Roxby, which is vacant and is of their gift, as they say, &c. The Prior says that the church is their right, as that which Ralph Paynell gave to them by charter, which they produced, which testifies this fact and the confirmation of his heirs. And the Abbot says that the same Prior never had seizin thereof, nor had he presented the last parson, but Walter de Scoteni, who gave to him the whole of the land which they have in Roxby, with the church of the same vill, by his charter which he produced, and which testifies this fact, and thereof prays a jury. And because Walter was not present, and it appertains to him to act in regard of the presentation, the Prior withdraws without a day, &c."

"*Lincolnshire.*—In assize of *darrein presentment* to the Church of Roxby, the advowson of which the Abbot of Roche claims against the Prior of Drax, and against the Prior of the Holy Trinity of York.

And the Prior of Drax comes and says that there ought not to be an assize thereof, because William Painell, of whose right and inheritance that church had been, gave the Church of Roxby to God and St. Nicholas, and to the canons serving in the territory of Drax by this charter, which he produces and which testifies this fact. He also proffers the charter of Richard de Courcy, who had to wife the daughter of the same William, confirming the gift of the same William and the charter of Robert de Gaunt, who had the same daughter to wife, confirming the same gift, and the charter of Walter de Scoteni, to whom the same Robert and his wife, heiress of the aforesaid William, had given that land where the church is situate, which testifies that Walter de Scoteni gave and by his charter confirmed to the Church of St. Nicholas and to the canons of Drax, whatsoever William had granted to the same canons in the vill of Roxby, namely, the Church of Roxby with all its appurtenances. But the Prior of the Holy Trinity produces the charter of Ralph Painell, father of the aforesaid William, who came at the conquest of England, and who gave to his church that church, and the charters of Alexander, Jordan, and William, his sons, confirming his gift, and the charter of Robert, then Bishop of Lincoln, and the confirmation of King Henry, great grandfather of the then King, and both Priors hold themselves to one answer. It was adjudged that Walter should be distrained to be present to manifest hereafter whether he be willing to warrant to the Abbot of Roche his charter or to the Prior of Drax the charter which he had made to him in the last instance, and in the meanwhile the jury to remain."

It is certain that Walter de Scoteni did not warrant the grant of the advowson to the Abbey of Roche, for the rectory continued in medieties respectively in the patronage of the two priories of the Holy Trinity and of Drax until the year 1292; but subsequently Robert the Prior and the Convent of the Holy Trinity granted their mediety of this church to the Prior and Convent of Drax.

An agreement was made before 1227 between Reginald Abbot of Roche and Alan Prior of Drax, viz., that the former granted to the latter two oxgangs of land with a toft in Roxby, for which the latter was to pay an annual rent of five shillings, and the Prior gave to the Abbot the water mill of Roxby with the pool and watercourse; and the Prior had liberty to have a horse mill within their own court to grind their own proper corn, but not that of his men, who should be obliged to do suit at their water-mill.

Philip Abbot of Roche released Thomas Prior of Drax from all suits at his court for what the latter had in Roxby.

Walter de Scoteni quitclaimed the annuity of £1 which the Abbot of Roche used to pay him.

According to an inquisition made at Lincoln before the justiciaries of the lord the King, namely, Sir William de St. Omer and Sir Warine de Chaucomb, in 1275, by twelve jurors of the wapentake of Manley, we find the following:—" Also they say that the Abbot of Roche holds one barony in Roxby for three knight's fees, which he had of the gift of Walter de Scotenai in the time of the lord King John, father of Henry last deceased, seventy years elapsed;

which barony, to wit, the said Walter held of Hugh Painel, and the same Hugh of Andrew Luterel, and the same Andrew of the lord the King in chief, and it is worth yearly one hundred marks, &c."

In 1287 John Paynel sought against the Abbot of Roche sixteen tofts and one carucate and a half of land, with the appurtenances in Roxby, which he claimed as his right by plea in court.

According to the "*Taxation of Pope Nicholas*," made about 1291, what the monks owned in Roxby was valued at £29 12s. 8d. per annum.

In 1292 John Paynel, by judgment of court, recovered against the Abbot of Roche one messuage and thirty-two bovates of land with the appurtenances in Roxby next to Stather, which the Abbot attempted to set at nought on account of errors therein alleged. This is also more fully recorded, as follows:—" John Paynell recovered before the justices of the Bench, first by default of the Abbot of Roche, one messuage and thirty-two bovates of land in Roxby, which judgement was confirmed by the justiciars before the King's counsel. And now both judgements are confirmed by the auditors of complaints, before whom the said Abbot complained of William de Brumpton, a justiciar of the Bench, that he had promulged the said first judgement in favour of and for the sake of upholding John de Kyrkeby, Bishop of Ely. In this judgement, because the Abbot said that in the time of the first judgement the first Abbot, his predecessor, who made default was dead, our lord the King enjoined that enquiry should be made by oath about his death. And the first said John proves by religious men, knights, and serving men worthy of credit, that the said Abbot who made default was alive when he made default. And the Abbot proves by his monks and other members of his community that he was dead. And it is said the said John gave the better proof, because the monks did not make their depositions as well as those whom John produced."

It will be seen by the following charters that the Abbot regained this property by purchase from Philip, brother and heir of John Paynel:—

Royal Charter.

"The King, to all &c., greeting. Inasmuch as it has been testified before us and our council that John Paynel, formerly in our court before our Justices of the Bench, by the award of our said court, recovered against Walter, formerly Abbot of Roche, one messuage and thirty-two bovates of land with the appurtenances in Roxby, by default which the said Abbot made in the suit that was between them in our aforesaid court by our brief *de recto* about the tenements aforesaid, *by which the estate of the said house is become much depressed;* we with the common council of our realm have determined this, that it be not allowed to religious men or others to enter upon any one's fee so that it come to a dead hand, without our licenfe and that of the chief lord from whom the thing is immediately held. Wishing therefore to do a special favour to Philip Paynel, brother and heir of the said John, we have given him licenfe, as far as in us lies, that he may give and assign that messuage and the aforesaid thirty-two bovates of land, with the appurtenances in Roxby, to our beloved in Chrift, Stephen, now Abbot of Roche, and the Convent of the same place, to have and to hold to them and their successors for ever; and to the said Abbot and Convent that they may receive the said messuage and land with the appurtenances from the said Philip by the tenor of the presents, we grant a special favour in like manner, being unwilling that the said John, or his heirs, or the said Abbot and Convent, or their successors, by reason of the statute aforesaid by us or our heirs should receive annoyance therefrom or in any way be oppressed, save, however, the services therefrom due and accustomed to the chief lord of the fee. In testimony, &c., witness the King at Westminster on the twentieth day of June."[a]

Charter of Philip Paynel.[b]

"To all the faithful in Chrift who shall see or hear the present letters, Philip Paynel, lord of Westrasen, greeting in the Lord. Know that I have received and had of the religious men, the Abbot and Convent of Roche, six hundred marks of good and lawful sterling money, in which they were bound to me for the surrender of the Manor of Roxby by a certain recognizance made in the court of our lord the King, A.D. 1293, and in like manner by divers writings made nevertheless between me and the said religious, concerning the said six hundred marks, of which six hundred marks fully and entirely within five years, as is contained in particular writings which they have in their possession, I call myself well and entirely paid and contented, and so I render the said monks quit of all expenses and losses for myself and my heirs and executors by these presents for ever; and the recognizance of six hundred marks and all writings whatever in any manner or time, however made, concerning them or part of them, I condemn and annul by these presents. And I and my heirs or executors will preserve the said religious free from harm against all men with respect to the said six hundred

[a] Patent Rolls, 21 Edw. I. Memb. 9.   [b] Dodsworth's MSS., vol. VIII. fol. 288 A.

marks, or from having any damages in respect of them for ever on pain of forfeiture of all our goods present and future. And be it known that the said Abbot and Convent have particular writings of the said payments in their possession and this writing of acquittance in full notwithstanding, so that it may not be understood by any one that I have twice levied the said six hundred marks. In testimony of which I have to the present letters placed my seal, and in testimony of the apposition of my seal I have procured the seal of the lord Prior of Drax and of Stephen * * * likewise to be placed to it. Given at the house of Drax * * * St. John Baptist, A.D. 1297."

In 1299 the King gave licence to Robert de Rothewell to give and assign to the Abbot of Roche two bovates of land with the appurtenances in Roxby; and to Ralph Brown of Roxby the same licence to give, &c., one bovate of land with the appurtenances in the same town to the said Abbot.[a]

In 1313 the King granted licence to Henry de Cokewald to give and assign to the Abbot of Roche one messuage, twenty acres of land, and two acres of meadow in Roxby, and to Hugh de le Wyk the same licence to give, &c., one toft and two acres and a half of land in Roxby, which said messuages, tofts, land, and meadow were of the fee of the said Abbot, and worth 23s. per annum.[b]

In 1339 the King granted licence, by a fine of forty marks, to John de Chaucumbe to give and assign to the Abbot of Roche one bovate and four acres of land with the appurtenances in Roxby, which were held from the aforesaid Abbot, and worth 6s. 8d. per annum.[c]

Hugh de le Wyk of Roxby gave the monks two acres of land in the same place in the South Field.

Thomas, the clerk of Flixburgh, and William de Coleton released the monks from the payment of two marks which they used to pay to them.

At the dissolution the annual income derived by the Abbot from Roxby, in rents, perquisites of court, &c., was £37 0s. 7d.; out of this the following fees were paid: £6 6s. 8d. to Thomas Lord Burgh, seneschal of Roxby; and £1 to Robert Thornabye, bailiff of Roxby.

Sandal.—In 1232 King Henry III. confirmed what the monks held in this place.

---

[a] Pat. Rolls 28 Ed. I. M. 73.   [b] Pat. Rolls 7 Edw. II. pt. 1. Memb. 8.
[c] Pat. Rolls 13 Edw. II. Memb. 44.

Sandbec.—On St. Giles' day, 1241, the monks obtained their first property in this place by the following charter:—

Charter of Idonea de Vipont.

"Know, all present and future, that I, Idonea de Vipont, in my widowhood and in free power over my body, have given, conceded, and by this my present charter have confirmed to God and the Blessed Mary and the monks of the Rock, the whole of my manor of Sandbec with my corpse, with the homages and services, as well of free men as of copyholders, and with all commons, liberties, and easements pertaining to the same manor everywhere within and without the said vill of Sandbec without hindrance, to be held and had for a pure and perpetual alms free and quiet from all services, customs, exactions, and demands. And I, Idonea, and my heirs will warrant the said manor of Sandbec with its appurtenances to the said monks, and will acquit and defend it for ever against all men. Moreover, for greater security I have affixed my seal to this writing. Witnesses: John de Croyton, Thomas de Bug, John de Stainton, Richard de Horbiry, Robert de Wickersley, knights; Walter, seneschal in the castle of Tickhill, Peter de Wadworth, William de Stainton, John de Monteby, Hugh de Scelhall, John de Wlvethwait."

(Seal, Idonea at full length, with a hawk upon her left hand.)

The right of the Abbot to this manor was disputed by Robert de Vipont, the second grandson of Idonea, as may be learnt from the following:—

Testification of Richard de Boyvill.

"To all who shall see or hear these letters, and especially to the twelve knights elected to make the great assize between the Abbot of Roche and Robert de Vipont, Richard de Boyvill in the Lord eternal health. Wishing to inform you upon the oath which is about to be made to you being present, I testify in truth by God, and by the baptism with which I have been baptized, and by the knighthood with which I have been dubbed, that on the day of St. Giles, in the year of our Lord 1241, my lady Idonea de Busli, of her own free will and full power of her body, with great deliberation of mind, gave to the Church of Roche the whole manor of Sandbec, with the ploughs and all other things pertaining to it, in the presence of many of her friends and faithful servants then and there present, Sir John de Croxton, Sir Thomas de Bury, Sir R. de Boyvill, knights; and Sir J. de Monby. On the morrow of St. Giles the charter of this donation was written and sealed with the great feal and private feal of the lady on the morrow of the nativity of the Bleffed Mary next following."

The right of the Abbot to this property was again queftioned in 1265, when an inquifition was taken by Robert de Ullay, &c., at Anfton, the jurors being William de Rhodes, Adam de Monte Acuto, &c., to examine whether the Abbot of Roche had intruded himfelf into the manor of Sandbec, which belonged to Robert de Vipont, by occafion of the troubles late had in England, when the jury found that the Abbot had not intruded himfelf, but was in feizin before the troubles, in the troubles, and after the troubles.

John, fon of Gilbert de Ewes, gave the monks fix acres and a half of land in Sandbec.

Hugh, Marfhal de Sywardthorp, gave his mill in Sandbec with the pool and watercourfe.

In 1535 the annual value of the property which the Abbot held in Sandbec was valued at £14 1s.; out of this he had to pay to the Hofpital of St. Leonard at York one fhilling, and to the Prior of Blythe, for a parcel of land in Sandbec, one fhilling per annum.

The following is an account of the timber belonging to the Abbot at Sandbec at the diffolution :—

County of York.[*]

"The manor of Sandbeck, in the fayd Countye, parcell of the poffeffyons of the late monafterye of Roche, in the fame countye :

"Trees growing aboute the fcyte of the feyd manor and in the hedges inclofing the lands perteyning to the fame wyll barly fuffyce to repayr the houfes ftanding uppon the fcyte of the feyd mannor and the feid hedges and fences, therefore not valued.

Ex^{r.} per me David Clayton."

At the diffolution the manor of Sandbec was granted to Richard Turke, gentleman, citizen of London, and in 3 Edw. VI. he had licenfe to alienate it to Robert Saunderfon and his heirs.

Stainsby.—In 1198 King Richard I. confirmed whatever the monks had in this place. At the diffolution they had property here, but of no great confequence, as it with three other places was only valued at 11s. 5d. per annum.

Serlby.—Matilda de Moles, before the year 1208, gave the monks all the lands which the men of Blythe held of Hugh de Moles, her brother, and afterwards of her in the fields of Serlby in the county of Nottingham.—*(See Torworth.)*

[*] Particulars for Grants. Mifcellaneous, No. 60.

Hugh de Moles with his body gave his mills in this place with the suit thereof. *(See Blythe.)* He also gave a fishery above and below the mills, with one oxgang of land and the service of 1s. from Alan de Clifton and his heirs, for one oxgang of land in the same territory; and of Norman, son of Robert, for another oxgang. The monks had no property here at the dissolution.

Sezacres.—From the confirmation of Pope Urban III. we find that William de Moles and William Fitz Gerard gave Sezacres with its appurtenances.

Shelley see **Thurstonland**.

Shepwick see **Walkeringham**.

Slade Hooton.—The Abbot of Roche obtained what he had here from Robert de Ripers in exchange for other lands, &c., as is shewn by the following:—

Charter of Abbot Richard and Robert de Ripers.

"Know, present and future, that it is thus agreed between Richard Abbot of Roche and the monks of the same place, on the one part; and Robert de Ripers on the other; viz., that the aforesaid Richard the Abbot and the monks, for themselves and for their successors, have given, conceded, and by this present charter confirmed to the aforesaid Robert de Ripers, for his homage and service, and for the exchange of his land of Slade Hooton, in addition to six marks of yearly rent, and for the exchange of two pieces of meadow in Walkeringham which the same Robert held, and for £100 sterling which he gave to the same with his own proper hands, their lands and meadows which they had in Wadworth and Alverley, and in Loversal, with the wood which they had in Wadworth, with the farm of the same wood and the mill, their mill, with the site and pools and waters, and with all kinds of suits everywhere pertaining to the aforesaid mill within the aforesaid vills and without, to be held and had by the same Robert and his heir and assigns and their heirs for ever, viz., in homages, in services of free men, in villanages with the villains and their suits and chattels, in wards, in relieves and escheats freely, peacefully, and hereditarily with all commons, liberties, easements, advantages, and with all other things and with all other pertenances to the aforesaid lands, meadows, mills, pools, and waters, and wood and wood farm everywhere pertaining within the said vills and without, without any hindrance. Saving, nevertheless, to the said Abbot and Monks and their successors their land in Wellingley, with its pertenances. But the aforesaid Robert and his heirs or assigns, or their heirs, render the aforesaid Richard and the monks and their successors only 27 pence per annum, to wit, 12 pence at the feast of St. Martin in the Winter, and 15 pence at Whitsuntide, for all services, exactions, and demands which respect or can respect the said Abbot Richard and Monks and their successors. There shall be done, nevertheless, by the aforesaid Abbot Richard and the Monks and their successors foreign services which pertain to the aforesaid tenements. But the aforesaid Richard and Monks, &c., shall not make or erect, nor by means of any of them cause to be made or erected, nor shall allow Peter de Wadworth nor his heir nor assigns, nor their heirs nor any of theirs, to make or erect any mill, to wit, neither water-mill nor wind-mill in the territory of Wadworth to the hurt or detriment or grievance of the aforesaid Robert or his heirs or his assigns, or their heirs. But the said Peter de Wadworth and his heirs shall have free multure of the whole of their malt and corn of their own proper homestead in the aforesaid mills for ever without let from any one, as is contained in the charter which the aforesaid Richard and the monks have of the aforesaid Peter. And the aforesaid Richard Abbot and his Monks, &c., all the aforesaid lands and mills, and pools and waters, and sites of the mills, and the wood and the wood farm, and the meadows, with all things and suits, easements, and with all pertenances to them everywhere pertaining, as was aforesaid against all people for the aforesaid service will warrant, acquit, and defend for ever. Now, for this donation, concession, confirmation, and exchange, the aforesaid Robert has given to the aforesaid Richard Abbot and Monks, &c., all his land which he had in Slade Hooton, with the villains and their goods and chattels and villanages and services of free men, with all pertenances as is aforesaid, without any restraint, and his meadow which he had in Walkeringham, and £100 sterling by rendering for the land of Slade Hooton to the lords of Tickhill 6*d*. per annum at Easter, and to Arnold Bisset and his heirs the services which pertain to the aforesaid land, as is contained in the charter which the aforesaid Robert had of the aforesaid Arnold, and which the same Robert freed to the aforesaid Abbot and Monks for the warrants and security of their agreement, and by rendering Adam, son of William de Walkeringham, for the aforesaid meadow 1*d*. per annum at the feast of St. Mary Magdalen, for all services. And that all the things which are contained in this writing may remain ratified, firm, and stable, as well the said Richard Abbot and Monks as the aforesaid Robert, the present writing made after the manner of a deed have with the impreſſion of their ſeals corroborated. Witneſſes: Simon de Heden, Robert de Wlrington, Richard le Blund of Blythe, Robert de Miſterton, Hugh de Moles, Henry de Darley, Richard de Louweder, Herbert de Wlrington, Gerard de Hedon, Jeffery de Turmiſton, Nicholas, ſon of Jeffery de Erdeſale, Thomas de Wlrington, and others."

The date of this charter is between 1238 and 1254.

Among the "*Particulars for Grants*"[a] we find the following:—

County of York.

"The manor of Hutton Slade, with Carre, Hutton Leveyt, and Hutton Robert, in the ſayd Countye, parcell of the poſſeſſyons of the late mon. of Roche, in the ſame countye."

"There be growing about the ſcytuations of xii tenements and cotages there and in the hedges incloſing the landes perteyning to the ſame lxxx okes and aſhes of lx and lxxx yeres growth, whereof lxv reſervyd for tymber to repayre the ſayd tenements and cotages and one corn myln there, and for ſtakes for hedgeboote to repayre and maynteyne the ſayd hedges and fences. And xx reſydue valuyd at iiij^d· the tree, which is in the holle vi^s viii^d·

Ex^r· per me David Clayton."

Smeaton.—From *Dr. Burton* we learn that Simon, ſon of Algar de Smeaton, with his corpſe gave half an oxgang of land here. This property, together with what the monks had in Scawſby, Campſal, and Aſkern, was valued in 1535 at 11s. 5d. per annum.

Snaith.—Edmund de Lacy, conſtable of Cheſter, granted and confirmed to the monks all that they held in his ſocage of Snaith, in the year of Grace 1158. *(See Tickhill.)*

Stainford.—The monks had property here in 1231. *Mr. Hunter* gives the following account of the foundation of a chapel at this place:—"On the day of Pentecoſt, 1355, an indenture was made between the Abbot and Convent of Roche on the one part, and Thomas de Rillington and ſix others, pariſhioners of the Church of Hatfield, on the other part, that the ſaid Abbot of Roche having the Church of Hatfield appropriated, granted and permitted that the ſaid pariſhioners and other the inhabitants of the town of Stainford might, by the Archbiſhop's licenſe, maintain at their own coſt a chaplain to celebrate divine ſervice in the Chapel of Stainford, newly builded, for the ſpace of three years daily, excepting on Sundays and other great feſtivals, whereon they were to repair to

[a] Miſcellaneous, No. 58.

the Parish Church of Hatfield. This agreement was confirmed by the Archbishop's vicar-general on November 17th, 1355."

The tithes which the Abbot of Roche derived from Stainford were valued at £5 per annum, out of which he had to pay 4s. 2½d. to the Provost of Stainford. The monks held their property here till the dissolution.

Stainredale see **Oneash**.

Stainton.—In 1202 Hugh de Stainton granted 30 acres of land, reckoned by the perch of 18½ feet, in the fields of Stainton, at Rokkehill, to the Abbot of Roche and his successors for a pure and perpetual alms. In such sort that the said Abbot or his successors make no building on the aforesaid 30 acres of land without the consent and will of the aforesaid Hugh or his heirs. And if the same Abbot or his successors lose anything of the same 30 acres of land by default of warranty of the aforesaid Hugh or his heirs, the said Hugh or his heirs shall make exchange of their land which lies on the side next the said 30 acres of land on the east to the extent that they have lost.*

The Abbot of Roche bought land in Stainton of Richard Baret, which was confirmed by John, son of Hugh de Stainton.

William Wasteneys, of Stainton, gave the monks half an oxgang of land here.

The property of the Abbot of Roche in this place is supposed to have exceeded 370 acres of wood and pasture. This calculation of course includes what he had at Lambcote Grange.

Stanhege see **Chatsworth**.

Stansal.—Among the evidences of Godfrey Higgins, Esq., of Skellow Grange, *Mr. Hunter* found a charter dated 1236, by which William Chaworth and William, the son of Eudo, chief lords of Wadworth, declare that they release all claims in lands of Sir Jordan Fitz-Payne, lord of Stansal, Wellingley, and Willsic, which the said Jordan has given to the monks of Roche in pure and perpetual alms, to wit, from that ditch which lies between Magilldhylls across as far as the bounds of Wadworth, and the fee of Wellingley and Stansal, and so runs from the arable land of Wadworth on the west until it comes opposite the town of Stansal on the east, lengthwise, and from the said ditch to another ditch which has been made in Littlemorye, from the south through the whole of that land which is in the western district as far as the arable land of Stansal and the bounds of Wadworth.

* Fines, Ebor. 4 John.

Jordan Fitz-Payne muft have made this grant before 1231, as it appears among the names of places confirmed to the monks in that year by Hen. III.

Stirrup.—Gerard de Stirrup gave turbary here before the year 1186. Stirrup is in Nottinghamfhire, and is not identical with Triftrop, as *Dr. Burton* has it in his "*Monafticon Eboracenfe*." The latter place is now called Streetthorpe, and lies near Doncafter.

In 1276 the Abbot of Roche held twenty acres of meadow and a toft and croft in Stirrup of the fee of Tickhill, the former being the gift of Hamel de Bugthorpe, in the time of Henry III.[*]

Robert Burton was bailiff of Stirrup at the diffolution, and received from the Abbot 10s. per annum.

In 1563 Robert de Hitchcock obtained poffeffion of that meffuage in Stirrup in the occupation of Richard More, late belonging to the Monaftery of Roche.

Streetthorpe.—At this place, which was formerly called Stireftorp, Triftrop, and Strifterop, the monks had property of which we learn the following from the "*Particulars for Grants*":—

County of York.

Grantee, Richard Stapleton. 6 *Edw. VI.*

All the rents and profits in Streetthorpe, in the County aforefaid, are worth in:—

The rent of one tenement, with all lands, meadows, paftures, and commons to the fame belonging, thus demifed to Brian Haftings, of Fenwek, by Indenture under the common feal of the late Monaftery of Roche, freely refigned, dated 24 Jan., in the 24th year of the reign of King Henry VIII., to have to the faid Brian Haftings, Elizabeth his wife, and Franc his fon, from the date of the prefents to the end and term of their lives, paying thence at the terms of St. Martin and Pentecoft equally £2 6s. 8d. per annum.

Memorandum. That this particler was delyvered to Sir Brian Haftings, knight, the 12th daye of Decembr, 6 Edw. VI., for a purchace.

Ex[r]. per Willm. Notte, Audit.

Strafford.—The monks paid to the bailiff of the King of the wapentake of Strafford 6s. 8d. per annum.

Templeborough.—The Roman encampment known by this name, which is fituated on the fouth bank of the Don about half a

---
[*] Hundred Rolls.

mile from Rotherham, came into the hands of the monks of Roche in the time of Hen. III. *Mr. Hunter* found among the Johnſton MSS. a charter by which Ralph, ſon of Richard de Savile, gave with his body to the Abbot of Roche a carucate of land in Brindſworth, which Peveril held, and Templeborough in the territory of Brindſworth. Witneſs, Peter de Wadworth.

Twenty years after the diſſolution the property which the monks had held here is deſcribed in an inquiſition of Lionel Rereſby, Eſq., of Thriberg, as "two mills and twenty acres of paſture called Templebarrow, with appurtenances in Ikkyls, held of the Queen as of her Monaſtery of Roche lately diſſolved, in ſocage, by fealty and rent of 13*s*. 4*d*. for all ſervices and demands."

Thorne.—William gave the monks the tithe of the eels taken at his fiſhery here, after the full tithe had been taken, which belonged to the monks of Lewis. The tithes here were valued at the diſſolution at £7 per annum.

Throapham.—The monks held property here at the diſſolution. *(See Laughton.)*

Thurnſcoe.—The monks had conſiderable property in this place before 1186, the gift of William Vavaſor.

They alſo had two carucates of land in Thurnſcoe, which belonged to William Paynel, and which he held *in capite* of the lord the King of the barony of Hooton.[a]

In 5 John, 1203, there was a fine between Galfred Luterel and Fretheſant his wife, and Iſabella, ſiſter of the ſaid Fretheſant, plaintiffs; and Oſmund Abbot of Roche, tenant of twelve bovates of land with the appurtenances, in Thurnſcoe. Verdict for the Abbot and his ſucceſſors, ſave foreign ſervice to the ſaid Galfred and Fretheſant and Iſabella, and the ſervice to the ſaid Fretheſant, which the aforeſaid land owes to them.[b]

In 20 Hen. III., 1236, there was a fine between William, ſon of Richard de Barnby, plaintiff; and Robert Luterel, whom Reginald Abbot of Roche called to warranty, and who made warranty to him of ten meſſuages, one mill, and twenty bovates of land, with the appurtenances in Thurnſcoe. Verdict for Robert Luterel.[c]

Andrew Luterel confirmed all that the monks had in Thurnſcoe.

In the thirteenth century the monks obtained the two following charters :—

[a] Hundred Rolls. [b] Fines, Ebor. Augmentation Office. [c] Ibid. No. 134.

Charter of Ralph de Rainville.

"Know all, &c., that I, Ralph de Rainville, of Thurnscoe, have granted, given, and by this my present charter have confirmed for the welfare of my soul and those of all my ancestors and heirs, to God and Saint Mary and the Monks of Roche, the attachment of the pond of their mill of Thurnscoe upon my fee of Holme, in pure and perpetual alms, free and quit from all service, exaction, and demand. And in accordance with which it shall be lawful for the said monks at their will to raise, strengthen, repair, and amend the said pond, as they shall think expedient, and to take land upon my fee of Holme as often as shall be necessary, without contradiction or impediment of me or my heirs, for raising and repairing the said pond. And I, Ralph, and my heirs will warrant, quit, and defend all the aforesaid to the said monks against all men for ever. Witnesses: Lord Robert de Wykereslay, knight; Peter de Waddeworth, Thomas de Lasci, Hugh de Lascy, Wm. de Tatewyc (Todwick), serving man; Johanna Whiethwait."[a]

Charter of Hugh, son of Hugh Lascy.

"Know all, &c., that I Hugh, son of Hugh Lascy, of Thurnscoe, have granted and by this my present charter confirmed to God, St. Mary, and the Monks of Roche all the land which my father granted to the same in exchange for ever at Hoxebrigge, and all the meadow which they hold of the gift of my father, as his charter testified. Moreover, I have remised and quitclaimed to the said monks from me and my heirs and assigns for ever all right and claim which I had or might have had in the meadow of the aforesaid monks, as it is bounded by the ditch before the gate of the grange of Thurnscoe after the manner of a farm or common herbage-ground. In such sort, however, that if any cattle of those of my heirs by reason of a defect in the ditch shall enter the said meadow we shall not quarrel about it, and for making greater security to the said monks in all the aforesaid, I have corroborated the present page by placing my seal. Witnesses: Jordan, son of Jordan de l'Isle, Jordan de Mar, Adam Paynel, Robert Lascy, Adam de Thurnscoe, Payn de Mar, Richard de St. Paul, John Grimbald."[b]

Hugh, son of Reiner de Darfield, gave the monks an oxgang of land here. Richard de Thurnscoe also gave another oxgang of land in this place.

---

[a] Dodsworth's MSS., vol. VIII. fol. 31 B. [b] Dodsworth's MSS., vol. VIII. fol. 32 A.

THE POSSESSIONS.

In 1316 the Abbot of Roche was certified purſuant to writ teſted at Clipſtone 5th March, as lord of the townſhips of Armthorpe and Thurnſcoe, and joint lord of Todwick. The Abbot had a charter of free warren here from Richard II. The property which the monks had at Thurnſcoe at the diſſolution was valued, together with 8*d*. perquiſites of courts, at £12 10*s*. 8*d*. per annum.

From the following "*Particulars for Grants*" we learn the deſtination of the monk's property here at the diſſolution:—

County of York.

Grantees, Doddington and Jackſon.

Thurnſcoe, Blitheſhaw manor, worth in the rent of one parcel of land, demiſed to John Anne, Eſq., by Indenture under the common ſeal of the late Monaſtery of Roche, as it is ſaid, to pay at the term of St. Martin only 5*s*.

Memorandum. The premiſs are no parcell of the aunchient inheritaunce of the crowne, nor of the duchies of Lancaſter or Cornwall, but came to the Kinge's Majeſtie's handes by ſurrender of the ſaid monaſtery.

23rd Dec., 1559. Jno. Gifford.   Per me, Antho. Rous.
At 28 yeres purchas.

County of York.

Grantees, Jno. Wright and Thos. Holmes.   7 Edw. VI.
The Manor of Thurnſcoe is worth in:—

	£	s.	d.
The rent of a grange there, called Thurnſcoe Grange, with the appurtenances, thus demiſed to Triſtram Feſh, by Indenture under the common ſeal of the late Monaſtery of Roche, dated 4 Nov., in the year of the reign of the late King Henry VIII., for the term of 21 years then next following, paying thence at the terms of St. Martin and Pentecoſt equally	2	0	0
The rent of a meſſuage and bovate of land, with the appurtenances there, in the tenure of Wm. Ellys, paying at the terms aforeſaid	0	13	4
The rent of a cottage and two acres of land, with the appurtenances there, in the tenure of Hugh Ellys, paying	0	6	0
Carried over	£2	19	4

	£	s.	d.
Brought forward	2	19	4
The rent of one messuage and one bovate of land, with the appurtenances there, in the tenure of James Ellys, paying	1	6	8
The rent of one messuage and one bovate of land, with the appurtenances there, in the tenure of the said Hugh Ellys, paying	0	13	4
The rent of certain lands there, in the tenure of the heirs of — Meres, paying	0	12	0
The rent of one cottage, with certain lands belonging to the same, in the tenure of the heirs of Wm. Ellys, paying	0	7	0
The woods not valued. Total.	£5	18	4

Thurstonland.—*Mr. Morehouse* thinks the manor of Thurstonland was given to the monks at the same time as the advowson of Hatfield by Earl Warren. At the dissolution the annual rents amounted to £8 19s. 7½d.; Thomas Green being steward, and Henry Gillott, bailiff here, and each receiving 20s. per annum. The grange of the monks possessed a right of stray and pasturage for twenty sheep upon the commons and waste lands in the lordship of Shelley, a privilege which no doubt had been granted by one of the early lords of Shelley.[a]

In 1532 John Walker, of Thurstonland, clothier, obtained a lease from the Abbot and Convent of Roche, of lands in Thurstonland, given under the seal of the monastery.[b]

In 1540 the King granted " to John Storthes, of Shyttylyngton, gentleman, all his manor of Thurstonland with all his rights, membres, and appurtenances, &c., late to the Monastrye of Roche, and now dyssolved, belonging, &c., and all other messuages, houses, byldyngs, mylnes, granges, londs, tenements, meadows, pastures, comons, waters, fysshyngs, lyng, and heth, &c., to hold of the said sovereign lord the King, his heirs and successors in cheff, by the suyt of the xx part of a knight's fee, and yelding, therefore, yerely 20s. to the King's Cort of Augmentacon of the Revenues of his Crowne."

Tickhill.—In the "*Monasticon Anglicanum*" we find the following :—

[a] History of Kirkburton.   [b] Ibid.

Charter of Edmund de Lacy.

"Know prefent and future that I, Edmund de Lacy, conftable of Chefter, have granted and by this my prefent charter confirmed to God and the Bleffed Mary and the Abbot and Convent of Roche of the Ciftercian order, all the gifts and fales made to them in my barony of Pontefract, in my conftabulary, in my barony of Tickhill and in my focage of Snaith, which they held at Eafter, 1258, according to the tenure of the charters of the donors and vendors, and this conceffion and confirmation I have made to them for the welfare of my foul and of my father, John de Lacy, and of Margaret my mother, and of Alice my wife, and of all my anceftors and heirs. Witneffes: Adam Abbot of Kirkftal, Sir John de Hoderode, fenefchal of Pontefract; Robert de St. Andrew, John Beke, knights; Sir Ofbertus, rector of Silkfton; Sir Robert de Nottingham, rector of Almonbury; Mr. William de Lichfield, rector of Braiton, and many others."

Tinsley see Winelepe.

Todwick.

The firft property which the monks had in this place was given them before 1186 by Ralph Tortemayns. This is given upon the authority of the "*Confirmation of Pope Urban III.*" In the Hiftory of the Manor, written by a monk of Roche, and printed in the "*Monafticon Anglicanum*," it is ftated that Ralph Tortemayns fold to the Houfe of Roche "Little Todwick," and whatfoever appertained to it.

William Tortemayns gave all his wood to the monks with the land on which it grew. He alfo confirmed the grant of pafture for eight fcore fheep in the common pafture in Todwick.

Gregory de Todwick and Alice his wife gave two acres of land in Todwick with their right to the advowfon of the church of the fame place.

Nicholas de St. Paul confirmed the grant of Gregory and his wife, and gave all his meadow lying between his houfe and the road towards the north in Todwick. He alfo confirmed the grant of ten acres of land and pafture for fixty fheep, given by his father (William de St. Paul), and gave all his land between Botyldwellwang and the grange towards the north of the way leading from Afton to Anfton; and on the other fide of the way towards the fouth he gave one acre and a half, with pafture for nine fcore fheep in Todwick, together with common pafture through his land for all the monks' cattle going from Todwick grange.

The monk's account, in the document above referred to, of the gifts of William and Nicholas de St. Paul, is as follows:—"William and Nicholas gave to the Houfe of Roche all their land between Botyldewellwange and the Grange, and all lordfhip and fervices pertaining to feven bovates of land, and alfo all the land, wood, and rent *quæ dirationavit* of Michael de Mawoners."

In 1316, purfuant to writ tefted at Clipfton, March 5, the Abbot of Roche was certified as joint Lord of Todwick.

All the above gifts were confirmed by Maud de Lovetot.

Charter of Maud de Lovetot.

"To all the fons of the Holy Church prefent and future, Maud de Lovetot, formerly wife of Gerard de Furnival, greeting. Be it known to your community that I, in my widowhood and in full power over my body, have given and by this my charter confirmed to God and the Bleffed Mary and the Monks of Roche, for the welfare of my foul and of my lord, Gerard de Furnival, and of all my anceftors and heirs, all the lands in the territory of Todwick, with their appurtenances, which Ralph Tortemayns and William Tortemayns, and William de St. Paul and Nicholas de St. Paul gave to the faid monks, to have and hold, as the charters which they have from them teftify. Witneffes: Robert, parfon of Mifterton, fenefchal; Ralph de Ecclefal, Philip Scrope, Walter de Heyr, Roger Whifton, William de Lindrick, Ralph de Bauuent."

In 1309 King Edward II. granted licenfe to Edmund de Waftenays to give and affign twenty acres of land with the appurtenances in Todwick to the Abbot and Convent of Roche, in exchange for twenty acres of land with the appurtenances in the fame place.

All the property which the Abbot had in Todwick was granted October 15th, 37 Hen. VIII., to William Ramfden and Ralph Wyfe, and John and Roger Wyfe, fons of Ralph. It is thus defcribed in the grant:—"All that grange of ours (the King's) called Todwick Grange, with the appurtenances in Todwick in our faid county of York, lately belonging and pertaining to the monaftery de Rupe, otherwife called Roche, in the faid county of York, now diffolved, and parcel of the poffeffions lately thereto belonging, and all the houfes, edifices, barns, ftables, dovecotes, gardens, orchards, lands, meadows, paftures, commons, and hereditaments of ours whatever in Todwick and elfewhere, wherefoever in our faid county of York, in any way appertaining or belonging to the faid grange, called Todwick Grange, or being with the faid grange demifed, let,

THE POSSESSIONS.

used, or occupied; and also all that messuage and tenement called the *Abbot's House*,ᵃ with the appurtenances, now or lately in the tenure of Janet Henfrew and Hugh Henfrew of Throapham, situated in the vill of Todwick, in our said county of York, formerly appertaining and belonging to the said late monastery de Rupe or Roche, and parcel of the possessions thereto lately belonging, &c., and which said grange called Todwick Grange and the rest of the premises in Todwick aforesaid now extend to the clear annual value of £5 10s. 8d. To have and to hold, &c., rendering from the said grange and the rest of the premises aforesaid 11s. 8d.ᵇ

Torworth.—There was a fine levied at Leicester the first Monday after the feast of St. Andrew, 10 John (1208) between Osmund Abbot of Roche, petent, and Thomas de Sandal and Matilda his wife, summoned to warrant to the said Abbot one bovate of land with the appurtenances in Torworth, whereof the said Abbot and Convent had the charter of the said Matilda in these words:—

Charter of Matilda de Moles.

"Be it known that I, Matilda de Moles, have given and by this my charter confirmed to God and St. Mary of Roche and the monks there serving God, one bovate of land with the appurtenances, in Torworth; viz., that which was Alexander Crassis, and one culture of land of thirty-eight acres in the territory of the said town, and pasture for a hundred sheep everywhere in the common pasture of the said town, and furthermore all the lands which the men of Blythe held of Hugh de Moles, my brother, and afterwards of me in the fields of Serlby and Torworth, and all the rents of those lands, &c."

From the "*Hundred Rolls*" we learn that the Abbot had in 1276 one hundred acres of land of the gift of Hugh and Matilda de Moles in the time of King John.

In 1246 there was a fine levied between "William" Reginald (?) Abbot of Roche, petent, and Adam de Holtal and Donysia, his wife, of six acres of land with the appurtenances in Torworth. Verdict for the Abbot.

In the time of Edw. III. the Abbot was summoned to answer to the lord the King on the plea by what warrant he claimed to

ᵃ The "Abbot's House" here mentioned still exists, in a ruined condition, in Todwick, and is known by the name of the "Old Hall." It is a good specimen of early English Domestic Architecture, and well deserving of a visit. In the wall of the gable on either side of the chimney is an oval-shaped aperture in the form of a "vesica piscis." At the upper angle of each is carved a beautiful little cross.

ᵇ I am indebted to W. H. G. Bagshawe, Esq., of Ford Hall, for these particulars.

hold his lands and tenements in Torworth in free and perpetual almoign, free and quiet from all gelds, &c. Verdict, that the Abbot for the present go thereof without a day, the right of the King being preserved.

In 1552 the property which the Abbot of Roche had possessed in Torworth was granted to two persons of the names of Green and Hall.

Particulars for Grants (Grantees, Green and Hall.)

Parcel of the possessions of the late Monastery of Roche, in the County of York.

Rents and profits in Torworth, in the County of Nottingham, valued in

	S.	D.
The profits of one field called Grangefield there, in the tenure of Robert Burton, paying thence per annum .	6	8
The profits of certain lands there, in the tenure of John Newcombe, paying thence per annum	0	6
The profits of certain land there in the tenure of Geoffery Bylton, paying thence per annum	0	6
The profits of two acres of land there, in the tenure of Carver, paying thence per annum	0	$3\frac{1}{2}$
The profits of three acres of land there, in the tenure of Geoffery Darell, paying thence per annum	0	9
The profits of three acres of land there, in the tenure of William Ingleby, paying thence per annum . . .	1	0
The profits of eight acres of land there, in three parcels, in the tenure of Robert Burton, paying thence per annum	2	0
The profits of five acres of land there, in the tenure of John Lewestye, paying thence per annum	1	3
The profits of four acres of land there, in the tenure of Hugh Thornell, paying thence per annum	1	0
The profits of certain lands there, in the tenure of John Smith, paying thence per annum	3	4
Clear yearly value	17	$3\frac{1}{2}$

Memorandum. The premysseys are no parcell of anye of the Kynge's Majestye's mannors or lordeshypps, neither do theye lye nye anye of his grace's howses, parkes, forestes, or chaces; and these benne the fyrste partyculars herof made unto annye personne, and there ys no more lande in Taworthe belonginge to the late Monasterye of Roche aforsayde.

Ex^r. 26 Januarii, 1552, per me, Willm. Rygges, Audit.

THE POSSESSIONS.

The clere yerelie value of the premifes above rememberyd is .. . . xvii^{s.} iii^{d.} ob.
Which rated at xxv yeres purchafe amounteth to . . . . xxi^{li.} xii^{s.} iii^{d.} ob.
To be paid within xx dayes nexte.

The Kyng to difchardge the purchafer of all encumbrances except leafes and covenants of the fame.

The tenure in focage laft part.

The iffues from the feaft of St. Michel the Arch.

The purchafer to be bounde for the valewe of the woodes.

Thoms. Norwicen.

At the diffolution the Abbot paid the Prior of Blyth one fhilling per annum for land in Torworth.

Wadworth.—Reginald Gurvy de Tickhill quitclaimed all his right in the mill at Wadworth.

Maud, relict of Matthew de Tickhill, gave two acres of land here.

Eudo, fon of Godfrey de Wadworth, gave lands to the monks in Wadworth, and confirmed what Maud, relict of Matthew de Tickhill, had given them.

Peter de Wadworth gave the monks forty-fix acres of his woodland lying on the weft fide of the wood extending from the weft field of Wadworth to the north. He alfo gave three oxgangs of land on the north fide of the north field; thirty-five acres and one rood in the weft field; and thirty-nine and a half acres and half a rood in the eaft field, in confideration of eighteen marks lent to him by the Abbot of Roche in his great neceffity, and alfo of fifty marks which he owed, and which the faid Abbot paid to Aaron the Jew, at York, and his brother. The witneffes to this deed were Ralph de Normanville, knight; Reginald de Kettleburgh, John de Armthorpe, H. de Bilham, Alexander de Stubbs, Peter de Roffington, Peter de Letwell, Ingeram de Stirap, Otho, fon of Mo. de Wilghefich (Wilfick), Adam Leming, and others.

Stillingflete's "*Abftract of the Acquittance of the Jews*" is as follows:—"The charter of Aaron, fon of Jofey, and of Leo, bifhop, and of Samuel, his fon, Jews of York. Be it known to all the faithful of Chrift, &c., that Peter de Wadworth and his heirs are acquit, &c. Moreover, be it known that we have quitclaimed to the Abbot and Convent of Roche three oxgangs of land and forty-fix acres which they have of the gift of the faid Peter, &c. In witnefs whereof we have put hereto our Hebrew letter and our feals."

The monks did this good act to their old benefactors, the Wadworth family, in the time of Henry III., during whose reign Peter de Wadworth lived.

William, son of John de Vavasour, quitclaimed in 1277 all his right in wards, escheats, &c., in Wadworth.

The monks held what they possessed in this place up to the time of the dissolution.

Walkeringham.—The monks had considerable property in Walkeringham, Lincolnshire, particulars concerning which may be seen in the following:—

Confirmation of King Edward II. of lands in Walkeringham.[*]

"The King to all to whom, &c., greeting.

"The grant, gift, and confirmation which Henry, son of Richard de Walkeringham, by his charter made to the monks of Roche of two tofts, 55¼ acres of land, and 11½ acres of meadow, with the appurtenances in Walkeringham, and of a certain plat of land with the Walcre, and of all the pasture which belongs to that bovate of land of the said Henry, which is called Wlger-oxgang, everywhere in the whole common pertaining to the vill of Walkeringham;

"The grant, also, and gift, and confirmation which the said Henry by another charter which he made to the said monks of one plat of land, with the appurtenances, in the aforesaid vill of Walcre, and two bovates and seven acres of land and meadow, with the appurtenances in the aforesaid vill of Walkeringham;

"The gift, grant, and confirmation which Richard, son of Henry, son of Richard de Walkeringham, by his charter made to the said monks of all that plat of land, with the appurtenances, in the said vill of Walkeringham, and with all things contained within the said plat, which he recovered from the said monks before the justices sitting at Nottingham;

"The grant, also, confirmation, and quitclaim which the said Richard by the same charter made to the said monks of all rents, lands, possessions, meadows, pastures, tenements, homages, services, wards, reliefs, and escheats, with all liberties and easements which they had by the gift and sale of the said Henry his father;

"The grant, moreover, gift, and confirmation which Adam, son of William de Walkeringham, by his charter made with the aforesaid monks of one toft with the appurtenances, in the said vill of Walcre, and with the passage to the said toft pertaining, and of 38

[*] Pat. 6 Edw. II. pars. 2. M. 7.

acres and one rood of land and meadow with the appurtenances in the aforesaid vill of Walkeringham;

"The grant, also, gift, and confirmation which Henry, son of Robert Arnewy of Walkeringham, by his charter made to the said monks of 5 roods and one selion* of land, and of all the land which the said Henry had at Frithesend, and of all the pasture which belongs to a half bovate of land, with the appurtenances in the whole common of Walkeringham;

"The grant, gift, and confirmation which Henry, son of Robert, son of Arnewy of Walkeringham, by his charter made to the aforesaid monks of all his land in Upper Walton, and of three selions and two acres of land, with the appurtenances, in the aforesaid vill of Walkeringham, and of all the meadow which the said Henry had in Monkeboye;

"The grant, also, gift, and confirmation which Henry, son of Robert Maumirr of Walkeringham, by his charter made to the aforesaid monks of three acres and a half of meadow and the mediety of one rood of meadow with the appurtenances in the said vill of Walkeringham, and of all the pasture which pertains to the mediety of one bovate of land everywhere in the whole common of the said vill of Walkeringham;

"The grant, moreover, and confirmation which the said Henry by the same his charter made to the aforesaid monks of all that culture in the field of Walkeringham, with all its appurtenances, which the said monks have of the gift of Roger, the chaplain.

"The remission, also, and quitclaim which the said Henry by the same charter made to the said monks of a certain yearly rent of $4d.$, which the said monks used to pay the said Henry for the culture aforesaid;

"The grant, moreover, gift, and confirmation which the said Henry by the same charter made to the aforesaid monks of the homage and whole service of Henry, son of Isabella, and his heirs, which the said Henry, son of Isabella, was wont to render to the aforesaid Henry, son of Robert, for the whole tenement which he held from the same in Walkeringham, and also of $12\frac{1}{2}$ acres of land and seven roods of meadow, with the appurtenances in Walkeringham;

"The grant, moreover, and confirmation which Adam, son of William de Walkeringham, by his charter made to the aforesaid monks of 4 acres of meadow at Drengefflete, which they had of the gift of Roger de Osberton, of the fee of the said Adam;

* A ridge of land lying between two furrows, uncertain in quantity.

"The grant, also, gift, and confirmation which the said Adam by the said charter made to the said monks of the whole service of Geoffery de Fulham and his heirs, which the said Geoffery used to do to him for a certain particle of land in a place which is called Morfurlung, and also of one toft, with the appurtenances, in Schepewykes, and of three acres and a half of land and meadow, with the appurtenances in Walkeringham;

"The grant, gift, and confirmation which Geoffery, son of Alan de Trent, by his charter made to the aforesaid monks of thirty acres and a half of land and meadow, with the appurtenances, in Walkeringham, with the homage of Walter de Misterton and his heirs, and all the service which he owed to him for two acres of land in Colmanhaghe, and also of the whole pasture which belongs to the mediety of one bovate of land everywhere in the whole common of Walkeringham, and all the service of Geoffery Fulholm and John, son of Roger, and their heirs;

"The grant, moreover, gift, and confirmation which the said Geoffery by another charter made to the aforesaid monks of four acres and one selion of land and three roods of meadow, with the appurtenances, in Walkeringham, and of all his meadow which he had at Helpol and Monkebothe and in the meadows of Walkeringham;

"We, holding these ratified and granted for us and our heirs, as much as in us lies, to our beloved in Christ the Abbot and Convent of the place aforesaid and their successors, grant and confirm as the aforesaid charters reasonably testify. In witness, &c., witness the King at Canterbury, 20th day of May, by fine of ten marks."

The monks had two pieces of meadow in Walkeringham from Robert de Ripers, for which they had to pay William de Walkeringham 6*d*. per annum.

King Henry VIII. by his letters patent, dated 11th November, 1544, granted to Sir Richard Lee, knight, and his heirs, the grange and farm of Walkeringham, with all the lands, meadows, and pastures late belonging to the Monastery of Roche.

Wallingwells.—*(Nottinghamshire.)*—The monks had property here at the dissolution. At this place was a House of Benedictine Nuns, founded about the same time as Roche. Its inmates consisted at the dissolution of a Prioress and eight professed.

Warelp.—The name of this place occurs in the "*Confirmation of King Henry III.*," 1231, as one in which the Abbot of Roche had property.

Wellingley.—Robert Fitz-Payne gave lands, and Jordan Fitz-Payne paſtures, in this place. King Richard I. confirmed to the monks the grange of Wellingley, and from that time up to the diſſolution it ſeems to have continued in their poſſeſſion.

Wickerſley.—Richard Fitz-Turgis de Wickerſley, one of the founders of Roche Abbey, gave the monks fifty loads of wood out of his wood in Wickerſley.ᵃ

Wilſick.—Jordan Fitz-Payne gave the monks land in this place.

Wineley.—In Stephens' continuation of the "*Monaſticon Anglicanum*" the following charter occurs:—

Charter of Walter Abbot and the Convent of Roche.ᵇ

"Know, preſent and future, that Walter Abbot and the Convent of Roche have granted and by the preſent charter confirmed to Robert, ſon of Roger de Tinſley, for his homage and ſervice two bovates of land, with the appurtenances, in the vill of Wineley, which he had of the gift of Walter his brother, to have and to hold to him and his heirs of the ſaid Abbot and Convent of Roche freely and quietly, paying thence per annum to the ſaid Abbot and Convent of Roche eight ſhillings in the grange of Roche, to wit, four ſhillings at Pentecoſt and four ſhillings at the feaſt of St. Martin in the Winter, for all ſervice ſave foreign, as far as belongs to two bovates of land of the ſaid fee in the ſaid vill. With ſuch underſtanding, however, that the ſaid Abbot and Convent are not bound to make warranty of the feoffament of the ſaid land to the ſaid Robert or his heirs. In witneſs whereof the ſaid Abbot and Convent and the ſaid Robert to the parts of this charter have alternately ſet their ſeals. Witneſſes: Johann de Stevinton (Swinton?) * * * Robert Bruerton, Peter de Lettewell, Galfrid de Helgheby. 1260."

(Much obliterated, and the Seals loſt.)

Owing to the obliterated condition of the original charter when this tranſcript was made, it is probable that the miſtake of writing "Wineley" for "Tinſley" has occurred. This alſo is the opinion of learned topographer, Samuel Mitchell, Eſq., of Sheffield.

Winterton.—Winterton, in Lincolnſhire, is mentioned in the "*Confirmation of King Henry III.*" as one of the places in which the monks had property. Whatever it conſiſted of it ſeems to have remained in their hands up to the time of the diſſolution, when it was valued at £1 1s. per annum.

ᵃ See page 5. ᵇ Tranſcript in the poſſeſſion of Sir W. Calverlay, Bt.

Winteringham.—Hamelin Bardolph and Katherine his wife, and Robert, fon of Eudo, gave the monks land in this place, which Hugh, fon of Ralph Bardolph, confirmed. Winteringham is fituated in Lincolnfhire, about three miles north of Roxby Grange. At the diffolution what the monks had here in pafture was valued at 10s. per annum.

Wpvelsworth.—This place is mentioned in the "*Confirmation of King Henry III.*" as one of the places in which the monks had property.

Woodhouse Mill.—The Abbot of Roche received £1 9s. per annum rent from the mill called "Wodhoufemyll."

York.—Agnes, the Priorefs of the Convent of St. Clement, at York, granted to the monks a certain piece of land leading from their orchard to the river Oufe, for which they paid £3 sterling.

Oblations, Alms, etc.

The oblations amounted at the diffolution to £1 per annum. This fum was diftributed yearly at the Supper of the Lord. The fum of £1 9s. per annum was expended in burning wax daily before the altar of the foundation of Richard Furnival, and 5s. was given yearly at the celebration of the obit for the foul of Thos. de Bella Aqua.

The Architecture,

Monastic Buildings, and their Remains.

THE ARCHITECTURE

HE architectural peculiarities and beauties of Roche Abbey have, until lately, been either misrepresented or neglected altogether. Not long since it was common for historians to devote nearly their whole attention to the possessions and genealogies of persons, and to content themselves with describing any buildings they might meet with, as of the earlier or later Gothic periods. Thanks, however, to the publication of books of sound information on the subject, and to the establishment of Archæological and Architectural Societies, the public have become more conversant with Architecture, and the pleasures of this magnificent art are now widely enjoyed. In proof of the ignorance we have mentioned, let any one take up a book describing the ruins of Roche Abbey Church twenty years ago. He will, almost certainly, find the two east walls of the transepts pointed out as the remains of the nave.

But besides being misrepresented by the pen, the architecture of Roche has received even worse treatment from the pencil. Drawings and engravings of the ruins may be met with, which can only be recognized by exercising the most vivid imagination and by referring to the name inscribed below. Round arches are pointed, and pointed arches are rounded. Windows are turned into doors, and doors into windows. In fact every sort of liberty is taken, including the rounding of the square abacus. But the artist has had to move on, as well as the topographer. Photography has appeared, and put to shame the clumsy daubs of former years. The difficulty of getting an exact representation of a building no longer exists. The most delicate and minute work may now be copied with marvellous exactness and ease. Photography gives us the form of arches, capitals, and mouldings; the position of every stone, beauty, flaw, crack, and stain.

It is left only to the imagination to obtain any idea of what the general appearance of the Abbey must have been, before it was "put to the spoil." (See p. 91.) We have the evidence, however, of William, Earl of Warren, who in 1345 admiring the magnificence of the stone work as well in the buildings of the said Abbot and Convent, as in their Monastery, made the monks a considerable grant. We have also the evidence of Cuthbert Shirebrook, who says that the Abbey at the time of its dissolution "was a very fair builded house, all of freestone; and every house vaulted with freestone and covered with lead." And we have sufficient still standing to prove how extensive and how beautiful the whole must have been: at all events we have every reason to be pleased with what remains, when we remember, that the only fragment left of Newminster Abbey, the Mother of Roche, is the north door.

In 1776, Mr. Brown, the landscape gardener, committed such havoc in the way of pulling down and covering up, that nothing less than an extensive disinterment can enable us to discover how much of the ruins of Roche remain underground. *Mr. Gilpin* gives us an account of these operations; "these ruins" he says, "and the scenery around them were in the roughest state, when Mr. Brown was employed to adorn them. He is now at work; and has nearly half completed his intention. This is the first subject of the kind he has attempted. Many a modern place he has adorned and beautified: but a ruin presented a new idea; which I doubt whether he has sufficiently considered. He has finished one of the vallies which looks towards Laughton spire: he has floated it with a lake, and formed it into a very beautiful scene. But I fear it is too magnificent and too artificial an appendage, to be in unison with the ruins of an Abbey. An Abbey, it is true, may stand by the side of a lake; and it is possible, that *this* lake may, in some future time, become its situation; when the marks of the spade and the pickaxe are removed—when its osiers flourish; and its naked banks become fringed and covered with wood. In a word, when the lake itself is improved by time, it may suit the ruin, which stands upon its banks. At present the lake and ruin, are totally at variance. Mr. Brown is now at work in the centre part of the three vallies, near the ruin itself. He has already removed all the heaps of rubbish, which lay around; some of which were very *ornamental;* and very *useful* also in uniting the two parts of the ruin. They give something too of more consequence to the *whole*, by discovering the vestiges of what once existed. Many of these scattered appendages also, through length of time, having been covered with earth, and adorned with wild brushwood had risen up to the windows, and united the *ruin to the soil* on which it stood. All this is removed: a level is taken, and the ruin stands now on a neat bowling green, like a house just built, and without any kind of *connection* with the ground it stands on. There is certainly little judgment shewn in this mode of improvement. The *character* of the scene is mistaken. If Mr. Brown should proceed a step further—pull down the ruin and build an elegant mansion: everything would then be right, and in its proper place. But in a *ruin* the reigning ideas are *solitude, neglect,* and *desolation*."[a] As Mr. Gilpin predicted, time has done a great deal, towards rendering Mr. Brown's work more in keeping with the ruin. All true lovers of Architecture will, nevertheless, always deplore the pulling down of detached fragments, and the heartless covering up of the ground plan, which we know still exists in great perfection. And for the present, we must content ourselves by hoping that the noble owner will, ere long, enhance a hundred-fold, the interest of the lovely spot he has the privilege to possess, by lifting the dark veil of earth which has for a century hidden from all eyes innumerable objects of interest and beauty.

Whatever may be the truth of the legend which attributes to Durandus a superstitious motive, in choosing the site for his Abbey, we have abundant proof, that there were not wanting many substantial reasons to confirm him in his selection. Among these may be mentioned, not only the beauty of the situation, for beautiful it must ever have been, from its natural combination of rock, wood, water, and meadow, even before it had received the attentions of Mr. "Capability" Brown; but also its complete seclusion from the outer world. Thus rendering it peculiarly suited to the requirements of the stern and rigid rule of the order of its occupants, one of whose special principles it was, in the selection of sites for their houses, that "they should never be constructed except in places separated from all converse and neighbourhood of men."[b] In both these respects it bears a striking resemblance to the parent Abbey of Fountains, as it does also with regard to another essential circumstance to an establishment of this kind, namely, an abundant supply of clear and excellent water. A further inducement to the monks to settle in this choice spot must have been the existence here of a splendid building stone, beautiful in colour, easily worked, and yet very durable, as is sufficiently testified by the admirable state of preservation in which the remains of the Abbey Church continue to

---

[a] Picturesque Beauty, vol. i. page 21.
[b] Cistercian Rule quoted by Mackenzie E. C. Walcott, in his "Church and Conventual Arrangement," from Harl. MS. 3708, f. 18.

this day, notwithstanding their exposure to the weather for so many centuries. The reputation, indeed of the Roche Abbey quarry, has long been widely spread, and so highly is it now esteemed, that when the new houses of parliament were about to be built, and search was made throughout the country, for the best materials for that purpose, the stone from this quarry was one of those ordered to be examined and reported upon.

It is evident, therefore, that these early Cistercians exercised no ordinary degree of judgment, no less than of taste, in selecting this place as the site of their future Abbey. And here, no doubt, they commenced as soon as their circumstances would permit, the erection of their conventual buildings. These, in all probability, may have been at first of a temporary character, until increasing wealth and prosperity enabled them, in that respect, to rival their parent and kindred houses of Fountains and Kirkstall, as seems to have been the case when Roche was brought to its full maturity and perfection.

As, it has been observed, the monastic remains of Roche Abbey are, at least as to what is visible above ground, of so limited an extent, it must be left very much to conjecture to determine what the buildings were when entire. Yet fortunately, our conjectures here need not be of a vague and wholly uncertain character. For, it is a well ascertained fact, that the arrangement of institutions of this kind, very much followed an established plan. And it is upon record as regards these Cistercian monasteries that they were, as far as circumstances permitted, built according to a fixed rule. We constantly read in the accounts which are preserved in the "*Monasticon Anglicanum*" respecting the establishment and the erection of the buildings of the monasteries, which were derived from the great Abbey of Fountains, that this was done "*de more*"—according to established custom, or "*secundum formam ordinis*,"—according to the form of their order. Now, though the remains here are certainly scanty, and those of the immediately parent Abbey of Newminster are reduced to the smallest fragment, yet in the kindred monasteries of Fountains and Kirkstall they are very ample. And from these we may, with considerable confidence, form an opinion as to what the general arrangement must have been at Roche.

From those examples then, as well as from others, we learn that the main offices of the Abbey were erected round a cloistered court, of which the nave of the church formed the northern side. That on the eastern side of the quadrangle were found, beyond the south transept of the church, first an apartment, which appears to have been a vestry, communicating with the church by a doorway, which yet remains at Roche. Beyond this veſtry, was the chapter-houſe, which in the early times of the erection of theſe abbeys, *i. e.*, in the 12th century, is always found in the parallelogram form: and of this building again, veſtiges have been diſinterred here ſufficient to verify this ſtatement. On the ſame ſide of the court at Kirkſtall are two vaulted apartments, the uſe of which is not very obvious; they are dark and dreary, and perhaps may have been places of confinement for refractory monks, or poſſibly merely ſtorehouſes. It ſeems not improbable that ſomething of the kind exiſted alſo at Roche, as the length of this ſide, as indicated by a corner maſs of maſonry ſtill remaining, muſt have afforded conſiderable ſpace beyond the chapter-houſe. At the ſouth-eaſt, no doubt, there would be alſo a paſſage. On the ſouth ſide of the court would, almoſt certainly, be found the Refectory, with its accompanying offices, as buttery, kitchen, &c. The weſt ſide of this court would, no doubt, be occupied by a large apartment, extending its whole length, and perhaps even beyond it, to the ſouth, as is the caſe at Fountains, where it is ſtill pretty perfect, and was alſo the caſe at Kirkſtall, as is plainly ſhown by the veſtiges which remain there. This noble apartment would reſt upon an undercroft, as in the examples juſt referred to, having a groined roof ſupported in the centre by a row of pillars. At Fountains the length of this erection, built at two different periods, is not leſs than 300 feet; of that at Kirkſtall about 175 feet. The upper chamber formed *one* of the dormitories in theſe Abbeys; for from the early account we have of Kirkſtall, preſerved in the "*Monaſticon Anglicanum*," it is evident there were two dormitories erected from the firſt foundation of the monaſtery, "*utrumque dormitorium, monachorum ſcilicet et converſorum*," *i.e.*, one for the monks and the other for the lay-brethren. And the ſame was probably the caſe alſo at Fountains and at Roche. On the weſt ſide of the cloiſter court, we may conclude, was the dormitory of the lay-brethren, a portion of which, ſeparated from the reſt, may have formed the ſleeping apartment of other dependents of the monaſtery, who no doubt were numerous, as the Ciſtercians were great agriculturiſts;[*] and alſo occaſionally, at

---

[*] It is remarked reſpecting the Benedictines, of whom the Ciſtercians were a reformed and ſtricter branch, in Stephenſon's Introduction to "Chronicon Monaſterii de Abingdon," publiſhed under direction of the Maſter of the Rolls, that "Benedict thought it good that men ſhould be daily reminded that in the ſweat of their face they ſhould eat bread, and day by day they toiled in the field, as well as prayed in the church. After having been preſent at the ſervice of Prime, the Monks aſſembled in the chapter-houſe, each individual received his allotted ſhare of work, a brief prayer was offered up, tools were ſerved out, and the brethren marched two and two, and in ſilence, to their taſk in the field. From Eaſter until the beginning of October they were thus occupied from ſix o'clock in the morning until ten, or ſometimes till noon. Beſides the monks, lay-brethren and ſervants were engaged, who received payment in coin. And as by degrees more land was brought into tillage than the monaſtery needed, the ſurplus was leaſed out to lay occupiers. Thus each monaſtery became a centre of civilization, and while the rude chieftain, intent on war or the chaſe, cared little for the comfort either of himſelf or his retainers, the monks became the ſource, not only of intellectual and ſpiritual light, but of phyſical warmth and comfort, and houſehold bleſſings."

least, of strangers. To this latter conclusion we seem led by the fact that at Fountains, where this part of the Abbey is found in a more perfect state than it exists elsewhere, one access is gained to this dormitory by a flight of steps placed on the *outside* of the cloister court. The dormitory of the monks, there seems little doubt, was an apartment which ranged over the chapter-house and other buildings on the eastern side of the court, and from this apartment access was gained to the choir of the church by a doorway opening upon a flight of steps within the south transept. These steps still remain at Fountains and Kirkstall, or at least the inclined plane on which they stood. And we may conclude that a similar arrangement existed at Roche, as we may observe that here a doorway, already referred to, leading from the south transept into the vestry, is not placed in the centre of this wall, but, as is also the case at Fountains and Kirkstall, considerably to the east side, in order, no doubt, to give room for the staircase.

Judging from the fragments of masonry which still remain and which appear to have formed the boundaries of the cloister court, its dimensions were about 180 feet on the east and west sides, and 125 feet on the north and south.

Beyond the court on the south-east it is evident that extensive buildings existed. A considerable block of masonry still remains at the distance of about 90 feet to the south of that, which we may suppose formed the south-east corner of the court, and which has been already alluded to. This masonry, it is probable, marks the boundary of the buildings in that direction. Here very likely may have been the Locutorium or monk's parlour, and to the east of this, the residence of the Abbot. This appears to have been the arrangement at Kirkstall: and there the foundation of a rather large building has been recently laid bare, to the north of what we may suppose to have been the Abbot's lodge. The plan of this building has been very much that of the nave of a church with a middle alley separated from aisles by an arcade of four arches on each side. It stood east and west, and had two entrances on each side of the latter end: it also shows vestiges of three, if not four, fire places. It seems probable that this was the Infirmary of the Abbey, as such was the usual arrangement of this monastic appendage. It is not unlikely that at Roche also the infirmary may be looked for in this direction, it being the usual one, although at Fountains it has been thought to have stood over the river immediately to the west of the great dormitory.

There is another considerable block of masonry remaining here, which stands to the south-east of the sites just referred to. This is said to be a fragment of the Abbey mill, and near it, beside the foot bridge, down in the bed of the stream, may be observed a beautiful Early English light clustered column. Again, to the south-west of the cloister court, there appear to have been other considerable buildings, the foundations of which it is stated, in dry seasons may be observed extending beyond the stream. It is probable that the Hospitium or guest house of the Abbey may have stood here.

The Abbey Gatehouse, of which there are considerable remains of great interest, will be described more at large hereafter, stands at some distance to the north-west of the church.

Such appears to have been the general arrangement of the monastic buildings at Roche. But their relative position and the plan of the whole Abbey precincts, together with its boundary wall, of which traces still remain, will be better understood by reference to Plate I.

The principal, indeed as already intimated, almost the only remains of this once extensive Abbey, are those of the church and the gatehouse, both of which are of great interest and excellence. These we will endeavour now to describe and to point out their architectural features.

The Church.

The church, when entire, must undoubtedly have been a very beautiful and noble structure, extending in length more than 200 feet, and having a breadth at the transepts of about 100 feet. Perhaps we may form the best idea of what it must have presented to the eye, by visiting the church of Kirkstall, which it certainly much resembled in its general plan and architectural character, though apparently a few years later in date. Kirkstall Abbey church, with the exception of a breach made on the north side by the fall of a portion of its tower, and the loss of some of its roofs, happily remains entire and unaltered, *with very slight exceptions*, as it came from the hands of its original builders. And a more noble and impressive structure it is scarcely possible to enter. It is true that it exceeds the church of Roche by about 20 feet in length, and in breadth of transept by about 18 feet. Still there having been the same number of arches on each side of the nave, the same bold lofty tower arches, arcades, and groined aisles, the general effect must have been very similar in both examples.

The ground plan of both these churches is that of a cross, with a tower at the intersection. The naves were spacious and lofty, the transepts without aisles, but having chapels on their eastern sides, here two in each transept, while at Kirkstall there were three; with short eastern limbs or structural choirs. (See Plate II.) The naves had each an arcade of eight arches with aisles, which no doubt here, as at Kirkstall, were groined. This also may have been the case with the nave itself, although it was not so at Kirkstall; and in that example neither the tower area nor the transepts appear to have been vaulted over, while at Roche such vaulting evidently existed, as may be seen from the shafts and springers which still remain. In both cases the choirs were groined over.

Of the noble church of Roche, as already intimated, only the eastern sides of the transepts, with a portion of their chapels and of the choir still remain. But these are sufficient to give us a knowledge of what the general architecture of the building must have been, and to enable us to fix its date with tolerable precision.

As regards what remains of the transepts, we have on each side two beautifully proportioned pointed arches of three orders, they rest upon bold clustered piers, with a vaulting shaft between them of the pointed boutell form, as are also the shafts which support the soffits of the arches, while the intermediate ones are either square or of the torus form. The form of the arches is that termed by *Rickman* the "drop arch,"* the centres being found within the width of the arch. They are also slightly stilted, their mouldings are formed of the pointed and round boutell used in alternation; and the abaci of the capitals are square, with a rather deep-cut moulding. Above the points of the arches is a bold stringcourse, passing round the vaulting shafts, and also round the pier of the central tower. Upon this stringcourse is an arcade of blank pointed arches, two over each principal arch; these are perfectly plain and devoid of ornament or shafts, having only the jambs slightly chamfered. Above these again is another stringcourse upon which, in each compartment, stands a round-headed window, also perfectly plain but having a dripstone. Above this string are the springers of the groined roof, which was evidently of very bold and good character: the diagonal ribs resting upon corbels which terminate in a conical form, and having capitals slightly enriched with foliage.

The arches of the transepts, as already intimated, opened into chapels, of these, those on the southern side are still entire, while those on the north are mostly in ruins. They seem to have been

---

* Ascertained by actual measurement, but only in a slight degree, and from the fact of the arches being stilted, a lofty character is given.

divided by a wall, raised only a few feet from the floor, and not as at Kirkstall, reaching to the roof. The most southern of the chapels has a round-headed window on its south side, beneath which is a piscina also with a circular head. And there can be no doubt that similar windows were originally found on the eastern sides of both these chapels, as well as of those in the north transept. Here, however, it is evident, that these original windows were superseded by insertions of larger dimensions, of the 14th century. A sufficient portion of the tracery of that next the choir still remains to afford pretty certain evidence of what the window was when entire. This will be found represented in Plate VII. fig 12. It seems very probable that one of these chapels was dedicated to the Virgin, and that in it was interred Matilda of York, Countess of Cambridge, who died A. D. 1440, having in her will directed that her "body be buried in the monastery of Roche, in the chapel of the blessed Mary, before her image, situated in the *southern* part of the church of the said monastery." She also directs that "there lie over her grave a stone of alabaster, raised aloft after the manner of a tomb, with an effigy."[a] It seems, very probable, that the figure of the noble lady may have rested on the wall, which divides the chapels: no other site being apparently available, for a tomb of such character, in areas of such limited dimensions as these chapels are. In support of this conjecture too, it is observable that the stone adjoining the central pier is cut away as if to receive the head of a figure.

The northern chapels seem altogether to have resembled those on the south side: in the one next the choir is a piscina like that in the south chapel, and round its arch and in the neighbourhood of it, are lines marked in a light red colour, with further plain indications that the stone work was also marked out in black lines. These are drawn upon a very thin coating of plaster, or rather of whitewash, which may be found also in other parts of the building.[b] These chapels were all groined over, and had bosses at the intersections of their ribs, some of which still remain.

The eastern limb or structural choir of the church, as already stated, is of short dimensions, extending in length only about 37 feet. It is without aisles or communication with the chapels. In these respects it agrees with the nearly coeval choirs of Kirkstall and Louth Park, and also with the original one at Fountains, which, however, was rebuilt, on a very enlarged plan, about a century after its first

---

[a] See p. 58.

[b] It was not uncommon, in early times, to whitewash the walls of churches, thus we are informed that in 1214, Robert de Lindsey, Abbot of Peterborough, "dealbavit" (whitewashed) the choir of that church.

erection. In all these cases the chorus cantorum, or choir for divine service, extended under the central tower, and probably a compartment or two beyond it. That such was the case at Fountains may be seen from the foundations of the stalls which yet remain there.

The eastern limb at Roche has had triple sedilia on the south side, which appear to have been surmounted by lofty canopies. These have entirely vanished: they appear not to have been original, but to have superseded sedilia under a single circular arch, as at Kirkstall, indications of such arch being here still discernable. To the east of these a plain niche of parallogram form contains a piscina, and probably also a lockyer. On the north side opposite the sedilia, are the remains of very rich canopied work of lofty dimensions. It is of the Decorated period, and may have been an Easter sepulchre, or perhaps a tomb of some benefactor.* To the west of this is also a shallow niche, also canopied, but of lower dimensions. This choir was lighted by round headed windows to the north and south, in the part which extends beyond the chapels, in three stages: in the western part, in the clerestory only. Beneath these, standing on a bold string, are two blank arches on each side, at the triforium stage, similar to those in the transepts, but somewhat richer, having shafts at their angles and moulded edges.

There is no means of determining what the arrangement of the east end was, as it has been entirely demolished. The choir was groined in two compartments, with quadripartite vaulting, the transverse rib in the middle resting on pointed shafts, which descend below the triforium stringcourse and terminate in conical shaped corbels, whose capitals are enriched with foliage. The diagonal ribs are supported by similar corbels.

Of the nave of this fine church, as already stated, very little now remains visible: though, doubtless, the whole of its basement lies buried beneath the soil, having been thus concealed by the levelling system of Mr. "Capability" Brown. The west end has, however, of late years been uncovered, and this, together with the fragments of three of the piers, enables us to determine its extent and the character of its architecture. (See Plate II.) Its length was 126 feet 6 inches, and, as we before said, it had an arcade of eight arches on each side, with side aisles. Its breadth was 30 feet 1 inch, that of its aisles, 14 feet 6 inches. The piers consisted of groups of eight

---

* Idonea de Vipont grand-daughter and heiress of Richard de Busli, the co-founder of Roche Abbey, gave *with her body*, to this house, the Manor of Sandbeck, and thus became a great benefactress. (See p. 140.) It is probable, therefore, that she would be buried in a place of special honour, near the high altar. May not this have been her tomb? She died A.D. 1241. Though certainly the canopy work appears of somewhat later date.

pointed boutells: whereof four were principal ones, and the remainder, placed in the angles, of smaller dimensions. The diameter of the piers was five feet. Their form will, probably, be more easily understood from the accompanying plan of their horizontal section, than from the more elaborate figure contained in Plate V. fig. 1.

There can be little doubt, judging from the remains of the transepts, that the piers and arches of the nave were very lofty and graceful in their proportions, and must have formed a very noble structure. The aisles were, most probably, vaulted, but as regards the nave itself, it may, perhaps, be questioned whether such was the case. We have no means of determining, with certainty, what was the arrangement of the upper stories. Very likely, however, the same general plan was followed as is found in the transepts and choir, namely, that of blank-arched triforium arcades, with single clerestory windows above.

From the excavations made at the west end, it is evident that the church was entered here by three portals: in this respect differing from the examples of Fountains and Kirkstall, which have each only one west doorway. The central and principal portal at Roche was of three orders, with nookshafts, the bases of which have small foot ornaments. The side doors seem to have been plainer.

The walls of the west end were about six feet in thickness.

As regards the style of the architecture and the date of this fine church, it has been already stated that it is of the character which is denominated Transitional Norman, which prevailed during the latter half of the 12th century. Of this style, however, there are several phases: shewing a gradual advancement from the pure Norman, till we arrive at the perfect Early English. A finer example of the earlier work of this period cannot perhaps be anywhere found than that which has already been so frequently alluded to, the church at Kirkſtall. There we have, with the exception of the pointed arches of the principal arcades, a perfect Norman building, ſhowing in its mouldings, capitals and other features, ſcarcely a veſtige of the following ſtyle. In that caſe we know from the records, which have been preſerved to us, that the church was begun ſoon after the ſettlement of the monks there in 1152, and that the work was carried on and completed at the ſole expenſe of the great patron of that houſe—Henry de Lacy. It was therefore, doubtleſs, erected earlier in the hiſtory of the convent, more continuouſly, and in a ſhorter period than that in which ſuch large ſtructures are uſually brought to a concluſion: while for the moſt part ſuch extenſive operations lag, or are for a time altogether ſuſpended from inſufficency of funds.

As regards this church of Roche, we have no reaſon to ſuppoſe that the brethren were ſo favourably circumſtanced: for although their patrons gave them lands, and granted them permiſſion to erect their monaſtery on which ſide of the water they pleaſed, we hear nothing of their having borne the expenſes of the buildings. It muſt, therefore, have been a conſiderable number of years before they were able to undertake the erection of ſo noble a church, having, doubtleſs, had to content themſelves, like the parent houſe of Fountains, for ſome time, with a much more humble oratory.* And this view of the caſe before us, is found exactly to accord with the architectural features of the remains of the church, no part of which, it is believed, can be aſſigned to a date earlier than about the laſt ten years of the 12th century. It ſeems, moſt probable, that it was erected during the Abbacy of Oſmund, under whoſe long, able, and active rule the houſe ſeems eſpecially to have proſpered and increaſed in wealth and poſſeſſions, and who obtained for it both from Pope Urban III and from Richard I, as well as from the Counteſs of Eu, the great ſuperior lady of the Tickhill fee, under which the land was held, confirmations of all its poſſeſſions and privileges. This Abbot preſided over the convent from A.D. 1184 to A.D. 1223.

The church, there is little doubt, was, according to the uſual cuſtom, commenced at the eaſt end: and here, accordingly, we find marks of the earlieſt character, ſuch, for inſtance, as a mixture of

---

* We read alſo with reſpect to the monks who were ſent out from Fountains to eſtabliſh a monaſtery at Barnoldſwic, (afterwards removed to Kirkſtall,) that the Abbot of the parent houſe, erected for them there, in the firſt inſtance, "*humble* offices, according to the form of their order." " Et miſſis fratribus officinas humiles erexit ſecundum forman ordinis." *Monaſticon Anglicanum*, vol. v. p. 531.

Again, as relates to Kirkſtall itſelf, it is recorded. "Abbas itaque—baſilican erigit in honore matris Dei ſemper virginis. Et diſpoſitis exordine humillibus officinis monaſterium ſuum mutato nomine Kirkeſtall nominavit. An. Dom. MCLII. *Ibid.*

the round and pointed shafts in the piers, with square edges at the angles: while the mixture entirely disappears when we get to the west of the crossing, where all the shafts of the pillars have assumed the pointed form. But even with regard to the earliest part, the tall and graceful proportions of the piers and arches, the lofty form of the latter, the pointed panelling of the triforium story, and the length and narrowness of the round windows, together with the character of the vaulting ribs and shafts, forbid our placing it early in the transitional period, which makes the simplicity and severity of its details the more remarkable, though strictly in accordance with the Cistercian rule.

The Gatehouse.

The only other considerable remain of the Abbey buildings, is a portion of the Gatehouse. This is situated at some distance to the north-west of the church. The lower story of this structure alone is preserved, which bears a considerable resemblance to the Gatehouse at Worksop Priory, and does not appear to differ much from it in date, both being of the Decorated period: and may be assigned to the early part of the 14th century. In one point the gateway of Roche does not resemble that of Worksop, inasmuch as it has a stone groined roof, while in the latter example, there is a beautiful original one of wood. This gateway is divided into two principal compartments of equal magnitude, being separated by the arch in which the gate hung, which had a smaller portal on the north side of it. Each of these compartments had others, into which they opened at their sides, all these varying in dimensions and the whole remaining perfect, with the exception of the one at the south-east angle, of which the greater part has perished. The compartments which remain are all groined over, having very bold diagonal and transverse ribs, the edges of which are merely chamfered. The ribs are supported by conical shaped corbels, and in the principal intersections have carved bosses. In the north-west corner of the inner compartment is a stone newell staircase, which led to the upper story. At the south-west angle of the gatehouse externally, there appears to have been a considerable mass of masonry, which possibly may have supported a staircase communicating with the outside, like the one at Worksop. The archways to the east and west are similar, each being about 15 feet in width, having obtusely pointed arches of three orders, the edges of which are merely chamfered, and are supported by shafts, which have plain capitals and bases. The eastern view of this building is given in Plate XIII; its ground plan Plate XIV; and the details of its architectural features in Plate XV. There can be little doubt that this gatehouse, when perfect, was a very fine building, exhibiting a noble simplicity and massiveness of structure, as may be inferred from what still remains, especially from the groined roof which is of a most marked character, and well worthy of observation.

The stables and farm buildings of the abbey, were probably to the north of the gatehouse, on the site where offices of the same character still remain.

An ancient key of copper, and various fragments of ornamental stonework have been from time to time disinterred, and doubtless an ample crop of similar objects still lie buried beneath the soil. Representations of some of these will be found in Plates XI and XII. Especially a fragment (Plate XI. fig. 1.) which contains a capital of a shaft of the great west door-way. Attention must also be called to the dedication cross, which is incised on the wall on the left side of the west door-way within, a representation of which forms the tailpiece to this section.

There is a large octagonal basin lying near the bridge which leads to the site of the mill. It has a hole through the centre of its bottom, and probably may have been for a fountain in the middle of the cloister court.

There are wells of beautiful water on the premises, especially "the Ladies' Well," or rather, most probably, "the Well of our Lady," which is situated a short distance from the site of the abbey court, though across the stream.

A great variety of mason's marks may be found in different parts of the buildings. Such as have been observed are given in Plate IX. as they may probably be of use, to those who are desirous of investigating that interesting subject.

Such are the only visible remains of the once noble and extensive Abbey of Roche. It must doubtless, when in its entire state, have presented a most striking and impressive effect to the spectator, when entering into its precincts, through the gatehouse, extending as it did quite across the valley, and being flanked on the northern side by its fine and lofty church. So extensive were its buildings that it seems evident even in the days of John, Earl of Warren, in the early part of the 14th century, it had out-grown the requirements of its inhabitants.[*] Or rather, perhaps, we should say, that the number of its monks had dwindled down considerably

[*] See p.p. 51, 112.

THE ARCHITECTURE, &c.

from what they had been in earlier times. For it is truly furprifing to contemplate the rapid increafe of this order of Ciftercians, on their firft eftablifhment, during the former half of the 12th century. This will be more clearly feen by reprefenting the matter in the tabular form of a pedigree, with the dates of the feveral oundations of Fountains and its offfhoots, thus:—

Such was the extraordinary rapidity with which the fame of the piety of the early Ciftercian brethren attracted numbers to their fociety, who flocked to their houfes "as doves to the windows." And not only did their numbers thus marvelloufly increafe, but their worldly poffeffions multiplied in like manner: and the great addition to their earthly wealth, no doubt, was attended with much of its ufual confequences, a departure from the primitive fimplicity and rigid piety of their order, and the introduction of an amount of laxity and luxury which the early Ciftercians fo earneftly efchewed. This increafing worldlinefs would naturally produce its ufual effect, the fervour of men's love towards the order, began fhortly to abate, and inftead of the wonderful increafe in the number of members and of houfes, which attended their firft introduction into the country, after the three earlier quarters of the 12th century, the foundation of an additional monaftery was of very rare occurrence. Inftead of "the good feed," as the early chroniclers of the order boafted, "taking root and bringing forth an abundant harveft" throughout the land, it would feem, that ere long, the blade began to wither away, till, at the time of the great cataftrophe, the number of the monks of thefe vaft eftablifhments had dwindled to a comparatively fcanty body, no more than eighteen brethren having been found here at the diffolution, and only about twice that number in the far larger parent Abbey of Fountains. At the kindred Abbey of Louth Park, Lincolnfhire, another offfhoot from Fountains, we are informed by *Tanner*, that in the reign of King Henry III there were no fewer than fixty-fix monks and one hundred and fifty converfi or lay-brethren, while at the time of the diffolution there were not above twelve religious in that houfe. Truly thefe eftablifhments had out-lived their day: and in their cafe was ftrikingly verified the dictum which comes to us from the higheft authority, "Now that which decayeth and waxeth old, is ready to vanifh away."[*]

Before taking leave of thefe interefting ruins and their beautiful environs, it would be ungrateful not to offer a tribute of thanks to the noble family within whofe domains they are fituated, for the kind privilege which has long been fo freely granted to the public to vifit them. It is indeed a rich treat, not only to the Archæologian and Architectural ftudent, but to every perfon who can at all take an intereft in what is beautiful in rural fcenery, to fpend a few hours in this choice retreat. And it is probable that there are few perfons refiding within many a mile of this spot, or who have ever vifited the neighbourhood, who have not, at one time or other, enjoyed the calm and tranquil pleafure of a brief fojourn here: and who will not efteem the day as one to be marked with the whiteft ftone, which has been spent, it may be in the fociety of friends who have now paffed away, in a fummer's ramble among the rocks, and "the high woodlands, which crown this happy valley," or in the enjoyment of a quiet, or, it may be a feftive hour, on the foft green fward, amidft fair Roche's

"White walls and filver springs."

[*] Heb. viii. v. 13.

Addenda.

ADDENDA.

A Flora of Roche Abbey.

THE situation of Roche Abbey is on the magnesian limestone, in a beautiful valley, bounded on the north by a range of perpendicular rocks, and on the south by the "King's Wood." Its fine carboniferous soil, its lake and waterfalls, its old stone quarries and rich banks, unite such a variety of favourable conditions that a Local Flora, worthy of notice, may reasonably be expected.

RANUNCULACEÆ.
R. ficaria. Little celandine, or pilewort.
R. acris. Upright crowfoot.
R. repens. Creeping crowfoot.
R. bulbosus. Bulbous crowfoot.
R. arvensis. Corn crowfoot.
Thalictrum minus. Meadow rue.
Helleborus viridis. Green hellebore.
Aquilegia vulgaris. Columbine.

BERBERIDACEÆ.
Berberis vulgaris. Barberry, in Kingswood and Hedges towards Tickhill, abundant.*

* Barberry used to grow commonly in hedges on the Abbey side of Tickhill; in the same neighbourhood mildew and blight on the cereals were usually mischievous, and the farmer naturally thought that barberry was the cause. A high botanical authority ridiculed the idea, on the ground that the blight on barberry (æcidium) was so different a vegetable to the (ustilago) on barley, or (tilletia) on wheat, that barberry could not be the cause. But facts prove that the spores of fungi, mixed up with the dust of the atmosphere, do mischief both to plants and animals, and we know the spores of one fungus stimulate the growth of the spores of another; we also see daily one fungus parasitic on that of another, and often a third upon that. It is therefore probable that the spores of the fungus on barberry, blown immediately on the wheat when in a moist condition, with rain or dew, would poison the juices of the plant, and so by weakening it, would render it an easy prey to the unwelcome parasites of mildew and blight.

CRUCIFERÆ.
Arabis hirsuta. Rock cress.
Thlaspi arvense. Penny cress.
Capsella bursa-pastoris. Shepherd's purse.

CISTACEÆ.
Helianthemum vulgare. Rock rose.

VIOLACEÆ.
Viola odorata. Sweet violet.
V. canina. Dog violet.

CARYOPHYLLACEÆ.
Lychnis flos-cuculi. Ragged robin.
L. githago. Corn cockle.
Stellaria nemorum. Wood stitchwort.

LINACEA.
Linum catharticum. Purging flax.

MALVACEÆ.
Malva sylvestris. Wild mallow.

TILIACEÆ.
Tilia europæa. Lime-tree.

HYPERICACEÆ.
Hypericum perforatum. St. John's wort.
H. montanum. Mountain St. John's wort.
H. pulchrum. Lesser St. John's wort.

GERANIACEÆ.
Geranium pratense. Crane's bill.
G. columbinum. Purple Crane's bill.

CELASTRACEÆ.
Euonymus europæus. Spindle-tree.

RHAMNACEÆ.
Rhamnus catharticus. Buckthorn.

LEGUMINOSÆ.
Ononis arvensis. Rest harrow.
O. campestris.
Trifolium repens. White clover.
T. pratense. Purple clover.
Medicago sativa. Lucerne.
M. maculata. Spotted trefoil.
Ulex europæus. Furze, whin, gorse.
Sarothamnus scoparius. Broom.
Onobrychis sativa. Saintfoin.
Vicia sylvatica. Climbing vetch.

ROSACEÆ.
Prunus communis. Blackthorn.
P. padus. Bird cherry.
Spiræa ulmaria. Meadow sweet.
Alchemilla vulgaris. Ladies' mantle.
A. arvensis. Parsley piert.
Agrimonia eupatoria. Agrimony.
Geum urbanum. Avens.
G. rivale. Water avens.
Rubus idæus. Raspberry.
Fragaria vesca. Wood strawberry.
Poterium sanguisorba. Burnet.
Potentilla fragariastrum. Cinquefoil.
P. Tormentilla. Tormentil.
Rosa canina. Dog rose.
R. inodora. Slightly-scented sweetbriar.
Pyrus aucuparia. Mountain ash.
P. malus. Crab tree.
Cratægus oxyacantha. Hawthorn.

ONAGRACEÆ.
Epilobium angustifolium. Willow herb.
Circæa lutetiana. Enchanter's nightshade.
Hippuris vulgaris. Mare's tail.

CUCURBITACEÆ.
Bryonia dioica. Red briony.

ARALIACEÆ.
Hedera helix. Ivy.

CORNACEÆ.
Cornus sanguinea. Cornel or dogwood.

UMBELLIFERÆ.
Sanicula europæa. Sanicle.
Angelica sylvestris. Angelica.
Heracleum sphondylium. Hog weed.
Daucus carota. Wild carrot.
Conium maculatum. Hemlock.
Bunium flexuosum. Earth nut.
Æthusa cynapium. Fool's parsley.

SAXIFRAGACEÆ.
Chrysosplenium alternifolium. Golden saxifrage.

CAPRIFOLIACEÆ.
Sambucus nigra. Elder.
Viburnum lantana. Wayfaring tree.
Lonicera xylosteum. The fly honeysuckle

RUBIACEÆ.
Galium aparine. Goose grass or bed-straw.
G. erectum. Upright bed-straw.
Asperula odorata. Sweet woodruff.

VALERIANACEÆ.
Valeriana officinalis. Valerian.
V. dioica. Small marsh Valerian.

COMPOSITÆ
Chichorium intybus. Endive succory.
Apargia hispida. Hawkbit.
Tragapogon pratensis. Goat's beard.
Carduus arvensis. Thistle.
C. pratensis. Meadow thistle.
Arctium lappa. Burdock
Gnaphalium sylvaticum. Cudweed.
Erigeron acris. Fleabane.
Pyrethrum parthenium. Feverfew.
Artemisia vulgaris. Mug wort.
Anthemis arvensis. Chamomile.
Achillea ptarmica. Yarrow.
Chrysanthemum leucanthemum. Ox-eye daisy.
C. segetum. Corn marigold.

ILICACEÆ.
Ilex aquifolium. Holly.

JASMINACEÆ.
Ligustrum vulgare. Privet.
Fraxinus excelsior. Ash.

APOCYNACEÆ.
Vinca minor. Periwinkle.

A FLORA.

GENTIANACEÆ.
Chlora perfoliata. Yellow wort.
Erythræa centaurium. Centaury.

CONVOLVULACEÆ.
Cuscuta europæa. Dodder.
Convolvulus arvensis. Bindweed.

SOLANACEÆ.
Solanum dulcamara. Bitter sweet.
Atropa belladonna, used to grow abundantly about Firbeck churchyard and *Hyoscyamus niger* at Stone, both have disappeared from the locality.

SCROPHULARIACEÆ.
Euphrasia officinalis. Eyebright.
Scrophularia nodosa. Figwort.
Verbascum thapsus. Mullein.

OROBANCHACEÆ.
Lathræa squamaria. Tooth wort.

LABIATÆ.
Mentha sylvestris. Horse mint.
M. arvensis. Mint.
Thymus serpyllum. Wild thyme.
Origanum vulgare. Marjoram.
Ballota nigra. Stinking horehound.
Lamium amplexicaule. Dead nettle.
Nepeta glechoma. Ground ivy.
Symphytum officinale. Comfrey.
Cynoglossum officinale. Hound's tongue.

PRIMULACEÆ.
Anagallis arvensis. Pimpernel.
Primula vulgaris. Primrose.
P. veris. Cowslip.
P. elatior. Oxlip.

PLANTAGINACEÆ.
Plantago media. Plantain.
P. lanceolata. Ribbed plantain.

POLYGONACEÆ.
Rumex pratensis. Meadow dock.
R. acetosella. Sorrel.
Polygonum bistorta. Bistort.
P. persicaria. Spotted persicaria.

THYMELACEÆ.
Daphne laureola. Wood laurel.

EUPHORBIACEÆ.
Euphorbia exigua. Spurge.
Mercurialis perennis. Dog mercury.

URTICACEÆ.
Humulus lupulus. Hop.
Urtica urens. Nettle.
U. dioica. Great nettle.

ULMCAEÆ.
Ulmus montana. Witch elm.
U. suberosa. Common elm.

AMENTIFERÆ.
Alnus glutinosa. Alder.
Betula alba. Birch.
Carpinus betulus. Hornbeam.
Quercus robur. Oak.
Fagus sylvatica. Beech.
Corylus avellana. Hazel.
Populus nigra. Black poplar.
P. tremula. Aspen.

CONIFERÆ.
Pinus sylvestris. Fir.
Taxus baccata. Yew.

TAMACEÆ.
Tamus communis. Black bryony.

HYDROCHARIDACEÆ.
Anacharis alsinastrum. Water thyme. This plant first appeared in the waters at Roche, about 1865; we noticed it in several places growing with great freedom, about half-a-century ago, and then it disappeared as mysteriously as it came.

TRILLIACEÆ.
Paris quadrifolia. Herb paris.

ORCHIDACEÆ.
Orchis pyramidalis. Tall orchis.
O. maculata. Spotted orchis.
Spiranthes autumnalis. Lady's tresses, on the old quarry spoil banks, opposite the farm house, from the high road down to the Abbey.
Neottia nidus-avis. Bird's-nest orchis.
Listera ovata. Twayblade.
Ophrys apifera. Bee orchis.
O. muscifera. Fly orchis.

AMARYLLIDACEÆ.
Narcissus pseudo-narcissus. Daffodil.

LILIACEÆ.
Convallaria majalis. Lily of the valley.

MELANTHACEÆ.
Colchicum autumnale. Colchicum.

ARACEÆ.
Arum maculatum. Wake robin.

JUNCACEÆ.
Juncus conglomeratus. Rush.
J. lamprocarpus. Rush.
Luzula pilosa. Wood rush.

CYPERACEÆ.
Carex digitata. Sedge.
C. fulva. Tawny sedge.
C. distans. Distant spiked sedge.
C. riparia. Great common sedge.

GRAMINACEÆ.
Phalaris arundinacea. Tall canary grass.
Anthoxanthum odoratum. Sweet vernal grass.
Phleum pratense. Catstail grass.
Alopecurus pratensis. Foxtail grass.
A. agrestis. Slender foxtail grass.
Agrostis canina. Bent grass.
A. vulgaris. Common bent grass.
A. alba. Fine bent grass.
Holcus lanatus. Soft grass.
H. mollis. Yorkshire fog.
Aira cæspitosa. Turfy hair grass.
A. flexuosa. Wavy hair grass.
A. præcox. Early hair grass.
Trisetum flavescens. Yellow oat grass.
Avena fatua. Wild oat.
A. pratensis. Meadow oat.
Poa annua. Annual meadow grass.
P. nemoralis. Smooth meadow grass.
P. trivialis. Rough meadow grass.
P. pratensis. Meadow grass.
Briza media. Quaking grass.
Cynosurus cristatus. Dogstail grass.
Dactylis glomerata. Cocksfoot grass.
Festuca ovina. Sheep's fescue grass.
F. sylvatica. Wood fescue grass.
F. gigantea. Tall fescue grass.
F. pratensis. Meadow fescue grass.
Bromus erectus. Upright brome grass.
B. asper. Rough brome grass.
B. sterilis. Barren brome grass.
Brachypodium sylvaticum. Wood brachypodium.
B. pinnatum. Upright brachypodium.
Triticum caninum. Dog wheat.

T. repens. Creeping dog wheat.
Hordeum sylvaticum. Wood barley.
H. pratense. Meadow barley.
Lolium perenne. Rye grass.
L. italicum. Italian rye grass.

EQUISETACEÆ.
Equisetum arvense. Horse tail.

FILICES (FERNS).
Ophioglossum vulgatum. Adder's tongue
Polypodium vulgare. Polypody.
Polystichum lobatum. Shield fern.
Lastræa filix-mas. Male fern.
Anthyrium filix fœmina. Lady fern.
Scolopendrium vulgare. Hart's tongue.
A few years back, in an old quarry, on the East side of King's Wood, this sportive fern altered from the common form of two heart-shaped lobes at the bottom of the frond, to one long lobe, full two inches, at a right angle from the mid-rib; the following year it returned to its normal form.
Asplenium trichomanes. Spleen wort.
A. adiantum-nigrum. Black spleen wort.
A. ruta-muraria. Wall rue.
Pteris aquilina. Brake.

MUSCI (MOSSES).
Anœctangium ciliatum. Hoary-branched beardless moss.
Bryum ligulatum. Thyme thread moss.
B. argenteum. Silver thread moss.
B. palustre. Marsh thread moss.
Dicranum bryoides. Lesser fork moss.
D. squarrosum. Drooping leaved fork moss.
D. scoparium. Broom fork moss.
Didymodon purpureus. Purple twin-toothed moss.
Encalypta vulgaris. Common extinguisher moss.
Diphyscium foliosum. Leafy double-bladder moss.
Funaria hygrometrica. Hygrometric cord moss.
Fontinalis antipyretica. The greater water moss.
Grimmia pulvinata. Grey cushioned grimmia.
Gymnostomum ovatum. Hairy-leaved beardless moss.

A FLORA.

Gymnostomum microstomum. Small mouthed beardless moss.
Hypnum alopecurum. Foxtail feather moss.
H. commutatum. Curled fern feather moss.
H. cupressiforme. Cypress-leaved feather moss.
H. loreum. Rambling mountain feather moss.
H. molluscum. Plumy-crested feather moss.
H. polyanthus. Many-fruited feather moss.
H. purum. Neat meadow feather moss.
H. rutabulum. Rough-stalked feather moss.
H. schreberi. Schreberian feather moss.
H. sericeum. Silky feather moss.
H. tenellum. Tender awl-leaved feather moss.
H. triquetrum. Triangular-leaved feather moss.
H. velutinum. Velvet feather moss.
Orthotrichum affine. Pale straight leaved bristle moss.
Polytrichum aloides. Aloe leaved hair moss.
P. commune. Common hair moss.
Tortula ruralis. Great hairy screw moss.
T. muralis. Wall screw moss.
T. subulata. Awl-shaped screw moss.
T. rigida. Rigid (aloe-like) screw moss.
Weissia calcarea. Calcareous Weissia.

MARCHANTIACEÆ.

Marchantia polymorpha. Common liver-wort.

JUNGERMANNIACEÆ.

Jungermannia asplenioides. Spleenwort scale moss.
Alicularia scalaris. Ladder scale moss.
Scapania nemorosa. Wood scale moss.
Madotheca platyphylla. Flat-leaved scale moss.

LICHENES.

Borrera tenella.
Callema nigrum.
Chroolepsus aureum.
Lepraria flava.
L. alba.

Lepraria viridis.
Lecidea parasemia.
L. rupestris.
L. ulmacola.
L. quernea.
L. ferrugineæ.
Lecanora albella.
L. vitellina.
Opegrapha atra.
O. scripta.
O. vulgata.
O. rufescens.
O. elegans.
Parmelia omphalodes.
P. pulverulenta.
P. olivacea.
P. parietina.
Peltidea canine.
Ramalina fraxinia.
R. fastigiata.
Scyphophorus pyxidatus.
Sphoma nigrum.
Thelotrema lepadinum.
Verrucaria epidermis.
V. cinerea.
V. gemmata.
V. nigrescens.
Variolaria faginea.
V. discoidea.

FUNGI.

Agaricus ceciliæ.
A. excelsus.
A. rachodes.
A. vaginatus.
A. melleus.
A. imbricatus.
A. nudus.
A. infundibuliformis.
A. fusipes.
A. personatus.
A. dryophilus.
A. stipitarius.
A. radicatus.
A. galopus.
A. iris.
A. mitis.
A. vulgaris stylobates.
A. speciosus.
A. mutabilis
A. fastigiatus.
A. trechisporus.
A. crustuliniformis.
A. longicaudus.

Agaricus semiorbicularis.
A. Rubi.
A. melinoides.
A. campestris.
A. arvensis.
A. cretaceus.
A. fascicularis.
A. velutinus.
A. fimiputris.
Æcidium berberidis.
Æ. compositarum.
Æ. crassum.
Æ. violæ.
Aregma bulbosum.
Bolbitius tener.
Boletus parasiticus.
B. edulis.
Bulgaria sarcoides.
Bovista nigrescens.
B. plumbea.
Clavaria amethystina.
C. rugosa.
C. umbrina.
Coprinus atramentarius.
Cortinarius callochrous.
Dothidea betulina.
D. ulmi.
Ergot. Common on the cock's foot grass.
Hirneola auricula-Judæ.
Hygrophorus distans.
H. eburneus.
Lactarius insulsus.
L. piperatus.
L. serifluus.
Lycoperdon cælatum.
L. giganteum.
Lycoperdon pyriforme.
Marasmius urens.
M. peronatus.
M. oreades.
M. insititius.
M. rotula.
M. graminum.
Morchella esculenta.
Nyctalis parasitica.
Paxillus involutus.
Peziza aurantia.
P. coccinea.
Phallus impudicus.
Polyporus lentus.
P. spumeus.
P. ulmarius.
P. vulgaris.
P. betulinus.
P. squamosus.
P. velutinus.
P. versicolor.
Rhytisma acerinum.
R. punctatum.
Russula heterophylla.
R. virescens.
R. nitida.
R. alutacea.
Sphæria berberidis.
S. bombarda.
S. confluens.
S. innumera.
S. ceuthosporoides.
S. mamæformis.
Thelephora terrestris.
T. versicolor.
Xylaria hypoxylon.

ADDENDA. 187

In addition to the Notices of Grants of the Monaſtic property of Roche given in the text, the following appear in the *"Inventories of Particulars for Grants preſerved among the Records of the late Augmentation Office,"* in Appendices to 9th and 10th Reports of the Deputy Keeper of the Public Records.

"Bellow, John, and John Broxholme, 10th June, 38 Henry VIII, Sec. 4, Requeſt to purchaſe,"—*Inter alia,*

"Farm at Staynton (York), late of the Monaſtery of Roche (York), Memorandum and Woods."—*Rep.* 9, *p.* 170.

"Brokyleſye, Robert, and John Dyon, 28th May, 36 Henry VIII. No requeſt." —*Inter alia,*

"Valuation of Farms in Wynterton (Lincoln), late of the Monaſtery of Rupe *alias* Roche (York). Memorandum, ſummary, and particulars of ſale of this "— *Ibid. p.* 177.

"Broxholme, John, and John Bellow, 30th September, 37 Henry VIII. Requeſt to purchaſe,"—*Inter alia multa,*

"Farm in the city of Lincoln, late of the Monaſtery of Roche (York)."—*Ibid. p.* 182.

"Butler, William, and others (No date), Henry VIII. No requeſt."—*Inter alia,*

"Woods pertaining to the Manor of Roxbye (Lincoln), late of the Monaſtery of Roche."

"Woods pertaining to Bramclyffe Graunge (York), late of the Monaſtery of Roche." *Ibid. p.* 183.

"Girlyington, Nicholas, 12th March, 35 Henry VIII. No requeſt."

"Farms in Roxby (Lincoln), late of the Monaſtery of Roche *alias* Rupe (York), and Woods."—*Ibid. p.* 213.

"Ramſden, William, of York, 20th February, 37 Henry VIII. Sec. 2. Requeſts to purchaſe,"—*Inter alia,*

"Farm in South Anniſton (York), late of the Monaſtery of Roche (York). Memorandum."—*Rep.* 10, *p.* 258.

"Sutton, Charles and John, 12th and 24th February, 36 Henry VIII.—*Inter alia,*

"Woods belonging to a Farm called Scotney, in Roxbye (Lincoln), late of the Monaſtery of Roche (York)."—*Ibid. p.* 281.

"Welbore, Michael, 13th December: Clyfford, George, 12th February, 36 Henry VIII. Requeſts to purchaſe"—*Inter alia,*

"Farms in Scawſby, Smeton, and Camſall (York), late of the Monaſtery of Roche (York). [The pen has been drawn through the Smeton entry.]"—*Ibid. p.* 296.

Page 159.   **Charter of Abbot Walter.**

This charter is ſtrangely included among thoſe of Kirkſtall Abbey, with which it has no connexion, in the *Monaſticon Anglicanum,* Edit. Caley, Ellis, and Bandinel.

May not the Wineley there mentioned be a contracted form of Wellingley? The Fitz-Paynes, lords of this latter place, were certainly cloſely allied to the family of Tinſley. They appear alſo under the name of De Hotens, from Hoton Roberts, where they held half a knight's fee of the crown: Henry de Tenneſlowe holding the other moiety.—*See Kirby's Inqueſt.*

Sir Henry de Tinfley, married Lucy, daughter of Sir Robert de Hoton Roberts.—*Hunter's South Yorkshire, p.* 399.

Page 169, 8th line from top.

It has been suggested that the hospitium, or guesthouse of the Abbey, was contained in this gatehouse, which seems to have been the case at Workfop, and in some other examples, but this opinion is open to considerable doubt here, for, in the first place in these Cistercian Abbeys, the hospitium generally formed a separate building of considerable magnitude, as at Fountains and Kirkstall, in the former of which there seem to have been two; and secondly, the arrangement here, on the ground floor at least, differs from the case of Workfop, inasmuch as the side compartments are not separated from the gateway, as they are in that instance where they form distinct apartments or offices, as would be required for a guesthouse. Here all is open, as if made for the shelter of a considerable concourse of people while waiting for some purpose; this would be likely to be the case with those who were expecting the distribution of the monastic alms. We may therefore, perhaps, with more probability, conjecture that the gatehouse at Roche formed the almonry, as well as the porter's lodge, of the Abbey.

That the gate was the usual place for the distribution of alms, both in monastic and private establishments is shewn by the following passage from a curious old poem much quoted in "*Parker's* Domestic Architecture of England," speaking of the *aumonere* or *elemosinarius*, it is said:—

> "All the broken mets he kepys y watz.
> To dole to pore men at ye gate."
>
> MS. Sloane, No. 1986 f. 43.

Page 172, 11th line from top, after the word "lockyer," add

Or it may be a credence, from "Credenza," *(Ital.)* a cupboard or shelf, on which the elements and sacred vessels were placed, before consecration. This, if not a separate table, was frequently formed of a shelf in the niche or ferestella, over the piscina. The arrangement found here is very unusual, though the same thing exists at Kirkstall under a round-headed arch.

Page 173, 5th line from bottom.

"About the last quarter of the 12th century:" thus the passage was originally written, but was altered as it stands in the text, in deference to the opinion of a very experienced and judicious Antiquarian.

ERRATA.

Page xvii, 14th line from top "Anflem" should be "Anfelm."
Page 4, 3rd line from bottom "Aorman" should be "Norman."
Page 22, last line of note "Pantage" should be "Pontage."
Page 114, 16th line from bottom "1355" should be "1535."
Page 156, 9th line from top "Lincolnshire" should be "Nottinghamshire."
Page 159, 7th line from bottom insert "the" before learned.
Page 174, 4th line from bottom "forman" should be "formam."

Index.

INDEX.

A

Aaron the Jew at York	155
Abbey of Sancta Maria de Rupe	xx
A B C, by William Thorpe	67
Abdy	99, 108
Aberdeen	42
Abingdon	55 (n)
Abbots of Roche, lift of	2
Abbot's Houfe	153
Abbot and Convent of Roche	155
———— Robert, of Whitby	7
———— of Newminfter, Letter from	60, 62
———— of Fountains Abbey	6
———— of Peterborough	171 (n)
———— Alexander, of Kirkftall	9
———— of Kirkftead	81, 151
———— of Newminfter	60
———— of Roche, Afton John de	55
"Abbreviatio Rotulorum Originalium"	110 (n)
Abftract of the Acquittance of the Jews	155
Act for the Diffolution of Smaller Monafteries	74
Acton in Suffolk, legend at	26
Acworth, Thomas	86
Acuto, Adam de Monte	141
Adam de Gigglefwick	50
Adam, fon of Ralph de Armthorpe	100
Addenda	181
Advowfon	126
Aggecroft	15, 17, 99
Agnes, daughter of Robert de Brunnington	100
Agreement between Abbot and Convent of Roche, Thomas Rillington, and others	114
Alan, the parfon of Maltby	120
———, Abbot of Roche	34
Albus, William	108
Alexander the IV., Pope, Bull of	31, 110
Almonbury	151
Algret	106
Alice, Countefs of Eu	17
Alteration in Cuftody of Seals of Religious Orders	45
Alverley	99, 120, 142
Alz, William de	10
Amabill de Brampton	109
Andrew, Saint	83
Anes	15, 21
Anne, John	149
Anne, William de	48
Annifton, South	187
Anfton	21, 120, 141
Anfelm	xvii
Antonie, John	71
Archbifhop of York	24, 25, 36, 37, 40, 43, 49, 54, 55, 58, 60, 62, 64, 66, 79, 114
Architecture, The	xvii, 163
Arcy, Henry de	111
Armthorpe, Henry de	100
————, John de	155
————, Ralph de	100
————, Thomas de	15, 100
16, 21, 28, 34, 35, 89, 100, 101, 125	
Arnaldus	4 (n)
Arncliffe	101
Arnethorpe	100
————, Thomas de	100
Arneldthorpe	100
Arnewy, Henry	157
Afhenbeech	101
Afheton, Arthur	134
Afhover	15, 16, 21, 101
Aske, Robert, at infurrections	78-80
———— executed at York	81
Askern	21, 101, 144
————, Maurice de	101
Atheling, Edgar	xvii
Afton	100
Aexoure	21, 101
Avenell, William	15
Avenal, William, Lord of Haddon	123
Averpenning	22 (n)
Augmentations, Court of	134
Augi, Countefs of	xx
———— Henry, Earl of	xxii

B

Bacon, William	121
Bagfhawe, W. H. G.	153
Balne	101
Banke	131
Bankewell, Simon de	54
Banks, James	89
Bauuent, Ralph de	152
Barbot, William	10
————, Richard	5
Bardolf, Hamelin	15
Bardolph, Hamelin	160
————, Katherine	160
————, Hugh	160
————, Ralph	160
Baret, Richard	10, 145
Bargo, Hugh de	23
Barker, Bobert	122
Barlings, Abbot of	81
Barnby	15, 16, 21, 32, 89, (n) 101, 102, 104
————, Benedict, Rector of	101
————, Richard de, William, fon of	147
Barneby, Gervafe de	5, 15, 32, 101, 104
————, Richard de	32, 102

Barneby, Hugh de	.	32
———, Alexander de	.	32
———, Thomas de	.	32
Barnoldſwick	.	103
Barnoldſwic	.	174 (*n*)
Bartlett, Cromwell's ſervant	.	70
Barton, Great	.	27
Barry, Richard	.	55, 126
Barvile, William de	.	103
Baſſett, William	.	123
Battle of Bannockburn	.	48
——— Boroughbridge	.	48
Bawtry	.	12, 21, 103
———, Richard de	.	106
Bayonne	.	37
Becket, Thomas à	.	9, 83
Beggam in Suſſex	.	68
Beke, John	.	151
Bella Aqua, Thos. de	..	160
Bell, Adam	.	93
Bellewe, John	.	123
Bellew, Thomas de	.	122
Bellſtring Lands	.	104
Bellow, John	.	187
Benedict, Saint	.	37
Benedictines	.	167 (*n*)
Benedictine Nuns	.	158
Beatrix, ſiſter of Roger de Buſli	.	xx
Bently, Lord of	.	xxiii
Bereus, Robert of	.	12
Beresford, Edward	.	122
Bergh, Roger de	.	122
Bernard, Saint	.	xviii
Bernehill	.	21
Berwick-on-Tweed	.	47
Bere, John	.	121
Betham	.	177
Bigod, Sir Francis	.	80
Bilham	.	103, 121, 126
———, Hugh de	.	126, 155
Bildewas, Abbot of	.	133
Bircheworth	.	117
Biſham Abbey	.	91 (*n*)
" Black Book " of the Monaſteries	.	74
Blackſtondelf	.	134
Bladeſworth, William de	.	104
Blakehills	.	26
Blitheſhaw	.	103, 149
Blodwith	.	22 (*n*)
Bloxolme, John	.	122
Blund, Richard le	.	144
Blythe	.	11, 12, 21, 87, (*n*) 103, 118, 141, 144, 153, xx
Blythe, Caſtle of	.	xx
——— Priory, Regiſter of	..	103
———, Prior of	.	103
Bodleian Library	.	87 (*n*)
Bohler, Mr. J.	.	vi
Bolgate	.	11
Boniface VIII, Pope	..	40, 133
Booth, Laurence	.	63
Botildewellewang	.	104, 151, 152
Bowes, Sir Robert	.	80
Boxley Abbey	.	83
Boyvill, Sir R. de	.	140
Braithwell	.	21, 104
———, Artrop de	.	104
Braiton	.	151
Bramclyffe	.	187
Bramley	.	16, 21, 104, 115
Brampton, Robert de	.	109
———, Michael de	.	109
Bramwith	.	15, 16, 21, 102, 104, 105
———, Nicholas de	.	32
Brancliffe	.	15, 16, 28, 34, 35, 100, 105, 125
Brathmere, Fiſhery of	.	114
———, ſee Hatfield	.	106
Brettvile, Robert de	.	108
Bridlington	.	105
———, Prior of	.	81
Brindſworth	.	147
Brinton, Robert	.	122
Britiſh Muſeum	.	82
Brochard, Girard	.	23
Brokyleſye, Robert	.	187
Brookhouſe	.	105
Broom Riddings	.	105
Brother Thomas	.	102 (*n*)
Brown, Mr.	.	164, 165, 172
———, Ralph	.	139
Broxholme, John	.	187
Bruce, Robert	.	46, 47, 48, 49
Bruerton, Robert	.	159
Brumpton, William de	.	137
Brunington, Robert de	.	100
Bruntat, John (?)	.	109
———, Eudo de	.	109
Bug, Thomas de	.	140
Bugthorpe	.	106
Bugthorpe, Hamel de	.	146
———, Nicholas de	.	106
Building of Roche Abbey	.	6
Bull of Pope Urban IV.	.	30
———, Alexander IV.	.	31
Burgh, Thomas Lord	.	139
Burgundy, Duke of	.	xviii
Burnet, Biſhop	.	72, 79, (*n*) 81, (*n*) 84
Burnell Family	.	126
———, William	.	130
Burton, Dr.	.	v, 15, (*n*) 36, 50, 56, 61, 110, 111, 144, 146
———, Richard	.	120
———, Robert	.	146, 154
———, William	.	65
Burton's "Anatomy of Melancholy"	.	82 (*n*)
Bury, Sir Thomas de	..	140
——— St. Edmunds	.	27, 40
Buſli, Ernaldus	.	xx, xxii
———, Idonea de	.	140
———, John de	.	xxii, 11, 12, 125
———, Jordan de	.	xxii
———, Richard de	xxi, xxii, 4, 5, 6, 9, 11, 15, 94, 110, 119, 120, 125, 126, 172 (*n*)
———, Robert de	.	10
———, Roger de	.	xx, xxi, xxii
Buteiler, William le	.	5
Butler, William	.	105, 187
Byland Abbey	.	45
Bylton, Geoffery	.	154
Bynd, of Eels defined	.	114 (*n*)

C

Callinglow	.	106
Calverlay, Sir W.	.	159 (*n*)
Cambridge, Counteſs of	.	58, 83, 127, 171
Cambridge, Earl of	.	xxiii
Campſall, Mr. W. H.	.	vi
Campſall	.	106, 126, 144
Canby, Mr.	.	94
Canterbury	.	47, 107, 158
Carliſle	.	44, 46
Carlton	.	106, 107
Carucages	.	21
Carr	.	107
Carter, William	.	86, 88
Carver	.	154

INDEX.

Carzon, Robert . . 32
Caſtage . . . 22
Caſtello, Gena de . 109
Caſtleſhaw . . 107
Catwick . . . 107
Cawood . . . 54
Cauz, Alfred le . 23
Cellarer of Fountains Abbey . 14
Chalons, Biſhop of . xviii
Chalons-ſur-Saone . xvii
Chaucer . . 50
Chaucomb, Warine de . 136
Chaucumbe, John de . 139
Chapel, Alan Fitz . 34
———, Henry de . 23
Chapter Houſe . . 86, 89 (n)
Charter Houſe . . 90 (n)
——— of Richard de Buſli . 4
——— of Richard Fitz Turgis . 5
——— of William, Earl of Warren . 28, 108
——— of John de Warren, Earl of Surrey . 51
——— of William de Roffington . 108
——— of Amabill de Brampton . 109
——— of William de Chaworth . 111
——— of Henry de Shelley . 117
——— of John Levet . 126
——— of Walter, Abbot of Roche . 122
——— of Adam Fitz Burnell . 125
——— of Warinus de Scargill . 131
——— of Philip Paynel . 138
——— of Idonea de Vipont . 140
——— of Abbot Richard and Robert de Ripers . 142
——— of Ralph de Rainville . 148
——— of Hugh, son of Hugh Laſcy . 148
——— of Edmund de Lacy . 151
——— of Maud de Lovetot . 152
——— of Matilda de Moles . 153
——— of Walter Abbot, and the Convent of Roche . 159
Chaworth, Henry de . 111
———, John de . 111
———, William de . 111, 145
Chatſworth . . 107, 145
Cheſter . . 144, 151
Chetham, Chriſtopher and Ralph . 134
Chriſt's Church College, Oxford . 68
Church, The . . 169
——— of St. George, Doncaſter . 109
Ciſteaux . . xvii, xviii, 47, 49
Ciſtercian Devotions . xix
Civita Vecchia . 31
Clayton, David . 131, 141, 144
Clifford, Henry, Earl of . 83
———, Robert de . xxii
———, Lord Roger . xxii
———, Lord Thomas . xxiii, 59, 83
——— Inquiſitions . 126
Clifton, Alan de . 142
Clinton, Lord . 122
———, Lord Admiral . 117
Clipſtone . . 103, 149, 152
Clyfford, George . 187
Cobcroft, Sir Robert . 91
Coc, Reginald . 108
Cokewald, Henry de . 139
Cole MS. . . 93
Coleton, William de . 139
Collys, Nicholas . 86, 88
Colmanhaghe . 158
Common Seals . 46, 118
Compendium of Diſcoveries at Roche, by Drs. Legh and Layton . 82
Coningsbrough, King of . 109

Coninſborough . xxiii, 15, 21, 34, 58, 104, 107
———, Lord of . xx
——— Caſtle . xx
Conference between Royal Army and Rebels at Ferribridge . 79
Confirmation of Counteſs of Eu . 17
——— of King Henry III. . 20
——— of King Richard I. . 16
——— of Pope Urban III. . 14, 151
——— of King Edward II., of lands in Walkeringham . 156
Corngilds . . 21
Cornwall, Duchy of . 149
Cotes, Allandel . 114
———, John . . 114
Council at St. Paul's, London . 45
Counhal, William de . 34
Counties . . 21
Courcy, Richard de . 135
Couſen, Joane . 122
Coventry . . 48, 82
Craſſis, Alexander . 153
Cramcumb, Godfrey de . 23
Craven, Hiſtory of . 7
Creſſi, William de . 18
Cromwell, Thomas 70, 71, 74, 78, 79, 80, 91, 92 (n)
Croxton, Sir John de . 140
Croyland Abbey . 6
Croyton, John de . 140
Crumbewell, John de . xxi, xxii
Cudworth . . 108
Cumberland, Earl of . 82, 83, 127, 129, 130
Cumberworth . 108
Cundal, Henry, Abbot of Roche 67, 72, 84, 86, 87, 88, 94
Cundall, Thomas . 86

D

Dadeſley . . xx
Danegilds . . 21
Darcy, Lord . . 79
Darell, Geoffery . 154
Darley, Henry de . 144
Deepcar . . 108
De la Roche . 125
De Rupe . . 125
De Hotens . . 187
Denſhaw . . 108
Derby . . 84, 99, 123
Deſcription of a Monaſtery . 69
——— Monk . 69
Dionyſius, Abbot of Roche . 9, 10
Diſcontent in the Roman Catholic Church in the time of Henry III. . 24
Diſſolution, The . 67
Docelin, Maſter, the Chancellor . 23
Doddeſworth, John . 82, 86, 87, 88
Doddington, Grantee . 149
Dodfworth 103, 104, 111 (n), 125 (n), 138 (n), 148 (n)
Domeſday Book . 12
——— Survey . xx, xxii
Doncaſter xx, xxiii, 21, 79, 80, 81, 83, 108, 109, 146
———, Deanery of . 94 (n)
Doncaſtre, John de . 132
Dover . . 47
——— burnt by the French . 39
Draft of an Act of Parliament after the Suppreſſion . 95
Drax, Richard . 86
———, Prior of . 135, 136, 139
———, Priory of . 136
Drengeſflete . 157

Drigwrt, Hugh de	15, 119
Dr. Layton's Letter to Thomas Cromwell	70
Drs. Legh and Layton and the Act of Suppreffion	77
Dromore, Bifhop of	61, 64, 65
Dugdale	xxi
Duningeton, William de	10
Duncroft	31, 110
Durandus	3, 4, 6, 8, 9, 37, 165
Durham	60
Dyon, John	187

E

Eaftwood, Rev. J.	vi, 91 (n)
Ecclesfield	91 (n), 108
Eccleshall, Ralph de	108
Ecclefal, Ralph de	152
Edinsor, Adam de	107
Edmund, brother of King Edward	38, 41, 43
———, Earl of Cornwall	43
———, Saint	82
Edward I. King of England	38, 39, 40, 41, 42, 100, 106, 125
——— II. "	46, 48, 100, 118, 152
——— III.. " Royal Charter of	112
——— III. "	xxiii, 127, 152
——— VI. "	146, 149
———, Prince	32, 33
Edwin, Earl	xx
Effarts	22
Eglifton Abbey	45
Ellrichethorpe	4, 5, 9, 10, 110
Ellercar, Sir Ralph	80
Ellis, Sir Henry	91 (n), 92 (n)
Ellys, William	149, 159
———, Hugh	149, 150
———, James	150
Elmifhall	125
Elizabeth, Queen of England	xxii
Elfi	xxi, 5
Elmfall	126
Ennufe	110
Engleis, Hugh le	12
Erdefale, Nicholas, fon of Jeffery de	144
Errata	188
Efpeke, Walter	xviii
Efton, John de	121
Eu, Countefs of	xx, xxii, 17, 99, 120, 125, 174
Eudo, Robert, Fitz	15
———, William, fon of	145
———, Robert, fon of	160
Everfham	33
Ewes or Ehus	110
———, John, fon of Gilbert de	141
Exeter, Thomas, Duke of	59 (n)
Execution of the Abbot of Barlings, at Lincoln	81
————————————Fountains, at Tyburn	81
"Excerpta é Rot. Fin."	xxii (n)

F

Fac-fimiles of the fignatures of the monks of Roche at the diffolution	86
Fairwath	16, 21
Farworth	110, 112
Fenwick	146
Ferribridge	79
Ferrars, Earl of	123
Fefh, Triftram	149
Feyrford, Matilda de	112
"Fines, Ebor."	145 (n), 147 (n)
Firbeck	104, 111
Fishlake	28, 111
Fitzwilliam, John, Lord	127
———, Thomas	121
Fitz-Payne, Robert	159
———, Sir Jordan	145, 146, 159
Fitz-John, Richard	xxii
Fitz-Turgis, Richard	xxiii
Flanders	47
Fleming, William the	119
Flemenfrith	22
Flixburgh	111, 135, 139
Flomenwith	22
Flora of Roche	181
Florence	26
Foffard's	12
Foljambe, George Savile	46
Fogfwell	5
Ford Hall	153
Forftal	22
Foffard, Nigel de	xxii
Fountains Abbey 6, 7, 14, 50, 92 (n), 166, 167, 168, 171, 172, 174 (n), 177	
———, Abbot of	81, 88 (n)
Foundation Charter of Richard de Bufli	4, 9
——————————of Richard Fitz-Turgis	5
——————————of John de Bufli	11
Franc-pledge	22
France	50
Freeman, John	91 (n)
Fretwell, Roger	104
Froude, quoted	78, 79
Frankland	131
Frithefend	157
Friar Mere	132
Fulham, Geoffery de	158
Fuller, Hugh	130
Furnival, Richard	160
———, Gerard de	19, 23, 152
Furneys, Richard de	107
Fyfhburn, Richard	86, 88

G

Gamul	4
Gamel, Filius Befingi	5
Garth, William	127
Gafcony	47
Gatehoufe, The	175
Gaunt, Robert de	135
Gavefton Piers	46
Gebod, Robert, fon of	111
Gerard, William Fitz	15, 142
Gerbode, William, fon of	104
George, fon of Lord Lumley	80
Gerwedon, Abbey	45
Gifford, John	149
Gigglefwick, Adam de	50
———, its well	50
Gilbert, the Chaplain	117
Gildingwells	111
Gilds	21
Gillott, Henry	150
Gilpin, Mr.	164, 165
Girlyington, Nicholas	187
Glaf, Robert, fon of	107
Gloucefter, the Earl of	26
Goderic-Riding	111
Gofeker	105
Grafton	74
Grandimont Order, Peter of the	xviii (n)
Grangefield	154
Grant, Royal	134
Gray John, Abbot of Roche	60
Greasborough	121

INDEX.

Green, Grantee	154
———, John	102
———, Thomas	89, 150
Grendon, Henry de	127
Grimbald, John	148
Guienne, Duke of	38
———, war in	39
Gunhale	100
Gunnora	xxiii
Guvry, Reginald	120
Gwarine, Abbot of Pontiniac	9

H

Haddon	123
Haimſoken	22
Haket, Ralph	122
Haloghby, Henry de	127
Hall, Grantee	154
Halyhton, Adam of	105
Hampol	125
Harleian MS.	165 (n)
Hartington, H.	123
Harold, Earl	xx, xxiii
Harworth	110, 112
———, Gamellus de	112
Haſtings, Brian	146
Hatfield	xxiii, 101, 110, 112, 150
———Park and Woods	114
Haugh	108, 115, 117
Haytſeld, Church of	113, 114, 144, 145
Heathcote	123
Heden, Gerard de	144
———, Simon de	144
Helgheby, Galfrid de	159
Helias, Abbot of Kirkſtall	18
Hellaby	115
Henfrew, Hugh	153
———, Janet	153
Hengwith	22
Henry I., King of England	xvii
——— II.	120
——— III., King of England	xxii (n), 100, 101
	105, 106, 110, 125, 139, 146, 147, 156
	158, 159, 160, 177
———Summons of	32
——— V.	xxiii
——— VI.	120
——— VIII.	70, 101, 102, 105, 110 (n), 122, 123
	128, 130, 131, 134, 146, 149, 152, 158
———, Abbot of Newminſter	18
———, Prior of Roche	7
Helpol	158
Herthwic, Robert de	105
Herſy, Baldwin de	108
———, Malveiſin de	108
Heſlington, John, Abbot of Roche	67
Heſley	115
Heſtwell	116
Hewett	131
Hewet, Robert	119
———, Agnes	119
Heyden, Richard de	34
Heyr, Walter de	152
Hidage	21
Higgins, Godfrey	145
Hillbrigthorpe	116, 125, 132, 133, 134
"Hiſtory of the Manor of Todwick"	94
Hitchcock, Robert de	146
Hoderode, Sir John de	151
Holme	116, 148
Holmes, Thomas, Grantee	149
——— Carr Wood	116

Holtheng	110
Holy Trinity, Prior of	136
Hooton	xxii, 116, 127
———, Slade	116, 144
———, Levet	116, 126, 127, 144
———, Jordan	116
———, Roger	116
———, Allen de	105
———, Barony of	147
——— Roberts	116, 118, 144, 187
———, Sir Robert de	188
Hope	116
Horbiry, Richard de	140
———, Ralph de	122
Hoſpital of St. John of Jeruſalem	113
Holtal, Adam de and Donyſia his Wife	153
Hoxebrigge	148
Hugh, the Clerk of Rotherham	10
"Hundred Rolls"	106, 120, 146 (n), 147 (n), 153
Hundeſdon, Lord	104
Hunt	131
Hunter, Mr.	xxiii (n), 104, 110 (n), 144, 145, 147
	188

I

Ichells	117
Ickles	117, 118
Idle, River	134
Idonea, Widow of Robert de Vipont	xxi
Ikkyls	147
Images burnt at Smithfield	83
Image of the Crucifix on a Rock at Roche	82
Index	191
Infangtheſ	22
Ingbirchworth	117
Ingleby, William	154
Injunctions given by the Commiſſioners on leaving Monaſteries	73
Innesby	117
Inſpections	22
Inſula, William de	105
———, Jordan de	116
Introduction	xvii
Inventory of Roche Abbey	88
Iſabel	xxi

J

Jackſon, Mr. Charles	vi
———, Charles	104, 120
———, Grantee	149
Jeffcock, Rev. J. T., F.S.A.	vi
Jeffry and Watt	93
Jeremiah, parſon of Roſſington	100, 126
Jervaulx, Abbot of	81
Jeroval Abbey	45
Jews at York	13, 155
John, King of England	101, 105, 106, 135, 136
	147, 153
———, the Foreſter	34
———, Abbot of Roche	42, 43
———, ſon of Phillip	23
Johnſton MSS.	147
Jordan, ſon of Phillip de Marr	121

K

Karleol, W.	23
Keeper, John	89
Ker, John	117
Ketelbergh, Reginald de	109, 155
Kilnhurſt	118
———, Roger de	118

Kilnhurſt, Thomas de	118
Kimberworth	xxi
"Kirby's Inqueſt"	100, 121, 187
Kirkburton, Hiſtory of	108 (n), 117 (n), 150 (n)
Kirkſtall	18, 19, 103, 166, 167, 168, 169, 170, 171, 172, 174 (n), 177, 187, 188
Kirkſtead	xxi, 177
Kiveton	103, 118
Knight's fee, defined	100
Knot Hill	132
Knott, legend of	26
Kyrkeby, John de	137
Kyveton, John de	103, 118

L

Laci, Henry de, Lord of Pontefraƈt	9
Lacy, Roger	18
——, Robert	148
——, Edmund de	144, 151
——, Henry de	116, 174
——, John de	151
——, Margaret de	151
——, Alice de	151
Lambcote	15, 16, 119, 145
Lambcroft	15, 119
Lancaſter	99
——, Thomas, Earl of	48
——, Duchy of	149
Landſdown MSS.	82
Langdon Abbey	70
Langley, Edmund de	xxiii, 52
Langthwaite, Hugh de	5, 109, 126
——, Richard de	121
Laſci, Thomas de	148
Laſcy, Hugh	148
Laughton	18, 43, 48, 105, 111, 120, 147
——, Lord of	xx
Layton, Dr.	70, 71, 72, 80, 81, 82, 83, 91 (n)
Lee, Sir Richard	158
Leek, John	106
Legend of Aƈton	26
—————— Roche	25
Legh, Dr.	70, 71, 72, 77, 80, 81, 82, 83
Leiceſter	153
Leirwith	22
Leming, Adam	155
Leon	109
Letter from the Abbot of Newminſter	60, 62
——— on the ſuppreſſion of Roche Abbey	89
Letewell, Peter de	155, 159
Levet	xxii
——, John	55, 126
——, Richard	116
——, William de	xxiii, 126, 127
——, Hammond de	116
——, Conſtantia	126
Lewes	28, 32, 52, 92 (n), 112
——, Monks of	147
Leweſtye, John	154
Leybun, Roger de	xxii
Librate	107
Lichfield	123
———, Biſhopric of	82
———, Mr. William de	151
Ligulf	16
Lincolnſhire	xxi, 91 (n), 111, 134, 135, 159, 160
———, Biſhop of	136
Lindric	43, 44, 84, 99, 120
	15, 17, 21, 120
Lindrick, William de	152
———, near Tickhill	120
———, Brook	120
Lindrick Common	120
————— Dale	120
Lindſey, Robert de	171 (n)
Liſt of Abbots	2
——— Subſcribers	viii
L'Iſle, Jordan de, Jordan ſon of	148
Liſa	177
Littel, Thomas de	117
Littlemorye	145
London	33, 40, 41, 42, 46, 102
Longſword, William	12
London, Dr.	90, 92
Louth Park	77, 171, 177
Louweder, Richard de	144
Loverſal	99, 120, 142
Lovetot, Maud de	152
Lowthwaite	4
Lucius, Pope	14
Ludham, Euſtachius de	106
Lumby	100, 120
Lumley, Lord, eldeſt ſon of	80
Luterel, Andrew	137, 147
—————, Galfred, and Frethefant Wife of	147
—————, Robert	147
Lyvet, James de	122
——, Richard	122

M

Magilldhylls	145
Maidſtone	83
Malcolm III.	xvii
Maltby	xxi, xxii, 4, 7, 11, 21, 120
—— Mill	116
——, Lord of	xxiii
Malgerio, Maſter	23
"Mancheſter Guardian"	134
Mandate from King Edward II.	48
Manſelyn of Doncaſter	116
———— of Brodfworth	116
Manvers, Leo de	15, 100, 105
Mapes, Walter	54
Maſter of the Rolls	167 (n)
Matilda of York	58, 59
Margens, Thomas	114
Mariſco, Henry de	100
Mar	21, 121
——, Roger de	15
——, Jordan de	148
——, Payn de	121, 148
Marr, Roger de	122
——, The Grange of	121
Marſh, Henry de	109
Mary, Queen of England	82
Maſon, William	104
Maude, daughter of Thomas, Lord Clifford	xxiii
Mauger, ſon of Roger de Stokes	115
Maumirr, Henry	157
Mawoners, Michael de	152
Medyltun, Thomas	86, 88
Meleton, William de	127
Melroſe, Chronicle of	18 (n)
Melſoe or Meux	177
Melton, William de	47, 49
Memers, Richard de	108
Merlay, Ranulph de	6
Merſſh, Robert de	127
Meteham, Thomas de	127
Michael, ſon of Leo de Manvers	100
Micklebring	121
———, Eugenia	121
Middleton	123
Mileri, William de	5

INDEX.

Misterton, Robert de . . 144
———, Walter de . . 158
———, Robert, parson of . 152
Mitchell, Mr. . . . 46, 159
Moles, Matilda de . . 141, 153
———, Hugh de . 141, 142, 144, 153
———, William de . . 15, 142
Molesme, Robert de . . xviii
"Monasticon Anglicanum" 110, 122, 150, 151, 159
166, 167, 174 (n), 187
" ——— Eboracense" . v, 36, 146
Monastery, description of . . 69
——— de Rupe . . 152, 153
Monkeboye . . . 157
Monkebothe . . . 158
Monk Bretton . . . 121
———, description of . . 69
Monks Bridge . . . 105
——— of Pipewell . . 7
——— of Salley . . . 7
——— of the Rock . 4, 7, 18, 125
Monby, Sir J. de . . 140
Monteby, John de . . 140
Montfort, Simon de . . 32, 33
Montforth, John . . . 118
Monyash . . . 121
Morton, Robert, Earl of . xx, xxii
Mores, Edward Rowe, Esq. . 110
More, Richard . . . 146
Morsurlung . . . 158
Morley . . . 121, 122
Mortimer . . . 33
Mortmain Act . . . 35
Morpeth, John, Abbot of Roche . 66
. . . 7
Morehouse . . 108 (n), 117 (n), 150
Moslay, Richard . . . 86, 88
Mowbray, John de . . 48
Moyle, Mr. . . . 130
Multhorpe, John . . 127
Munkegate, Peter de . . 29

N

Newhum . . . 16
Newhall . . . 21, 122
Newland . . . 122
Newerth . . . 115
Newminster Abbey . 7, 18, 66, 164, 177
———, John, Abbot of . . 60
———, Robert, Abbot of . 7
Newmarch, Adam de . 5, 6, 15, 122
Newmarches . . . xxiii
Newcombe, John . . . 154
Newsome . . . 15, 122
New Visitation of Religious Houses ordered 81
Neuflet . . . 114
Nevil, Geo. Reg. . . . 59 (n)
Nicholas, clerk of Laughton . 120
———, parson of Tickhill . 12
Norfolk, Duke of . . 79, 80, 81
Northumbland, Duke of . . 101
Northampton . . . 46
North, Edward . . . 130
Normandy, Robert, Duke of . xvii
Norwich, Galfrid de . . 29
Normanville, Ralph de . 122, 155
Norwicen, Thomas . . 155
Nostel, the Prior of . . 121
"Notes and Queries" . . 27 (n)
Notte, William . . . 146
"Nottinghamshire, History of" . xxii
. . xx, 106, 123, 146, 158

Nottingham xx, 41, 84, 103, 115, 122, 141, 156
———, County of . . 154
———, Sir Robert de . . 151

O

Oblations, Alms, &c. . . 160
Odenell, son of Nicholas D'Aubeney . 105
Odo, Filius Johannis . . 5
Oldcotes . . . 16, 21, 123
———, Philip de . . . 122
Oneash or Anes . 15, 21, 99, 106, 121, 123, 145
Ormesby, William de . . 41
Orm . . . 16
Osbertus, Sir . . . 151
Osberton, Roger de . . 157
Osmund, Abbot of Roche 13, 14, 16, 17, 18, 19, 20
25, 101, 105, 120, 147, 153, 174
Outfangthef . . . 22
Oxford . . . 68
———, Earl of . . . 79
Oxgang . . . 99, 107

P

Painell, William . . . 135
———, Hugh . . . 137
———, Jordan . . . 5
Parcel of the Possessions of the Monastery
of Roche . . . 128
Paris, Matthew . . 12, 25, 26 (n)
Parker's Domestic Architecture of England 188
Parks, John Del . . . 114
Pannage or Pawnage . . 22
Particulars for Grants 101, 102, 104, 106, 117, 120
122, 128, 130, 141, 144, 146
149, 154, 156, 187
Passage . . . 22
Patent Rolls . . . 138, 139
Paul's Cross . . . 83
Paul, Nicholas de Saint . 99, 151, 152
———, St. Richard de . . 148
———, St. Robert de . . 29
Payne, Robert Fitz . . 12, 15
———, Geffery Fitz . . 115
Payn, Robert, son of . . 111
Paynell, Ralph . . . 135
———, John . . . 137
———, Phillip . . . 138
Paynel, Adam . . . 148
———, William . . . 147
Pension to the Abbot of Roche . 87
Penrice . . . 83
Percy, William . . . 28
Peter, John Fitz . . . 114
Petre, Doctor William . . 87
Peterborough, Abbot of . 171 (n)
Philis's Hole . . . 27
Philippa, Queen of England 52, 53, 113, 114
Philip, Abbot of Roche . 34, 35, 136
———, King of France . 38, 41
Piers Ploughman's "Vision and Creed" 55
"Pilgrimage of Grace" . . 78
Pipewell . . . 7, 177
"Placitorum Abbreviatio" . 31
Plantagenet, Richard . . 59
Pleas . . . 21
———, Roll of . . . 135
Plesley, Simon de . . 15, 101
Podensac, Governor of . . 39
Pocklington . . . 106
Pollington . . . 100
"Polyolbion" of Drayton . . 50

Pontefract	79, 117, 151
Pontiniac	9
Pontage	22
Pope, the	20, 24, 25, 33, 50, 73
———, Nicholas	123
Portman, John	92 (n)
Portsmouth	39
Possessions, the	99
Premonstranses Order	45
Prior of Blythe	141
——— of Drax, the	25
——— of York, the	25
——— of Workfop	43
Profits of Rectory of Hatfield	115
Prophetic Parable	56
Pryme, Mr. De la	94

Q

Queen Philippa's gift to Roche	53
Questions asked by the Commissioners on Visiting Monasteries	72
Quick	132

R

Radcliffe-on-Trent	103, 118
Rainville, Ralph de	148
Ralph the Priest	10
———, Bishop of Chichester	23
———, son of Nicholas	23
———, son of Robert Fitz-Payne	12
Ramsden, William	128, 131, 152, 187
Raftal, Mr.	xviii
Rawmarsh	108, 115, 118
Raveni, Willielmus Filius	5
Reference to Plates	xii
Reginald, Abbot of Roche	19, 20, 25, 105, 147, 153
——— the Bailiff	109
——— the Presbyter de Doncaster	126
——— the Tailor	109
Reins, Robert	82
Reresby, Lionel Esq.	147
Reprisals	115
Rhodes, Peter de	121
———, William de	141
Richard I., King of England	12, 16, 20, 23, 100, 141, 159, 174
——— II.,	149
———, Abbot of Roche	28, 29, 34
———, son of Hugh	23
——— the Granger	34
Richmund, Roger	23
Rice, Ap. Dr.	70, 71
Rickman	170
Rievaulx, Abbot of	81
Rillington, Thomas	114, 144
Riparus, Robert de	99, 120
Ripers, Robert de	142, 158
Risby	17, 21
Robert, Abbot of Roche	43, 44, 46, 47, 48, 56, 57
———, son of Glai	15
———, Saint	7
——— the Cellarer	29
Robin Hood	93
Robynfone, John	82, 86, 88
Roche, Adam de la	116
———, William de	122
Rochester, Bishop of	83
Rochdale	101, 108, 116, 131
Rodmerchewyet, Hugh de	106
Roger, son of Hugh Fitz Walter	100
Rokkehill	145
Roll's House	81, 96 (n), 106 (n), 125 (n)
Rome	24
Romburgh	68
"Rood of Grace"	83
Rossington	100, 115
———, Jeremiah de	109
———, Peter de	109, 116, 155
Rothwell, Robert de	139
Rothell, parfon of	117
Rotherham	29, 89, 99, 105, 117, 147
———, S de	43
Rot. Fin.	xxi (n)
Rous, Antho	149
Roxby	13, 15, 21, 89, 134, 135, 136, 137, 138, 139, 160, 187
Royal Charter	106, 118, 137
Rufford Abbey	45
Rupe, Monastery of	134
———, William de	29
Rupibus, William de	23, 29
Rumsey	xvii
Ryevall, Abbot of	133
Rygges, William	154
Rypun, Nicholas de	32
Ryvall	xviii

S

Saddleworth	134
Sake	22
Salley	177
Sally, Abbot of	7 (n)
Sandal, Thomas de	32, 126
———, Madilda	153
Sandall	21, 139
Sandbeck	xxi, 11, 33, 89, 140, 141, 172 (n)
Sandebi, William de	10
Sanderson, John	110
Saunderson, Robert	141
———, Sir Nicholas	xxii
Sarah, relict of Richard de Bawtry	106
Savile, Richard de, Ralph son of	147
Sbyson, Thomas	29
Scalzebi, Robert de	5, 6, 15, 122
———, Knight of	10
Scarborough	80
———, Earl of	vi, xxii, xxiii
Scausby, Hugh	12
Scawsby	21, 141, 144, 187
———, Adam de	109
Scelhall, Hugh de	140
Schepewykes	158
Schofelde, Lord Thomas de	132
Scoreby of Marr	16
Scoteni, Walter de	15, 135, 136
Scotage	21
Scotney	187
Scotland	47, 48, 49
Scroby	44, 60
Scrope, Philip	152
Scutage	21
Seals of the Abbey	45 46, 118
Seal of the Cell of Roche	110
Secretum of the Abbey	45, 46
Selesai, Henry of	108
Serlby	103, 141, 153
Sezacres	15, 142
Shaw, G. Esq.	132 (n)
Sheffield	87 (n)
Shelley	142, 150
———, Henry de	117
Sheldon, Thomas	123

INDEX.

Shepwick	142
Shepley, Mathew de	18, 108
Shires	21
Shirebrook, Cuthbert	89, 164
Shyttylyngton	150
Shrewsbury, Earl of	79
Sibylla	xvii
———, de Sancta Maria	29
Silkstone	151
Simon de Montfort	33
——— de Baukewell	54
——— Fitz Simon	117
———, Precentor of York	29
Skellow	126
———, Grange	145
———, John de	126
Slade Hooton	5, 99, 107, 120, 142, 143
Sloane, MS.	188
Smeaton	144, 187
———, Alan	117
———, Simon son of Algar de	144
Smetheton, Alan de	32, 34
Smithfield	83
Smith, Mr. Theophilus	vi
———, John	154
Smythe, Thomas	86
Snaith	144, 151
Soke	22
Sonke	21
Southerfell	26
"South Yorkshire"	xxiii (n), 110 (n), 188
Spalding Abbey	45
Spencer	104
Sprotbrough	121
Sprotburgh, Lord of	102
Stacye, Rev. J.	vi
Stainton	16, 21, 119, 145
———, Hugh de	5, 145
———, Hugh, John son of	145
———, John de	140
———, William de	140
Stainforth	21
Stainsford	144, 145
———, John Fitz Peter de	114
———, Provost of	145
Stainredale	145
Stallage	22
Stanhop	49
Stanhope, Sir Edward	xxii
Stanfal	21, 145
Stanhege	107, 145
Stapelton, Lord Robert de	131, 132
Stapleton, Robert de	117
———, Richard	146
Statute relating to Seals of Monasteries	45
Stather, North and South	111, 137
Staynton	187
———, John de	122
Stelle, Robert	89
Stephen, Abbot of Roche	37, 40, 41, 138
———, King of England	xix, 4
———, Cardinal	18, 25, 120
Stephenson, Thomas	120
Sterndale	123
Stevinton, Johann de	159
Stillingflete	155
Stirap, Ingeram de	155
———, Gerard de	16, 146
Stirrup	16, 21, 146
Stokes, Thomas	127
Stone Edge	132
Storthes, John	150
Stowe	53
Strafford	146
Strie, William	109
Stristerop	146
Streetthorpe	146
St. Paul, Robert de	29
— Agatha Abbey	45
— Clement at York, Agnes, Prioress of	160
— Mary of Roche	153
— Andrew, Robert de	151
— Roche	125
— Mary's, York	68
— Paul's London	45
— John's Church, Laughton	120
— Omer, Sir William de	136
— Leonard, Hospital of, at York	141
Stubbs, Alexander de	32, 155
Styrrup, Ralph de, Robert son of	112
———, Robert de	112
Suffolk	26
Summons to Stephen, Abbot of Roche	38, 39
——— to Parliament	32, 38, 39, 43, 44, 47
Suppression of Monasteries	94 (n)
——— of Roche Abbey letter on	89
Surrey, John, Earl of	51, 52, 112
Surrender Deed of Roche Abbey	84
Surdeval, Richard de	xxii
Surtees Society	28, 59 (n)
Sutton, Charles	187
———, John	187
Swain, Fitz Swain	7
Swaincroft	134
Swayn, Adam Fitz	16
Swift, Mr. W.	vi
Swinton	122, 159
———, Raynder de	122
———, William de	122
Sykes, Dr.	vi, 109 (n)
Symon, son of Symon	15
Sywardthorp, Hugh Marshal de	141

T

Takewith	16
Tange	21
Tanner	101, 177
Tatewyc, William de	148
Taxation of Pope Nicholas	137
Templeborough	117, 146, 147
Tenneslowe, Henry de	187
"Testamenta Vetusta"	59 (n)
"——— Eboracensia"	59 (n)
Testification of Richard de Boyvill	140
Theam	22
Themantale	21
Theodare, a Monk	19
Thethingpenning	22
Thomas, Abbot of Roche	36
———, the Granger	32
———, son of Artrop de Braithwell	104
Thomas, William Fitz	101
Thoc, Thomas	32
Thornsham, Robert, Steward of Anjou	23
Thorne	28, 147
Thornhill, Robert	110
Thornell, Hugh	154
Thornabye, Robert	139
Thoroton, Dr.	v, xxii
Thorpe	37
———, William	67
Thoresby's MSS.	18, 53
Thriberg	147
Throapham	120, 147, 153
Thundercliffe Grange	xxi

ROCHE ABBEY.

Thurstonland	89 (n), 142, 150
Thurne, Thomas, Abbot of Roche	64
Thurnscoe	15, 16, 21, 103, 116, 126, 147, 148, 149
———, Adam de	148
Tickhill	xx, 11, 12, 17, 18, 21, 48, 103, 106, 112, 143, 144, 146, 150, 151, 174
——— Castle	xx, xx, 48, 121
———, Roger de, Abbot of Roche	11, 12
———, Reginald Guvy de	155
———, Mathew de, Maud, relict of	155
Tikill, William, Abbot of Roche	62, 63
Tilli, Ote de	104
Tinsley	151, 187
———, Sir Henry de	188
———, Robert de	159
"Tin Trumpet" quoted	69
Todwick	15, 21, 94, 104, 148, 149, 151, 152, 153
——— Grange	151
———, "Old Hall" at	153 (n)
———, "History of the Manor" of	151
———, "Little"	151
———, Gregory de	151
Toffred, Abbot of Croyland	6
Toft defined	100
Toll	22
Torr	110
Tortemayns, Ralph	15, 151, 152
———, William	151, 152
Torworth	16, 21, 103, 118, 141, 153, 154, 155
Tower Hill	81
Trent, River	49, 52, 111, 134
———, Alan de	158
Tristrop	146
Trithings	21
Turbary	21
Turgis, Richard Fitz	4, 5, 6, 94, 125, 126, 127
Turke, Richard	102, 105, 141
Turlaveston, Ralph de	10
Turmiston, Jeffery de	144
Twell, Thomas	86, 87, 88
Twing, Robert	25
Tyrrell, Henry	128, 130, 131

U

Ulecotes, Philip de	18
Ullay, Robert de	141
Upland, Jacke	23
Urban, Pope III.	14, 16, 30, 116, 117, 119, 123, 125, 135, 142
——————— IV.	107
Urnethorp, Hugh de	117

V

Vallambrosa	26
Vallis Dei or Vaudry	177
"Valor Ecclesiasticus"	101, 105
Vavasour, William	15, 99, 147
———, John de	156
Verona	16
Verum, Richard de	123
———, William de	123
Vesci, Lords of Rotherham	xxiii
Vickers, Mr. G. Naylor	vi
Vipont, Robert de	140, 141
———, Idonea de	xxii, 140, 172 (n)
Viteri Ponte or Vipont, Robert de	xxii
Vivian, Archdeacon of Derby	23

W

Wadworth	15, 21, 111, 120, 142, 143, 145, 155, 156
Wadworth, Peter de	13, 109, 140, 143, 147, 148, 155, 156
———, Eudo de	111, 155
———, Godfrey de	15, 111
———, Ralph, Priest of	111
———, Hugh de, Abbot of Rocke	13, 16, 135
Wakefield	133
———, John, Abbot of Roche	58, 59, 60
Walcott, Mackenzie E. C.	165
Walcre	156
Wales	47, 84
Walent, Henry	117
Wallbran, Mr.	92 (n)
Wallingwells	158
Wall, Robert	81
Walker, John	150
Walkersall	118
Walkeringham	110, 120, 142, 156, 157, 158
———, Richard de	156
———, Roger, Chaplain of	157
———, William de	143, 156, 158
———, Adam de	157
———, Henry de	156
Wakling, John de	108
Walsingham	83
Walter, son of Leon	109
———, Abbot of Roche	30, 137
Walton, Upper	157
Warmsworth, William de	109, 110
Warpening	22
Warren, the Goldsmith	88 (n)
———, William, Earl of	18, 28, 34, 41, 108, 111, 112, 114, 164
———, John, Earl of	50, 51, 52, 92, 112
———, William de	xx, xxiii
Warely	21, 158
Warwick	92 (n)
Wasteneys, William	145
Wastenays, Edmunde de	152
Wastenayes, Lord Edmund de	132
Watt	93
Waverley	xviii
Weighton Common	79
Welbeck Abbey	45
Welbore, Michael	187
Wells, Thomas	86, 88
Well, the "Ladies"	176
Wellingley	15, 16, 21, 111, 143, 145, 159, 187
Wentworth	117
———, W. de	43
———, Thomas	117
Westminster	38, 39, 44, 46, 78, 119, 138
Westrasen	138
Westnis	100
Wetelay	117
Wheland, John	82
Whalley, Abbot of	133
Whiethwait, Johanna	148
Whitehall	83
Whitehead, Henry	133
Whitaker, Dr.	7
"White Monks"	xviii
Whitwell	15, 107
Whiston Roger	152
Wickersley	5, 21, 159
———, Richard de	9, 116, 126
———, Robert de	116, 140, 148
———, Richard Fitz Turgis de	159
Wilfick	145, 155, 159
Wilson, Henry	82, 86, 88
———, W.	104
William, Abbot of Roche	49
———, Chaplain of the Castle of Tickhill	12

INDEX.

William, fon of Richard de Barnby	102	Woodhoufe Mill	160
———, fon of Gilbert de Catwick	107	Workfop	xx, 94 (n), 175, 188
———, fon of Henry de Marifco	100	———, Prior of	19, 43
———, fon of Edward III.	52	Worcefter	33
———, fon of Richard de Bufli	10	Wortley	xxi
———, Sir William Fitz	100 (n)	Worthley, Henry de	103
——— the Fleming	16	Wrigley, John	134
——— the Conqueror	xxii	Wright, Jno.	149
Williams, Sir John	122	Wulfagh	108
Will of Matilda of York, Countefs of Cambridge	58	Wyk, Hugh de le	139
		Wynkyn de Worde	12 (n)
Wilkynfon, John	119	Wynterton	187
Wilghefich, Mo. de Otho, fon of	155	Wyn, Miles	100 (n)
Winchefter	23	Wyfe, Ralph	152
———, Bifhop of	xix, 22	———, John	152
Windfor	47	———, Roger	152
Wineley	151, 159, 187	Wyvelfworth	21, 160
Winterington	15, 17, 21		
Winterton	159	Y	
Winteringham	160		
Wlger-Oxgang	156	Yorkfhire	xxii. 84, 99, 120
Wlrington, Robert de	144	——— Churches, notes on, by a Monk of Roche	94
———, Herbert de	144		
———, Thomas de	144	York	xx, 60, 79, 80, 81, 82, 112, 135, 160
Wlvethwait, John de	140	——— Fabric Rolls	28, 29
Woburn	177	——— Cathedral Church	29
Wolfpit	5	——— Caftle	82
Wolvethwait, John de	110, 111	———, St Mary's Abbey	7
Wolfey, Cardinal	68, 70	———, Matilda of	171
Woodhall	121		

ROBERT WHITE, PRINTER, PARK-STREET, WORKSOP.

www.ingramcontent.com/pod-product-compliance
Lightning Source LLC
Chambersburg PA
CBHW021401230426
43666CB00006B/596